A HISTORY OF WEST AFRICA

To The Nineteenth Century

BASIL DAVIDSON is an eminent British author and journalist who has a particular interest in the history of Africa, upon which he is a recognized world authority. His books include THE LOST CITIES OF AFRICA, BLACK MOTHER, THE AFRICAN PAST, AFRICA: THE HISTORY OF A CONTINENT, and WHICH WAY AFRICA: THE SEARCH FOR A NEW SOCIETY. He is an active contributor to numerous journals and periodicals in both England and America, and recently spent some time at the University of California at Los Angeles as a visiting lecturer on African history. Mr. Davidson has travelled regularly in Africa for many years studying evidence of ancient African history and observing current history in the making.

F. K. BUAH, M.A., is Headmaster of the Tema Secondary School in Ghana and is the author of HISTORY FOR GHANA SCHOOLS, OBJECTIVE QUESTIONS AND ANSWERS IN HISTORY, and A NEW HISTORY FOR WEST AFRICAN SCHOOLS AND COLLEGES.

J. F. ADE AJAYI, B.A., PH.D., is Professor of History at the University of Ibadan, Nigeria. His books on African history include CHRISTIAN MISSIONS IN NIGERIA 1841–91, MILESTONES IN NIGERIAN HISTORY, and YORUBA WARFARE IN THE NINETEENTH CENTURY (with R. S. Smith).

A HISTORY OF
WEST AFRICA

To The Nineteenth Century

BASIL DAVIDSON

WITH F. K. BUAH

and the advice of J. F. ADE AJAYI

MAPS BY K. C. JORDAN, F.R.G.S.

ANCHOR BOOKS
DOUBLEDAY & COMPANY, INC.
GARDEN CITY, NEW YORK

dedicated with affection to
my friends and colleagues of the
University of California at Los Angeles
and especially
James S. Coleman
and
Robert R. Griffeth

CONTENTS

Part two

The civilisation of the sixteenth century   105
A D 1500 – 1600

    sixteenth century   173

    The stratification of society   174
    Masters and servants   176
    Kinds of service   179
    Methods of government   181
    Kings, nobles, governors   182
    Professional armies   185
    Law and order   188
    Clash of beliefs   190

15 New pressures from outside   193

    Changes in North Africa: the Turkish empire   193
    The coming of the Europeans to West Africa   197
    A new partnership   201
    Beginning of the Atlantic slave trade   202

    Part three

    The seventeenth and eighteenth centuries   207

16 A period of great change   209

    The sea-merchants   211
    European rivalries   212
    Growth of the Atlantic slave trade   214
    Firearms   216
    Cause and effect   218

17 Benin, Oyo, and the delta states   219

    Benin   219
    Decline of the empire of Oyo   221
    The delta states   223
    Government in the delta   224
    The trade of the delta   226

LIST OF MAPS

Mefrε Sika,	*I call Gold,*
Sika ngye so.	*Gold is mute.*
Mefrε Ntama,	*I call Cloth,*
Ntama ngye so.	*Cloth is mute.*
Onipa ne asεm.	*It is Mankind that matters.*

INTRODUCTION

■

EARLY TIMES

1 THE BACKGROUND OF HISTORY

Africa through the ages

To understand the African present it is necessary to understand the African past. Is this, perhaps, an unforgivably banal statement of the obvious? It would be so, of course, were it not for the fact that many have denied the possibility of understanding the African past; or, if they have not entirely denied it, they have thought that the African past is scarcely worth understanding because it contained no large and influential processes of human development.

The scholarship of the last few decades, but especially of the last few years, has revealed these negative attitudes to be the fruits of illusion. Whatever we may have thought or believed, there now stands clear the truth that Africans possess a history of their own that is both interesting and long. If much remains to be unravelled by the skill of future historians—and these pages will show this again and again—much is already recovered. So manifestly is this the case that African history can now be recognised as a valid and even indispensable chapter in the general history of man. And the African present, by the same token, becomes explicable in terms of the African past: to a very great extent, moreover, only in those terms.

This short book is intended as an introduction to an important part of the African side of the story of mankind for all who enjoy reading history, and who find in history a liberation of the mind. Its limits are those of West Africa in space, and the eight centuries A D 1000–1800 in time. These limits are imposed by the practical needs of covering a great deal of factual ground in a conveniently brief narrative. One has to remember, at the same time, that what happened in West Africa is finally explicable only

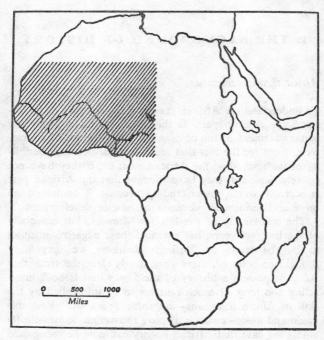

1   West Africa

when account is taken of what happened in the rest of the
continent, and, with varying intensity, in the rest of the
world as well.

This inter-dependence is an essential point. Although
West Africa is in some respects the richest and most interesting of all the regions of Africa from an historical
point of view, its past development needs to be placed in
continuous relationship with neighbouring regions, especially North Africa. For it has never been true that West
Africans have lived in complete isolation from their neighbours. On the contrary, at certain points they have lived in

close relation with them. Allowing for this reservation, however, it seems reasonable to consider the area shown in Map 1 as representing an historical continuum in space and time. Enclosed within it there lies an historical reality of unfailing interest and drama.

Even so, why AD 1000–1800? The dates, admittedly, are arbitrary. Nothing occurred at either of them which can justify drawing a broad line between what went before and what came after. Yet they are permissible dates for beginning and ending this book, I think, not only because of their convenience but also because of the reality they enclose. By AD 1000 the West African scene was fully launched upon that vast process of Iron Age development which was to carry these many and varied peoples from one phase of social growth to another. If Ancient Ghana was already at its zenith and would soon decline, battered by enemies from without and rebels from within, the factors then in play were at work throughout the whole wide region, whether in the shadeless grasslands of the north or the crowded forests near the coast. And by AD 1800, eight momentous centuries later, these factors of Iron Age growth were already beginning to give way to new factors injected from beyond the seas.

These eight centuries are in every way a big period. They form the heart of the West African story. Crucially formative, they offer in their diversity a forceful and vivid picture of human destiny, whether in good times or in bad, in failure or success, in setback or advance. These are the years that have really mattered here. But to place a framework round this picture of an evolving African civilisation we begin with a sketch of earlier times and end with an outline of some new developments after 1800.

Two other preliminary points: one large and the other small. Is it reasonable to speak of "African civilisation"? Shouldn't one rather speak of many African civilisations, with those of West Africa forming only a part, though certainly an important one? Perhaps: yet the term used in this book is more than merely convenient. There is as much justification for speaking of African civilisation as of European or Asian or American civilisation; and it is in this broad and tolerant sense that our use of the term should be taken. It has the advantage, besides, of stressing that the history of each of the major regions of Africa belongs properly to a much wider continental whole.

The other point, a small one, is that Christian dates are used throughout these pages, although many of these dates were conceived in the chronology of Islam. Readers may care to note that the Muslim calendar begins in A D 622. An *approximate* indication of the period of an Islamic date may be had from a Christian date by subtracting 622. But the qualification is important because the Muslim year is a lunar year, and therefore shorter than a Christian year. Other variables add to the difficulty. Those who wish to know the true Muslim equivalents of Christian dates are referred to one or other of the available conversion tables. Perhaps the handiest of these is Dr. G. S. P. Freeman-Grenville's *Muslim and Christian Calendars,* published in 1963.

Geographical divisions of West Africa

There is an obvious and close connexion between the ways in which people have developed in the past and the kind of countryside and climate they have lived in. So the history of West Africa, as of any other part of the world, is closely connected with its geography.

West Africa is divided by nature into a number of belts of varying land and climate. These belts run between west and east, with the Atlantic Ocean at one end and the valley of the river Nile and then the Red Sea at the other end. Looking at them from north to south, in other words, they form a number of zones.

A soil map of West Africa shows five main zones of different soils. These range from the desert of the Sahara to the red-brown tropical soil and the laterite soil that form, between them, much of the region's surface. A rainfall map shows even more belts or zones, reckoning these by the average amount of rain that falls every year in each of them. In the southern Sahara this average is less than ten inches a year. In western Guinea and the Niger delta, at the other extreme, the average rainfall is more than ten times as much.

These wide differences in environment are manifest in everyday life. Anyone who makes a journey from the Sahara down to the coast will pass through belt after belt of differing vegetation, ranging from open plains to dense forest. There are very many such variations. For our purposes, however, they may be grouped together into two principal zones: the land and climate of the open plains of the north, and the land and climate of the forest and coastal areas of the south. The first of these is *Western Sudan;* the second is *Guinea.*

One should remember, at the same time, that each of these principal zones of different land and climate contains many lesser zones: the waterways of the great Niger river-system, the Niger delta itself, the mountain ranges of eastern Nigeria and western Guinea, the islands that lie along the coast of Sierra Leone, the course and estuary of the Gambia river, and many others.

Besides these two main zones we should also note another zone of historical importance. This is formed by the open country between the Pra river in modern Ghana and the Yewa river in modern Nigeria. Here it is that the grasslands of the north push down almost to the coast, thus splitting the great forest belt of West Africa into two parts.

Different zones have different advantages and handicaps. The West African forest belt is wonderfully good for growing valuable crops, yet bad for cattle. The plains of the north are good for cattle, but no good for certain valuable crops like cocoa. Soil and rainfall both play their part.

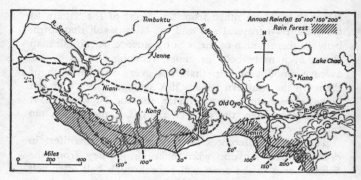

2   Rainfall in West Africa

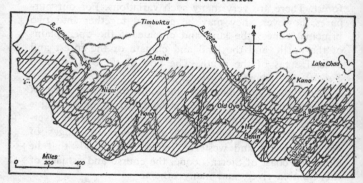

3   The total area affected by tse-tse flies

So, for example, do a number of insect pests. Of these, perhaps the most influential on history has been the tse-tse fly, which causes a fatal disease in cattle (*nagana*) and also in human beings (*trypanosomiasis*, better known as sleeping-sickness). Of the twenty-one known varieties of tse-tse fly, about eight are really dangerous vectors of disease; and several of them, mainly *Glossina palpalis* and *Glossina morsitans,* appear to have been common in many parts of West Africa from the earliest times of human settlement. A central point about the tse-tse fly is that it has severely limited the areas in which people could keep cattle and horses, or develop the use of ploughs and other forms of animal-drawn equipment.

These natural variations have led to many contrasting ways of life. They help to explain why Hausa farmers and their neighbours have been so successful with raising cattle; or why Ijaw fishermen of the Niger delta, to take another example, have proved so skilful in catching fish; or why Akan farmers, to offer a third example, have founded their wealth on the growing of forest crops. And all these variations in ways of living and of working have gone hand-in-hand with different ways of community life, different methods of government, different ideas about how to keep law and order, and much else besides. Natural variations, in short, have helped to lead to social variations.

Way of life of early men

Recent discoveries have suggested that Africa may have been the birthplace of humanity. Some scholars now believe that it was in Africa that early types of men, very different from ourselves, first developed the use of tools, and that this occurred some two million years ago. Though the evidence for this rests so far on the recovery and analysis of fossil bones in the East African Rift Valley region, it seems clear that early types of *homo* were by no means limited at that time to eastern Africa, and several important fossils are known for the central, southern, and western regions as well. The present view is that the first toolmaker was *australopithecus,* a manlike creature about four feet six inches tall who lived in small settlements in high savannah country good for hunting game, who was quite skilled in the making of crude stone implements, but who did not yet have the use of fire.

Equipped with the beginnings of technical skills in the

manipulation of tools and weapons, these early types of
men made progress over the forgotten centuries of the
Early Stone Age. Natural selection slowly played its part.
By about a million years ago there were many more types
of *hominid*, manlike creatures who were certainly not apes
but also not yet fully human; and they had spread over
much of Africa as well as over much of the rest of the
world. Gradually they grew stronger and more efficient in
their fight for survival. At the same time they continued to
grow more numerous.

About sixty thousand years ago, apparently, man in
Africa acquired the use of fire. Not long after that, maybe
a mere twenty thousand years, natural selection finally
produced its masterpiece, *homo sapiens* himself. A point
to hold in mind here is that the evidence now available
suggests that certain main features of what may possibly
be called "racial difference" were already in existence as
much as forty thousand years ago. Language will have
taken early shape at this period, too, though the splitting of
a few "original mother tongues" into the main language
groups of modern Africa appears not to have begun until
some ten thousand years ago. On points such as these,
however, we are still on doubtful ground.

Homo sapiens greatly improved the available technical
equipment. But he remained a hunter and gatherer of
food, living in very small communities and moving from
one place to the other nearly all the time, until some eight
or nine thousand years ago. Then comes his major revolutionary discovery after stone, tools and fire: the possibility
of growing food, rather than merely hunting for it or collecting it from wild plants.

Food growing in the Neolithic or New Stone Age had
immense consequences. It enabled people to live quite
differently from before, although the change, perhaps needless to say, was neither swift nor sudden but the work of
many generations. Little by little, it became possible for
people to settle in one place for months at a time, and

afterwards for years at a time, and eventually for all their lives. This was a process, one should note, which occurred at different times in different places.

First invented in the Middle East, the habit of living by agriculture, by growing food instead of hunting game and gathering wild plants, was adopted by Africans of the Nile Valley some six thousand years ago. Africans of other regions started agriculture in somewhat later times. Knowledge of how to farm and raise cattle spread gradually across the open plains. It came last of all to the dense forest lands of West and Central Africa; here it dates to less than three thousand years ago, and its further extension southwards after that was closely linked, as we shall see, to the development of iron weapons and tools.

At this point there should be noted an important natural difference between the Africa of New Stone Age times and the Africa of today. West Africa today is divided from North Africa and the Nile by the Sahara Desert. But this was not always the case; in New Stone Age times, this vast and often terrible desert was a rich and fertile land. The Sahara then was clothed with tall trees and green pastures. Broad rivers flowed through it. Game and cattle were plentiful there. Fish abounded.

From one end of the Sahara to the other, from Mauretania in the west to Egypt in the east, scientists have found stone tools and bone harpoons and fishing hooks, as well as pictures and drawings on rock of animals and men and gods. All these were made and left behind by many settlements and groups of vanished people. The Old Sahara may indeed be reasonably seen as a cradle of early African civilisation. Far from being a natural barrier between the peoples of West and North Africa, the Old Sahara joined these peoples together. All could share in the same ideas and discoveries.

Many travellers journeyed through the green Sahara in New Stone Age times, often by means of horse-drawn chariots or carts. Ancient rock pictures of these horses and

vehicles have been found along two main trails between
North and West Africa. One of these trails passed through
Mauretania in the western Sahara, while the other went
through the central Sahara between the middle section of
the Niger river and modern Tunisia. We can be sure that
new ideas and discoveries were taken back and forth by
these old travellers.

Around 2000 BC there began a long and eventually
disastrous natural change. The climate gradually became
much drier. The Sahara received less and less rain. Its
rivers began to fail and, little by little, its farming peoples
had to move away and find new homes. Some went northward, and helped to form the Berber peoples of North
Africa. Others pushed eastward to the margins of the fertile valley of the Nile. Others again came southward into

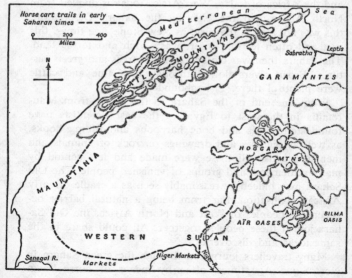

4 Chariot trails in early Saharan times

West Africa. By about 500 B C this complicated movement of peoples was already in the past, and the Sahara had become the dry and stony wasteland that we know today. The horse made way for the camel, widely used from about two thousand years ago, because the camel, with its broad feet, could move better over sand and could walk from well to well further than the horse.

The southward movement of peoples may have helped to bring the discoveries of the New Stone Age into West Africa. But it would be wrong to conceive of this process as mere diffusion from north to south: there was certainly a great deal of West African invention. There is evidence, even though it does not yet add up to proof, that the peoples in the Western Sudan were beginning to grow rice, and perhaps one or two other crops, as much as 5000 years ago. It is also obvious that methods and tools for growing food that were suitable in the northern plains had to be adapted for use in the forest. The peoples of the forest, in short, learned how to modify and adapt the discoveries of agriculture to their own kind of country. They made their own agricultural revolution.

Early peoples of West Africa

Who were those peoples of West Africa who adapted and invented new methods of farming and metal-working several thousand years ago? The answer is that they were the descendants of Stone Age peoples who had already been living in West Africa for a very long time, and also the ancestors of the modern inhabitants of West Africa.

Many West African peoples have legends and traditions which say that their ancestors came from another homeland in the distant east or north, or from some part of West Africa other than where they live today. A few of these traditions will be examined later. In central Guinea, for example, the Akan and the Nzima say that their ancestors

came from far in the north. The Ga and Ewe hold that
theirs came from the east. The Yoruba of eastern Guinea
likewise have a tradition which explains that their ancestors originated far in the east. What value do such traditions really have?

Nearly always, these legends and "memories" must be
taken as referring only to very small groups of incoming
ancestors. When they really occurred, such movements will
have been made only by a small minority of people, by a
few clans or families, or by a few warriors under strong
leaders who, leaving their homeland, entered new territory,
merged there with the more numerous peoples whom they
found, and began a new tradition about where all these
people had come from.

We shall find plenty of examples of the way in which
West African history has repeatedly combined what was
new with what was already very old. We shall see how new
ideas, merged with old ideas, launch new ways of government. We shall see how new skills, combined with old
skills, promote new methods of earning a livelihood. And
it may be useful, at this stage, to think of this constant
combining of what is new with what is old, this interplay of
history, as being like the action of a West African weaver.
He stretches first of all his long threads, tying them to a
stake in the ground or perhaps a tree trunk. He pulls them
taut and sits to his loom. Then he threads his shuttle and
begins weaving it back and forth between the stretched
threads. Out of this interplay there comes a cloth. The finished cloth is composed of the two sets of threads, and yet
it is something entirely new. It is different from any of the
threads, and it is also more than any of them.

If one uses this illustration to explain the history of West
Africa, as one could use it to explain the history of any
other region of the world, then the long threads represent
the inhabitants of West Africa, together with the beliefs,
ideas, skills and customs they have worked out for themselves. The shuttle threads are all the new beliefs, ideas,

skills and customs that have come into West Africa from
time to time, or have been invented or created in West
Africa. Woven together, all these threads make what may
be called the cloth of history.

Through the course of time the cloth of history in West
Africa, as elsewhere, has been constantly rewoven in a rich
process of change and development. New designs and patterns have repeatedly appeared in it. This has been the
never-ceasing process of change by which many traditions
about the distant origins of various peoples have come into
being. But what we have to remember here, as we embark
on this study of the past, is that nearly all the inhabitants
of West Africa are in fact the descendants of peoples who
have lived in this region since the earliest appearance of
man.

The importance of iron

The discovery of agriculture wove many new patterns and
designs into West Africa's cloth of history. Another event
of comparable influence was the discovery of how to use
metals. This, too, had many profound consequences and
caused significant changes in the way people lived.

The ancient Egyptians, like some of their Asian neighbours, were using copper and gold more than five thousand
years ago. This was long before other Africans had acquired any knowledge of the use of metals. But copper and
gold, though excellent for making jewels and pots, were
not much use for hunting, warfare, or tilling the soil. They
were too soft. Egyptian and Asian metalworkers then discovered how they could obtain a harder metal if they mixed
copper with tin. The result was bronze, which is harder
than copper. The disadvantage still remained that copper
and tin, like gold, were rare metals. Kings and famous
warriors could afford bronze weapons and golden jewels.
Ordinary folk could not.

Some time around 1500 B C an Asian people called the Hittites, who lived in the country that is Turkey today, evolved techniques for the smelting of iron, using ore which calls for a much higher temperature than gold, copper, or tin. This was a discovery of crucial value for two reasons. First of all, iron was a metal out of which hard tools and weapons could be forged. Secondly, iron was plentiful. Once men had understood how to use iron, good tools and weapons could eventually be made in large quantity by many different peoples.

One people after another of the ancient world adopted the use of iron. These peoples are said by historians to have entered their Iron Age. So far as Africa is concerned, iron began to be commonly used in the countries of the Nile Valley, along the coast of North Africa, and in Ethiopia, soon after about 600 B C. West African peoples first entered their Iron Age—had begun, that is, to smelt ore and make their own iron tools and spears—a little later, the most likely date being between 300 and 200 B C.

The main evidence for West Africa's earliest Iron Age comes from Nigeria. Scientists have shown how people who lived in the region of the joining of the Niger and Benue rivers began using iron more than two thousand years ago. They have been able to demonstrate this from the evidence of iron-working left behind by these people, who also modelled skilfully in terra cotta (baked clay). The name given to this early Iron Age way of life in central Nigeria is the Nok Culture, after the village of Nok where some of the evidence was first discovered. The Nok Culture may be regarded as the beginning of the West African Iron Age, at least until further discoveries are made in other areas of West Africa.

The importance of iron was so great in those distant times that the reasons for it should be reviewed in more detail. The first reason was that it gave West Africans better weapons and tools. Iron-pointed spears were more effective than sharp sticks or stones. Iron-headed hoes, probably

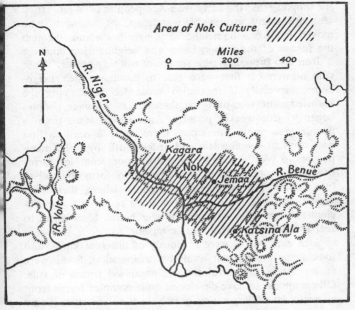

5 Approximate known area of Nok Culture

invented some time after iron-pointed spears, were better than stone or wooden ones. Iron-headed axes could fell trees and shape wood much better than stone axes.

These improvements in equipment led to the production of more food. Having more food, people lived better than before. They became more numerous. But more people needed more land. Here lay a second reason why iron was important, and why its use marked the opening of a new stage of development. With iron spears and iron tools, Africans could attack some of the great natural barriers of their continent. They could penetrate the deep forests, open new trails, defend themselves against wild animals, and generally move about with more safety. There are grounds for thinking that the early Iron Age peoples of West Africa sent out many groups of wanderers, of *migrants* who moved from one homeland to a new homeland, through the forests of the Congo basin and neighbouring lands.

Iron also brought a new source of military power. Those who mastered it first were able to dominate their neighbours, especially if they also succeeded in keeping the knowledge of iron-using to themselves. Stronger peoples began to rule weaker peoples. And, at the same time as people grew more numerous, there came a need to find new ways of keeping law and order. Little by little, many peoples in West Africa embarked on more complex forms of political organisation. They began to form themselves into states. This happened especially where there was growth of trade. This growth of trade required more efficient rules of behaviour among neighbours. Men began to feel the need for organised government.

Such early states were obviously of different kinds, and took shape at different levels of organisation. Some were embryonic in their evolution of organised forms of rule. Others appear to have developed quite complex forms from an early date. They varied greatly in their structure. Some gave rise to chiefs and kings with a clear executive authority. Others discovered no such need. Yet in all of them there was the use of a number of organisational systems which were to continue through the centuries, though very diverse in their particular applications. These included systems of kinship loyalty; segmentation into clans and other groupings by family relationship; and, here and there, the development of "age-sets" composed of men (and to a lesser extent also of women) who were born in the same year, or in the same two or three years, and were vowed to special duties and social obligations.

It may be remarked that no useful evidence of special skill or accomplishment should be read into relative degrees of traditional organisation in social and political matters. Those peoples who had kings were not therefore giving proof of greater intelligence or enterprise than those who had none. The existence of strong central governments was no proof of superiority in social values. What this diversity really reflected was the wide variation of environment and opportunity in which all these scattered peoples lived. They faced different problems. These problems they had to solve in different ways.

Among these variables in political development, the possibilities of trade were undoubtedly of early and continuous influence. Those peoples who lived on the main trails of developing trade tended to form themselves into states with a central king or government. They found they could operate better in this way. But other peoples who lived far off these trails, and so had little interest in trade, tended to rest content with much looser forms of rule. They tended to go on living by the old family and clan customs of earlier times. One may even make a rough rule on this important subject. This is that the production of goods for trade, and trade itself, were main causes in the early formation of states. Many of the early states grew out of prosperous market-centres, settlements, and towns.

Early states

The earliest of West Africa's large states seems to have been known as Aoukar. Later ages have called it Ghana, although this was really the title of its king or emperor. North African and other Arabic writers began mentioning Ghana during the ninth century A D. Soon after A D 800, Al-Fazari named it as "the land of gold." In about A D 830 Al-Kwarizmi marked it on a map. Before looking at what is known of the history of this interesting and long-famous empire, there are a few things to say about it which illustrate its relationship to the use of iron.

It seems likely that the origins of Ancient Ghana go back much further than A D 800, and that this old state and em-

pire grew out of its peoples' need to help and protect their
trade. The heart of Ancient Ghana lay in its market-centres.
These were placed in the grasslands to the north of the
upper waters of the Niger and Senegal rivers. Their commercial position was an unusually strong one. They stood
at the southern end of the trading-caravan routes which
crossed the Sahara from North Africa. But they also stood
at the northern end of the trading routes which came
northward from the gold country of the south-west—the
modern regions of northern Guinea and southern Mali.
The traders of these market-centres bought gold and ivory
from the traders of West Africa, and sold these goods to
the traders of North Africa in exchange for Saharan salt
and North African goods. Being powerful in trade, they
needed to be powerful in government. They greatly succeeded in this, and for a long time they flourished as a
powerful if loosely organised political unit.

But what took place in the lands of Ancient Ghana, in
the north-western region of West Africa, also took place
elsewhere. Other trading states were formed along the
course of the Niger river. Still others emerged in neighbouring regions. By the time our main period begins in
about A D 1000, the peoples of West Africa had already
passed through many stages of social and political experience. Their Iron Age development had brought them to
the threshold of five great centuries of growth.

Such is the scene to be held in mind as we approach the
history of these centuries. This was a large and varied region in slow but steady process of change. Many people
still kept to their old ways and ideas, quietly tilling a patch
of ground or patiently casting their nets for fish, their world
no wider than the life of their village, their family, or their
clan. Yet already, even though they could not know it, the
winds of a different future were beginning to blow among
them.

All this was the subtle work and interplay of a developing civilisation. Yet this civilisation did not live entirely

by itself, cut off from contact with other civilisations. It was part of a larger African development. Although the Sahara was now a dried-up wilderness, West Africa remained in touch with North Africa and with the lands of the Nile Valley. Those ancient contacts were never broken. They ensured that these three great regions—West Africa, the Nile Valley, and North Africa—should develop together even though, because of the grim Sahara lying between them, they also developed separately. One can make little sense of West African history unless this picture is constantly in mind: three great regions learning from each other, teaching each other, trading with each other through the centuries.

A comparison of West Africa then with West Africa today—a very difficult comparison to make—shows many contrasts. There were far fewer people. And although most of them lived by growing food, their crops were much less varied. They had no maize in those times, no pineapples, no sweet-potatoes. They had as yet few towns, and no great cities. But even then, a thousand years ago, many important features common to a later West Africa were already in existence. Many religious beliefs, social manners, customs, habits, and methods of organisation had already come to birth.

The sources of historical knowledge

It may reasonably be asked how anything of value can be known about what happened in those distant times. Except in a few trading towns and cities, where Muslims were present, West Africans had no knowledge of the art and use of writing and of written records.

Much about those distant times still remains vague or lost to us, and perhaps will always be so. Yet we have three valuable sources of information, and each has yielded a great deal of historical knowledge. The first is archaeology.

This derives from Greek words that may be roughly translated as meaning "the study of what is old." But archaeology has come to have a special meaning. It calls for the study of the material remains and ruins of the past, of the tools, weapons, pots, house-foundations, ancient settlements and towns that vanished peoples have left behind them. Archaeology has already provided good information about the past of West Africa; as it develops, it will certainly provide much more.

The second source of historical knowledge is oral tradition. This is the history—part legend and part truth—which generations of ancestors have passed down by word of mouth. West Africa, like other regions of Africa, is rich in such historical traditions, in oral history as distinct from written history. Many West African peoples set aside a special group of men whose task it was to learn, remember, recite and afterwards teach to their sons and successors the historical traditions which they, in turn, had received from their forefathers. These remembered traditions can be sometimes very helpful. But they have to be taken with care. For they may also tell of things which did not happen, or did not happen in the way they are said to have happened, or not for the reasons that are given in the story. We shall notice some examples in the course of this book.

Then there is a third source of knowledge about the distant past of West Africa. This is generally less valuable than the other two, but now and then it is more valuable. It consists in the books that were written by North African and Arab travellers and historians, some of which are of fundamental importance both for an understanding of the general picture and for the splendidly vivid detail they occasionally provide. Much later, Europeans also began to write books about West Africa in Portuguese, English, French, Dutch, and other languages; and a few of these memoirs and records are also full of useful information.

Generally, then, we already have a grasp of the West African past that is fairly reliable in outline after about

A D 1000. Though often lacking in the detailed precision which indigenous written records provide in Europe during the Middle Ages, the broad lines are sufficiently clear. As the years go by, moreover, the detail multiplies. From about A D 1400 it is even copious at certain times and places.

PART ONE

■

FIVE DYNAMIC CENTURIES
AD 1000–1500

2 WEST AFRICA IN ABOUT AD 1000

Some general notes

Three major factors dominate the movement of society in the centuries between AD 1000 and 1500. They are the spread and great expansion of metal-working, especially in iron weapons and tools; secondly, the steady growth of trade and of production for trade in certain staple items, both inside West Africa and between West and North Africa across the Sahara; thirdly, the parallel foundation of large market-centres and trading cities in the plains of the Western Sudan, along the banks of West Africa's principal rivers, and in the forests and coastland of Guinea.

Such developments, and some others of less influence, were of course linked together. Iron tools and weapons helped to expand production, whether of crops or minerals or other goods, and to provide new sources of military power. These in turn promoted the growth of trade. And the growth of trade went hand-in-hand with the rise of markets, towns and cities.

Many West African communities were more or less profoundly influenced by this network of social and economic pressures. They worked out new ways of organising their community lives, and of enforcing law and order. Some of them went ahead without chiefs and kings and central governments, while others founded large states and empires. Cities grew in number, size, and wealth, and became the home of new kinds of craftsmen and traders, politicians, priests, soldiers, writers, and men of learning. With their export of ivory and gold, these trading cities and the states which often grew around them became an indispensable part of the whole wide organisation of international trade that was composed of western and northern Africa, southern Europe, and western Asia.

This long and repeatedly fruitful period has been called a golden age of West African development. The term is fanciful. There were plenty of rough and bitter years, sudden incursions of cruelty and chaos, times of arbitrary rule and persecution of the weak; the story of man is no gentler here than anywhere else. Some peoples prospered; if they did, it was often at the sorry expense of their hapless neighbours. Others suffered; if so, it was not only from the empire-builders but also from unlucky circumstances in their habitat or failure of internal organisation. Those who lived on the trade routes, or near them, were drawn irresistibly into the mainstream of change, either as rulers or as ruled. Those who were far away in the forests and hills had little part in all that, but at least they had the advantage of living largely undisturbed.

Yet the term "golden age," if taken with the necessary pinch of salt, is not entirely romantic. It is true that these centuries witnessed the transformation of West African life into a richly varied social and political fabric. It is true that this civilisation was the parent of modern West Africa. It is true that some splendid things were done. Travelling through the fourteenth-century empire of Mali, the Moroccan Ibn Batuta found "complete and general safety in the land"—and the land of Mali stretched then for many weeks of horseback travel through the grasslands of the Western Sudan. "The traveller has no more reason than the man who stays at home," he wrote from personal experience, "to fear brigands, thieves or violent gangs." Such far-ranging security revealed a major achievement in community organisation, and it was by no means the only one of its kind.

The record is nothing if not complicated. In order to study it with a minimal confusion of names and dates, three useful though arbitrary regional divisions seem wise.

They are shown in Map 6: western region, central region, and eastern region.

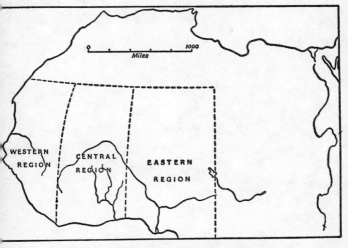

6 Regional divisions adopted in this book

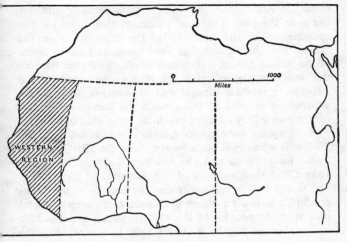

7 The western region

3 THE WESTERN REGION

Introduction: The Sudan

In the western region we include the empire of Ancient
Ghana in the grassland plains that lie around the upper
waters of the rivers Niger and Senegal, as well as all the
forest country and coastal country from modern Senegal
to the frontier of modern Liberia.

These grassland plains of the western region are the
most westerly part of the Sudan. They look northward to
Mauretania and Morocco, and eastward to the rest of the
Sudan. But what exactly is meant by the *Sudan?* This useful

word has Arabic origins. West Africans certainly did not use it in the past. They had names of their own for the countries which the Arabs called the *Bilad as-Sudan,* the "country of the blacks" that lies immediately to the south of the Sahara Desert. Taken as a whole, the Sudan runs all the way from the valley of the Nile to the shores of the Atlantic in modern Senegal and Mauretania. It is a vast area whose peoples all share much the same kind of history, because they all share much the same kind of country.

Geographers have roughly divided the Sudan into two "halves": into the Eastern Sudan, from the Nile Valley to about Lake Chad, and the Western Sudan, from about Lake Chad to the shores of the Atlantic.

Yet it is well to remember that the peoples of the Western Sudan have always been in contact, often a very fruitful one, with the peoples of the Eastern Sudan and the Nile Valley, just as they have always been in contact with the peoples of the Sahara and North Africa, and with the peoples of the forest lands of Guinea. The records of both "halves" of the Sudan—Eastern and Western, with an approximate dividing line at Lake Chad—really belong together, although the Western Sudan has a special and important history of its own.

The specialness of this history—and it emerges, of course, from all regions of West Africa in varying degree—rests like any other history in the personal, individual and emotive qualities and characteristics of the peoples concerned, whether the nameless many or the few leaders whose identity is known and whose deeds and reputations are at least outlined in the records that we have. But the specialness also rests in the interplay of the three major factors already mentioned: metal-working, production for trade, and markets for exchange. These factors acquired a profound influence on many of the peoples of the Western Sudan in ancient times, high on the list of reasons why being the long-distance trade across the Sahara. It was out of this contingency of circumstances, this socio-

economic motor of effective change, that there emerged
the notable political organisation of Ancient Ghana.

Early trade

Old West Africa possessed two kinds of wealth that were
greatly desired by the peoples of the far north and east,
whether in Africa or Europe or Asia. These were gold and
ivory. The trans-Saharan trade in these and other goods
entered a time of expansion when Muslim Arabs enclosed
the lands of North Africa in a new social, political, and
religious system during the eighth century A D, and, in so
doing, promoted a wide system of trade throughout North
Africa and the Near East of Asia.

But Ancient Ghana, like other states of West Africa, also
had one great need which the peoples of the Sahara, or
the peoples beyond it, could help to supply—salt. It is probably true that salt was no less valued by the peoples south
of the desert, because of their hot climate and relative lack
of local supplies, than was gold by the peoples who lived
north of the desert.

So the basis of trade between the Western Sudan and the
Berbers of the Sahara lay in the exchange of salt for gold.
But this was only the basis of trade. The total system was
much wider. For the Saharan Berbers sold the goods they
bought from the Western Sudan to the traders of North
Africa, and the traders of North Africa sold them again to
Europeans and Asians. European and Asian goods came
down into West Africa by the same methods. Needless to
say, there were other items of trade besides gold and salt.
West Africa, for example, also needed copper, silks, and
more metalware (such as pots and pans and swords) than
West Africans could make themselves. West Africa also
supplied ivory and kola nuts. Both sides sold and bought
slaves although West Africans, having a less stratified economy than their North African neighbours and consequently

a smaller need of wageless labour, sold more slaves than they bought.

All this trade led to the founding of cities. Most of these cities were especially concerned with the trade across the Sahara. They began as small trading settlements, but grew bigger as more traders came and went, and became centres for craftsmen who worked in leather, wood, ivory, and metals. City governments became necessary, as well as men trained to be put in charge of keeping accounts, of maintaining law and order, of ensuring the safety of citizens. Then the rulers of these cities began to extend their power to ever wider regions of neighbouring countryside. Gradually the cities grew into states, and the states into empires.

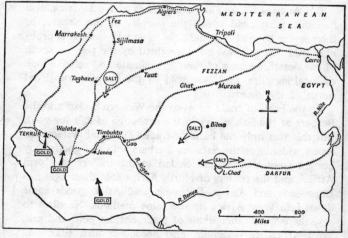

8   Trade and trading routes across the Sahara in early times

This long historical process—from trading settlements to trading empires—also occurred to the north and east of the Sahara. Trading settlements and cities duly appeared in the stony lands of the Sahara itself. These were Berber cities. Some of them are alive to this day: Agadès, Ghat, and Murzuk, for example. Others, like Walata and Tichitt, still exist but have lost their wealth and importance. Others again, such as Audaghost and Sijilmasa, have entirely disappeared. All these towns were founded for the trans-Saharan trade.

The same process of city-founding and empire-building went on to the south of the Sahara. Here, too, some of the great cities of the Western Sudan, such as Kumbi and Tekrur, have disappeared; while others, such as Timbuktu, Gao, and Jenne, have survived. And the main business of these old cities of the Western Sudan was likewise to conduct the trade that came and went across the Sahara, and was fed by the wealth of West Africa.

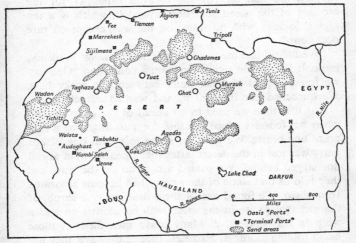

9   The terminal and oasis "ports" of Saharan caravans

Crossing the Sahara

It was hard and dangerous to carry on this trade. Ibn
Batuta has left a vivid description of how he crossed the
desert in 1352. He tells how he travelled down from Fez
to Sijilmasa, then one of the greatest of the market-centres
on the northern side of the Sahara. There in Sijilmasa he
purchased four months' supply of food for his camels. Together with a company of Moroccan merchants who were
also travelling to the Western Sudan, he journeyed on to a
place called Taghaza, a principal salt-producing centre of
the great desert. At Taghaza, he tells us, "we passed ten
days of discomfort, because the water there is bitter and
the place is plagued with flies. And there, at Taghaza, water
supplies are laid on (by the caravan captains) for the
crossing of the desert that lies beyond it, which is a ten
nights' journey with no water on the way except on rare
occasions."

"We indeed had the good fortune to find water in plenty,
in pools left by the rain," Ibn Batuta continues. "One day
we found a pool of fresh water between two rocky hills.
We quenched our thirst at it, and washed our clothes.

"At that time we used to go ahead of the caravan, and
when we found a place suitable for pasturage we would
graze our beasts. We went on doing this until one of our
party was lost in the desert; after that I neither went ahead
nor lagged behind. We passed a caravan on the way, and
they told us that some of their party had become separated
from them. We found one of them dead under a shrub, of
the sort that grows in the sand, with his clothes on and a
whip in his hand . . ." Many brave men died on those
harsh trading journeys. Nameless though they are, they too
deserve their place in West African history.

The trade continued in spite of all dangers and difficulties. It brought many changes to all the peoples who had a

part in it. This was the trade that shaped the growth of great political structures in the Western Sudan. Without it, they might never have been formed; nor could they otherwise have prospered and grown strong.

Foremost among these early states and empires was Ghana.

4 THE EMPIRE OF GHANA

Traditions of origin

Our three main sources of knowledge about the past—
archaeology, oral history, and the books of North Africans
—speak repeatedly enough about Ancient Ghana, but tell
tantalisingly little about the tone and texture of its life.

We can be sure of some of the things they tell us; others
must be left in doubt. What we can be sure of is that early
West Africans who lived to the north of the upper waters
of the Niger river formed themselves into a strong trading
state before the ninth century, and spread their power into
an early empire. This empire exercised domain over many
neighbouring peoples. It commanded a large region of
trade, security, and strong government, and lasted for several hundred years. It was deeply respected by travellers
who came within its borders, and by others, living far
beyond those borders, who heard or read of it.

We can be fairly sure, too, that the peoples who formed
this state and empire spoke one of the languages of the
Mande group, languages that are spoken today by many of
the peoples of the western region (and also by some of the
central region). These founders of Ghana, who were probably Soninke, had good trading relations with the Berber
chiefs and traders who lived to the north of them, in oasis
towns in the Sahara; and it was through these that they
conducted trade across the desert.

Their empire was called Aoukar. The word *ghana* was
a title, which meant "war chief," and was borne by the
king of the country. The king was also known as *kaya
maghan*, king of the gold, evidently because he controlled
the export of that precious metal. Late in the eighth cen-

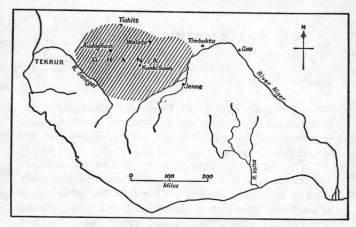

10 Ancient Ghana

tury A D, if not earlier, North Africans began to call this empire Ghana* after the title of its ruler.

How long did Ancient Ghana endure as a state? If we accept that its beginnings were in the fourth or fifth century A D—a date that is far from sure, but seems to be supported by traditions as well as by the evidence relating to gold imports into Roman North Africa—then we can say that Ghana survived for nearly a thousand years. Not until about A D 1240 did this great structure finally crumble and disappear. Useful and detailed information about the latter years of Ghana is available in books written by North

---

* There are two reasons why the modern state of Ghana, though situated far away from Ancient Ghana, has the same name. One is that the old traditions speak of a movement of some of the people of Ancient Ghana southward into the region of Asante. Another reason is that the modern leaders of Ghana wished to celebrate the independence of their country—formerly the Gold Coast—by linking their new freedom to the glorious traditions of the past.

African and Spanish Arab authors in the eleventh and
twelfth centuries A D. One of these books—the *Kitab al-
Masalik wa'l Mamalik* of al-Bakri—offers a brilliantly clear
picture of the court of the emperor of Ghana in about A D
1065, and of the way in which that emperor, whose name
was Tenkaminen, organised his power and wealth.* One
may perhaps note, to situate it in a wider history, that it was
completed in 1067, just a few months after the Norman-
French invasion of a north European island, then little
known, called England.

Growth of Ghana

From this account of Al-Bakri's one can guess a good
deal of what had happened during earlier times. It appears
that many of the North African and Berber traders of the
Sahara accepted Islam after the Arab conquest of the
eighth century. They abandoned their old religions and became Muslims. They were made welcome at the capital of
the emperor of Ghana, who was not a Muslim but a believer
in Ghana's own religion, probably the religion of the
Soninke, and were allowed to build a town of their own.

The "town of the Muslim traders" was six miles away
from the emperor's own town with its surrounding settlements. While the latter were built in the traditional materials of West Africa—hardened clay, thatch, and wooden
beams—the more successful Muslim traders preferred to
build their houses in stone, according to their own customs
in North Africa. It is not exactly known where the capital
was when Al-Bakri wrote his book. In the course of
Ghana's long history, the king's capital was undoubtedly
moved from one place to another. But we can add a good
deal to Al-Bakri's picture by studying the remains of

* Al-Bakri did not visit Ghana himself, but collected information from many travellers who did.

Ghana's last capital, which lay at Kumbi Saleh about two hundred miles north of modern Bamako. Here too there was a town where the king of Ghana lived, and another nearby town where the Muslim traders had their houses and stables. At the height of its prosperity, before A D 1240, this city of Kumbi was evidently the biggest West African city of its day, and may have had as many as fifteen thousand inhabitants or even more.

So long as they observed the laws of Ghana and paid their taxes, the traders from the north were assured of safety and hospitality. This was a partnership in long-distance trade that endured for a very long time. Its safety depended on the strength of the emperor and his system of government. Al-Bakri has left us a masterly description of all that. King Tenkaminen, he wrote, "is the master of a large empire and of a formidable power." So powerful was this king, indeed, that he could put "two hundred thousand warriors in the field, more than forty thousand of them being armed with bow and arrow." But the real strength of the Ghana armies, as we know from other North African sources, came from their power in iron-pointed spears. Their weapons, like their organisation, were stronger than those of their neighbouring peoples; and this was the strength which underpinned their political supremacy.

Working from eye-witness accounts received from Muslim travellers, Al-Bakri describes the pomp and majesty of this powerful ruler in these words:

"When the king gives audience to his people, to listen to their complaints and to set them to rights, he sits in a pavilion around which stand ten pages holding shields and gold-mounted swords. On his right hand are the sons of the princes of his empire, splendidly clad and with gold plaited in their hair. The governor of the city is seated on the ground in front of the king, and all around him are his counsellors in the same position. The gate of the chamber is guarded by dogs of an excellent breed. These dogs never leave their place of duty. They wear collars of gold and silver, ornamented with metals. The beginning of a royal audience is announced by the beating of a kind of drum they call *deba*. This drum is made of a long piece of hollowed wood. The people gather when they hear its sound . . ."

The brilliance of these old glories was long remembered among the peoples of the Western Sudan. Five hundred years later, a writer of Timbuktu called Mahmud Kati entertained his readers with the legends of those ancient days. In a book of outstanding historical value, the *Tarikh al-Fattash,* the "Chronicle of the Seeker," he tells how a certain king of Ghana of the seventh century, called Kanissa'ai, possessed one thousand horses, and how each of these horses "slept only on a carpet, with a silken rope for halter," and had three personal attendants, and was looked after as though it were itself a king. These old legends, magnified and embroidered with the passing of the years, also tell how the early kings of Ghana used to give great banquets to their subjects, feeding ten thousand at a time, and dispensing gifts and justice to all who came. Such legends show something of the grandeur of Ghana's reputation in its years of power and magnificence.

Government of the empire

If one looks carefully behind the travellers' information collected and written down by Al-Bakri and other Arab writers, and behind the legends that were afterwards rehearsed in countless homes through many years, several large developments in ways of life emerge from the mists of time. These were undoubtedly of high importance, and must be clearly understood.

With the growth of Ghana, and of other states like Ghana, the peoples of West Africa were inventing new methods of living together, of governing themselves, of raising money to pay for government, and of producing wealth. These ways repeatedly stressed the need for a single strong authority or government which could rule over many lesser authorities or governments. This central authority could only, in the thought and customs of the times, be a king. In states like Ancient Ghana, the power of government increased still further. Important kings became kings over lesser kings—in our terms, emperors. At the heart of the explanation of why this happened there was the growth, as already suggested here, of international trade. Occupying the lands to the north of the upper waters of the Niger, the old Ghana rulers and their people enjoyed a position of great force and value. Their towns and trading settlements became the intermediaries or middlemen between the Berber and Arab traders of the north and the gold or ivory producers of the south.

It was this middleman position which made Ghana strong and prosperous. It was this that gave its rulers gold and glory. It was this that paid its armies, and this that made its civilization shine with a light whose dazzling brilliance we can still glimpse in the Arabic texts. Little by little, the people of Ghana and their rulers felt the need for a strong government not only over themselves, but also over their neighbours, so that they could ensure peace and order throughout a wide region of the Western Sudan. For only in this way could they make the best use of their middleman position. And at the same time as they felt this need, they also had the chance of realising it. They were skilled workers in iron. They were able to use iron weapons against neighbours who generally had few or none.

As time passed, the ruling men of Ghana, the Soninke, people of the Mande language group, extended their political control. They strengthened their middleman position by bringing lesser states like Tekrur (in modern Senegal) under their sway. They pushed their borders southward in the direction of the land of the gold producers, and they also pushed their influence northward into the Sahara. They acquired authority over south-Saharan cities like Audaghost, one of those famous markets which has long since disappeared. In this way the emperors of Ghana wielded power, commanded wealth, and were numbered among the greatest men of their time.

Their system of government expanded with their success in trade. As it expanded, it became more complicated. A king and his counsellors could rule over a small country. They could not control a large one unless they could also rule through lesser kings and counsellors. Even with the swift horses of the Western Sudan, a king's orders would have gone too slowly through the land and would not have been obeyed. So the king of Ghana needed governors whom he could place in charge of distant provinces.

By this escalation of cause and effect there grew up a number of lesser governments (under lesser kings or governors) which all owed loyalty and paid taxes to a single central government. No doubt it was a crude and relatively haphazard system. Ordinary folk ran many dangers. They were often bullied or plundered. But the steady growth and conduct of trade over a wide region meant peace and security over a wide region; and many people of Ghana must have benefited from this. The formation of Ghana and its growth into a large empire may thus be said to have marked a decisive stage in social development, and to have signified a large political and economic achievement.

Revenue and wealth of Ghana

Before leaving this subject it will be helpful to look a little more closely at how these powerful kings ruled, maintained their public services, and met the costs of keeping law and order. For they established ways of government which were afterwards to appear again and again in the Western Sudan.

Where did King Tenkaminen and the emperors who

ruled before him find the wealth to maintain many soldiers, for example, and to feed and arm them? Where did they get the means to make rich gifts to strangers from other lands? Questions like these take us back to the economic system of the Ghana empire. And Al-Bakri, happily enough, helps us to the answers.

The ruler of Ghana, Al-Bakri tells us, had two main sources of revenue. These were taxes of two kinds. The first of these was what today we should call an import and export tax. This tax consisted of sums of money (or more probably their equal in goods) which traders had to pay for the right to bring goods into Ghana, or to take other goods out of the empire. "The king of Ghana," wrote Al-Bakri, "places a tax of one dinar of gold on each donkey-load of salt that comes into his country." But he also "places a tax of two dinars of gold on each load of salt that goes out." Similar taxes, higher or lower in value as the case might be, were applied to loads of copper and other goods.

The second kind of tax was a form of production tax. It was applied to gold, the most valuable of all the products of the country.

"All pieces of gold that are found in the empire," says Al-Bakri on this point, "belong to the emperor." But this regulation was more than a means of collecting royal wealth. It also appears to have been a way of keeping up the price of gold. If the emperor had not insisted on taking possession of all pieces of gold, Al-Bakri explains, then "gold would become so abundant as practically to lose its value."

Ancient Ghana, in short, adopted the monopoly system that is employed in our own times for another precious commodity, diamonds. Most diamonds are mined by a handful of big companies, which work hand-in-hand with each other and have agreed among themselves not to put all the diamonds they mine upon the market, for if they did, they would drive down the price. Instead, the diamond companies sell their diamonds in dribbles and trickles, according to the demand for them. And their price accordingly stays high. The old emperors of Ghana acted not too differently with regard to gold.

They were able to do this because of Ghana's strong trading position. West African gold was important to Europe as well as to North Africa and the Near East. In earlier times the Europeans had obtained the gold they needed, whether for money, ornaments, or the display of personal wealth, from mines in Europe or in western Asia, but these were becoming worked out at about the time of the rise of Ghana.

And so it came about that the gold used in North Africa and Europe was largely supplied, century after century, by the producers of West Africa. Even kings in distant England had to buy West African gold before they could order their craftsmen to make coins in this prince of metals. It was on this steady demand for gold that the states and empires of the Western Sudan founded their prosperity. West Africa's miners and prospectors, ore-crushers, goldsmiths and traders: these, first and foremost, were the men who made that prosperity possible.

Ghana began the trade in gold. As time went by, other peoples envied Ghana's success. When Ghana disappeared in the thirteenth century, its place was eventually taken by another great empire built on the same foundations and by much the same methods. This was the empire of Mali, even larger and more powerful than Ghana had ever been. Mali carried the organisational progress made under Ghana to a new level of development.

The fall of Ghana

Between the fall of Ghana and the triumph of Mali there occurred a long and puzzling interlude of political confusion.

In the eleventh century, Ghana was attacked by Berber warriors from the north-west, from the Mauretanian Sahara. These Berbers were hard and hungry folk driven by troubles of their own, mainly poverty, into striving for a share in the wealth of more prosperous neighbours. What seems initially to have set them on the move was an invasion of wandering Arabs who came westward into North Africa, looting cities and plundering farms. These Arabs defeated the Berbers and ruined much that they had built. The Berbers of the far west began to look for a new means of livelihood.

The solution they found, as so often in history, took a religious form. There arose among them a devout and characteristically severe Muslim leader called Abdullah ibn Yasin. He is said to have established himself on an island in the river Senegal, whence he began to preach a religious war against non-Muslims. He and those who followed him became known as the people of the hermitage, Al-Murabethin, or the Almoravids. Gradually, ibn Yasin brought the Berber communities of the far western lands under his authority. In 1056, moving northward into Morocco, the Almoravids captured the then great city of Sijilmasa. From there they went further to the north, eventually conquering the rest of Morocco and southern Spain.

Another wing of the Almoravid movement meanwhile marched against Ghana. Its leader, Abu Bakr, put himself at the head of a Berber confederation, made an alliance with the people of Tekrur, whom we shall discuss in a moment, and waged a long war against Ghana. In 1054 he took the city of Audaghost. In 1076, after many battles, the Almoravids were able to seize the capital of the empire.

But these invaders, like others after them, could not hold the West African lands they had taken. There were many revolts. Abu Bakr was killed while attempting to suppress one of these in 1087. By this time, however, the Ghana empire had fallen apart. Its emperor had authority over

only a few of its former provinces. Great changes were on
the way.

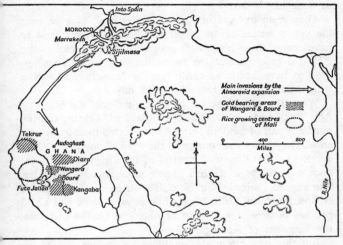

11   The Almoravid invasions

The successor states of Ghana

In this time of troubles, set in motion by the Almoravid
Berbers but soon drawing other peoples into action, a
number of smaller states strove for mastery over the frag-
ments of the old empire. One was the state of Tekrur. Another was Diara. A third was Kaniaga. In some of these,
a new name now enters on the scene, that of the Peul
(or Pullo in the singular) whom in English, following
Hausa usage, we call Fulani (or Fulah in the singular).

These Fulani were to make several big contributions to
West African history. The most dramatic of these will be
described later on. Meanwhile we should note that the

Fulani were and are a West African people of a somewhat
different physical stock from most of their neighbours, but
who spoke (and speak) a language related to the languages
of Senegal.

They seem to have originated in the lands that lie near
the upper waters of the Niger and Senegal rivers, and to
have shared these lands with peoples like the Soninke who
played a great part in the formation of Ghana. They appear to have begun as cattle-keeping farmers, and this is
what many of them remain to this day.

When the wide structure of Ghana suffered the blows of
Abu Bakr and his armies, the Fulani of Tekrur (in the
northern part of modern Senegal) reasserted their independence. They in turn set out upon the road of conquest. After
about A D 1200 they took control of the kingdom of Diara,
once a province of Ghana. Their most successful leader,
Sumanguru, seized Kumbi Saleh, then the capital of
Ghana, in about 1203. Meanwhile other Fulani and allied
peoples became powerful in another old Ghana province,
the kingdom of Kaniaga.

But this new attempt at building an empire out of the
ruins of Ghana met with no better fortune than the Berber
efforts led by Abu Bakr. Two developments brought
Sumanguru's enterprise to defeat. The first was that the
Muslim traders of Kumbi, Ghana's last capital, rejected
Sumanguru's overlordship. For reasons that were no doubt
partly religious and partly commercial, they quit Kumbi
and travelled northward, there to form a new trading centre at Walata, far beyond the reach of Sumanguru's soldiers. Secondly, in about 1240 or maybe a few years earlier,
Sumanguru was challenged by the Mandinka people of the
little state of Kangaba, near the headwaters of the river
Niger. The two armies fought each other at a famous battle at Kirina. Sumanguru was defeated and soon afterwards killed. His chiefs and generals retreated to Tekrur,
where they and their successors continued to rule for many
years.

Sumanguru's defeat opened a new chapter in history. For the little state of Kangaba was the heart and core of the future empire of Mali. It was to be the Mandinka peoples who would now bring peace and order to wide regions of the Western Sudan.

5 THE EMPIRE OF MALI

Kangaba

The old traditions of the Western Sudan suggest that Kangaba, the little state that was later to grow into the mighty empire of Mali, was founded some time before A D 1000. What is certain is that the Mandinka people of Kangaba were also middlemen in the gold trade during the later period of Ancient Ghana. They were important among those who carried northward the gold of Wangara and Bouré, the gold-bearing country that is now the northern part of the Republic of Guinea, to the market centres of Ghana. It is even very probable that it was through these gold-traders of Kangaba that the rulers of Ghana and their agents were able to secure their main supplies of gold.

In later times the traders of Mali, the Dyula or Wangara as they are still called, were to become famous for their skill and enterprise. There is reason to think that they were similarly active in the days of Ancient Ghana as well. It is likely that while Kangaba was a subject country of the Ghana empire, perhaps sending yearly gifts to its ruler in exchange for friendly protection against enemies and rivals, the traders of Kangaba enjoyed positions of privilege within the empire.

There was here a two-sided interest. The government of Ghana needed gold, and it was largely from Wangara that Ghana's gold had to come. But the traders who dealt in the gold of Wangara also needed a market, and it was above all in Ghana that they could find this market.

When the empire of Ghana was riven in pieces by attacks from without and revolts from within, this peaceful system of two-way interest was destroyed. All was then in the melting-pot of new rivalries for power. Eventually, as we have seen, Sumanguru prevailed. Once Sumanguru had mastered Kumbi and the main caravan routes, it was with him and his agents that the Mandinka of Kangaba had to conduct their business. Yet Sumanguru was never able to set up a firm and lasting system of law and order over the lands he had conquered. Others challenged his power. The caravan routes ceased to be safe and peaceful. And no doubt the people of Kangaba, whose livelihood was thus threatened and who were increasingly oppressed by Sumanguru, were troubled by all this. In about 1230, at any rate, they decided to enter the struggle themselves. They made a bid for independence; and they won.

Sundiata and Mansa Uli

The legends tell the story in more colourful and personal terms. They speak of Sumanguru's harsh taxation, of his bad government, of his seizure of Mandinka girls. These abuses caused the Mandinka to revolt. Fearing reprisals by Sumanguru, who had a frightening reputation for dangerous witchcraft, the ruler of Kangaba fled. But the situation was saved for him by a brother, Sundiata Keita, whom he had exiled. Returning from exile with an army which he had raised with the help of the ruler of the Meama, who lived near Lake Faguibine on the middle reaches of the Niger, Sundiata gathered friends and allies, increased his forces, gave them fresh heart and courage, and marched boldly against the dreaded Sumanguru.

"As Sundiata advanced with his army to meet Sumanguru," say the old legends, "he learned that Sumanguru was also coming against him with an army prepared for battle. They met in a place called Kirina [not far from the modern Kulikoro]. When Sundiata turned his eyes on the army of Sumanguru, he believed they were a cloud and he said: 'What is this cloud on the eastern side?' They told him it was the army of Sumanguru. As for Sumanguru, when he saw the army of Sundiata, he exclaimed: 'What is that mountain of stone?' For he thought it was a mountain. And they told him: 'It is the army of Sundiata, which lies to the west of us.'

"Then the two columns came together and fought a terrible battle. In the thick of the fight, Sundiata uttered a great shout in the face of the warriors of Sumanguru, and at once these ran to get behind Sumanguru. The latter, in his turn, uttered a great shout in the face of the warriors of Sundiata, all of whom fled to get behind Sundiata. Usually, when Sumanguru shouted, eight heads would rise above his own head."

But Sumanguru's witchcraft, the legends recall, proved less powerful than the witchcraft of Sundiata. Thanks to this, Sundiata prevailed. Sumanguru was struck with an arrow bearing the spur of a white cock, fatal to his power, and "Sumanguru vanished and was seen no more . . . [but] as for Sundiata, he defeated the army of Sumanguru, ravaged the land of the Susu [allies and subjects of Sumanguru], and subjugated its people. Afterwards Sundiata became the ruler of an immense empire . . ."

The capital of Kangaba at this time was at a place called Niani, a city that has long since disappeared but was located near the river Niger, not far from the frontier of modern Guinea and modern Mali. And from about this time the name "Mali," which meant "where the king resides," generally absorbed the name Kangaba, and the empire of Mali was born.

Sundiata, who founded this empire by winning the independence of Kangaba and then extending its power beyond Kangaba's narrow frontiers, was by no means the first ruler of his dynasty. The founder of this line of kings is called Barmandana in the traditions. He is said to have ruled in about 1050, though little or nothing is known about him and the date must be taken with reserve. Dyigui-Bilali ruled in the second half of the twelfth century, and was followed by Musa Keita who was in turn followed by Nare

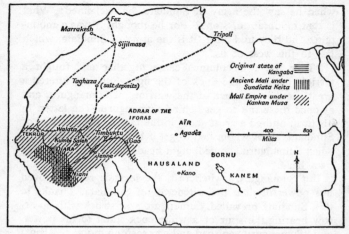

12   The expansion of the empire of Mali

Fameghan; but all these, unlike Sundiata, are misty figures.

Sundiata (sometimes known as Mari Diata) came to the throne in about 1230 and reigned until about 1255. He was succeeded by Mansa Uli (1255–70), who followed in the conquering path of his great predecessor. Under these kings Mali secured or regained control of the gold-producing lands of Wangara and Bambuk, invaded and subjected most of Diara to the north-west, pushed its influence down the course of the Niger to the shores of Lake Deba, and emerged as the true imperial successor of Ghana.

Mansa Kankan Musa

But having gone as far as this, the rulers and armies of Mali went further still. The great political problem in the western region of the Western Sudan was how to bring peace and order into the confusion which had followed on the collapse of Ghana. The problem was tackled, and largely solved, by a Mali emperor whose name became more famous even than that of Sundiata. This was Mansa Kankan Musa, who carried Mali to the height of its power and thrust its fame far across the world.

Mansa Musa came to power in about 1312. By the time of his death, in 1337, Mali had grown into one of the largest empires in the world.* What Mansa Musa did was to repeat the success of Ghana on a still more ambitious scale. He already had firm control of the trading routes to the gold lands of the south, as well as some authority within those lands. Now he brought the lands of the middle Niger under his control, and enclosed the key trading cities Timbuktu and Gao within his empire. He imposed his rule on southern Saharan trading cities like Walata, and pushed his armies northward until their influence was felt as far as the salt deposits of Taghaza on the other side of the desert. He sent them eastward beyond Gao to the very frontiers of Hausaland, westward into Tekrur and the lands of the Fulani and Tucolor, and brought those countries, too, under his dominion.

Through twenty-five successful years Mansa Musa progressively enclosed a large part of the central and western regions of the Western Sudan within a single system of law and order. He did this so well that Ibn Batuta, travelling through Mali some twelve years after the great emperor's death, could find "complete and general safety in the land." It was a grand political success, and it made Mansa Musa into one of the greatest statesmen of his time.

The Dyula or Wangara traders of Kangaba grew in strength with the widening power of Mali. Their trading groups began to spread into many parts of West Africa,

* The year of Musa's death is often given as 1332. But the great North African historian, Ibn Khaldun, whose writings remain the best source of information on the dates of the rulers of Mali, has recorded that Musa was still alive in 1337.

pushing their enterprises far down into the forest lands as well as across the plains of the north.

This was also a period of large Islamic expansion in the Western Sudan. Unlike the rulers of Ghana, Mansa Musa had accepted the new religion. Many lesser rulers followed him. So did some of their peoples. Other rulers and peoples remained loyal to their own religions, but Islam steadily widened its influence. More and more West Africans went on pilgrimage to Mecca. More and more Arabs and Egyptians came to visit Mali. Trade and Islam grew together, and both prospered.

Mansa Musa himself made a famous pilgrimage to Mecca in 1324. His magnificent journey through the Egyptian capital of Cairo was long remembered with admiration and surprise throughout Egypt and Arabia, for Musa took with him so much gold, and gave away so many golden gifts, that "the people of Cairo earned incalculable sums" thanks to his visit. So lavish was Musa with his gifts, indeed, that he upset the value of goods on the Cairo market. Gold became more plentiful and therefore less valued, and prices accordingly rose. The North African scholar Al-Omari, who lived in Cairo a few years after Mansa Musa's visit and wrote the words just quoted, declared that of all the Muslim rulers of West Africa Musa was "the most powerful, the richest, the most fortunate, the most feared by his enemies and the most able to do good to those around him." Behind these words of praise one may glimpse the power and reputation that Mali drew from its control of a very wide region of trade in precious goods such as gold, salt, ivory, and kola nuts.

Mali was now a world power, and recognised as such. Under Mansa Musa, Mali ambassadors and royal agents were established in Morocco, Egypt, and elsewhere. Mali's capital was visited by North African and Egyptian scholars. On returning from pilgrimage, Mansa Musa brought back with him a number of learned men from Egypt. These settled in Mali and Timbuktu. One of them, called As-Saheli, is said to have designed new mosques at Gao and Timbuktu, and built a palace for the emperor. The fashion of building houses in brick now began to be popular among wealthy people in the cities of the Western Sudan.

Niani, the capital of all this empire, has long since disappeared. Yet as late as the sixteenth century, the Moroccan traveller Leo Africanus could still describe it as a place of "six thousand hearths," and its inhabitants as "the most civilised, intelligent, and respected" of all the peoples of the Western Sudan.

Decline of Mali

But the very success of this far-reaching empire was also a reason for its decline. The onward movement of civilisation, the spread of metal-working and of trade, the growth of the ideas of kingship and of strong central government, the pressures of wealth and commercial rivalry—all these and similar influences stirred many peoples in West Africa. Some of these saw that there were new advantages in being free to run their own affairs. The ruler and people of the city of Gao, for example, who had to pay taxes to the emperor of Mali, became determined to be rid of these taxes. They believed they could do better on their own, and others thought the same.

The truth seems to have been that Mali had outgrown its political and military strength. Only supremely skilful leadership at the centre could now hold these far-flung provinces together. Mansa Musa had possessed that skill. His successors, generally, did not.

Yet Mali remained a powerful empire until soon after 1400. Then it ran into a host of troubles. Gao rebelled. The Tuareg of the southern Sahara, always hoping to win control of the market cities of the Western Sudan, seized Walata and even Timbuktu. The peoples of Tekrur and its neighbouring lands, notably the Woloff, threw off the con-

trol of Mali. Others in the south-western region of the empire, especially the Mossi in what is now the modern Republic of Upper Volta, began to harass the emperor's
governors and garrisons. Later on, after the Portuguese arrival on the West African coast, a ruler of Mali appealed
to them for help, though in vain. By about 1550 Mali had
ceased to exist as a state of any importance.

The peoples of western Guinea

This is the place to say a few words about the early history
of the peoples who now occupy the lands of western Senegal, Gambia, the Portuguese colony of Guinea, Sierra
Leone, and Liberia.

Most of these peoples lived at what was then the back
door of West Africa. Their lands mostly lay outside the
big political changes and developments of the Western Sudan. South of them there was nothing but the empty ocean,
crossed then by no ships from other continents. We may
imagine that they lived quiet lives, keeping to their ancient
ways, warring with each other from time to time as one or
other of them began to look for new land to cultivate, but
generally content with their ancestral methods of social and
political organisation.

Adapted already to Iron Age ways, these people had developed their own farming and fishing, their own skills in
metal-working, their own arts of dance and music and
sculpture. They had also evolved methods of living together
with a minimum of friction or conflict. But their early history is obscure. Deep in their forests, safe in their steep
valleys, they remained on the margin of the busy world.

Western Senegal, where there are no forests or steep
valleys, made an exception. The peoples who lived there
were always influenced by the clash and conflict in the
neighbouring plains of the Western Sudan. Tekrur, lying
along the south bank of the Senegal river, was part of

Ghana. Afterwards it was part of Mali. Later again, its peoples regained their freedom of action. Towards A D 1300, a people moving westward from the Sudan formed the state and then the empire of the Woloff. Mingling with the Serer, already in the land, they became an important people; and they have remained one to this day. They formed three big provinces or states: Walo, Cayor, and Baol. Pushed back by the Woloff, some of the Serer moved south again, collided with a branch of the Mande-speaking peoples, went further on, and founded the small kingdom of Sine-Solum along the north bank of the Gambia river.

Not much later, the Susu people came into conflict with

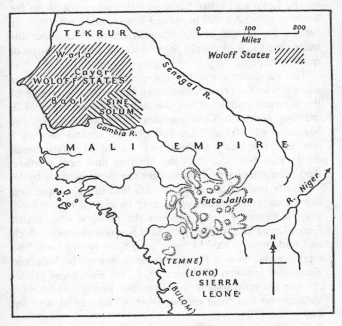

13 The peoples of western Guinea

the Fulani, with whom they had sometimes been friendly, and formed a state of their own in Futa Jallon, the hilly region that lies in the centre of the modern Republic of Guinea. Other Susu moved on down to the coast, where most of them live now, while a branch of the Fulani won control of Futa Jallon, where they have likewise remained until the present day.

These scattered facts may suggest an impression of constant movement and collision. Yet it is useful to remember that all these events were spread across many years. There will have been long interludes of peace and quiet.

In Sierra Leone, the Baga, Temne, and Gola peoples were joined by the Kissi and the Bulom, and afterwards by the Loko and other Mande-speaking peoples along the Scarcies river. All this happened before, and probably long before, the middle of the fifteenth century. At about the same time the Kru people became strong along the coast of modern Liberia.

This relatively uneventful life along the coast, and on the islands near the coast, came to an end after the middle of the fifteenth century. Then the ships of Europe arrived in growing numbers. Their captains began knocking on the backdoor of Africa. They brought the coastal peoples a new and previously undreamt-of chance of international trade. But they also brought firearms and new warfare. And soon afterwards they brought the overseas slave trade.

This is not yet the place to look into the consequences. But an early European report may be quoted briefly here, since it throws a sharp light on the political situation of Sierra Leone in about 1500; and this was a situation which had undoubtedly existed for a long time before that. The report comes from a Portuguese book written by Valentim Fernandes between 1506 and 1510, but Fernandes probably got his information from another Portuguese, Alvaro Velho, who had lived on the West African coast between 1499 and 1507.

Fernandes makes it clear that small states had already

emerged along the Sierra Leone coast. He mentions villages which had kings of their own, and explains that these kings also had counsellors. "If the king wants to go to war, he gathers the elders and holds his council. And if it appears to them that the war is unjust, or that the enemy is very strong, they tell the king that they cannot help him, and give orders for peace in spite of the king's disagreement."

This early report also shows that some people were not only more powerful than others, but also more prosperous. "The houses of the poor are made of stakes stuck in the ground, hardened with mud and covered with thatch. [But] the houses of the rich are made of hardened clay and brick, well whitewashed in the interior, and outside covered with chalk or white clay, and the interior is very well adorned, and these are the best houses in all Guinea." This dividing-up of society into people of differing power and wealth is a point of central importance, and one to which we shall return in Chapter 12.

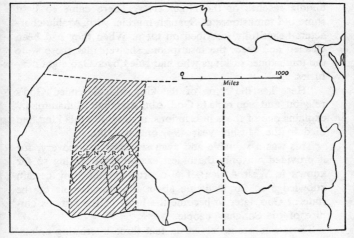

14 The central region

6 THE CENTRAL REGION

In this section we embark upon the early history of the peoples of the central region of the Western Sudan and Guinea, remembering, once again, that it is a geographical division which is only for the convenience of study. Much of the central region was in fact part of the empires of Ghana and Mali, or felt their influence.

Rise of the empire of Songhay

In 1939 an important archaeological discovery was made at the village of Sané, near the ancient city of Gao on the

middle reaches of the Niger river. There came to light
some old tombstones of Spanish marble, with Arabic characters beautifully inscribed on them. When they had been
cleaned and read, the inscriptions showed that these were
the tombstones of kings who had ruled over Gao eight centuries ago.

"Here lies the tomb of the king who defended God's
religion, and who rests in God, Abu Abdallah Muhammad,"
explains one of these inscriptions, adding that this king had
died in the Muslim year 494, or A D 1100.

This was a valuable and even sensational discovery, for
it provided not only the oldest examples of writing so far
known in West Africa: it also provided the only certain
knowledge so far available about the foundations of the
state of Gao, later to become the heart of the famous empire of the Songhay people.

These tombstones reveal in fact three interesting points.
They show that Gao, by the eleventh century, was prosperous and strong enough to have become a state ruled over by
its own kings. They prove that its kings had accepted Islam.
And they indicate that Gao had extensive trading links with
North Africa, for the tombstones in question had been
brought from Muslim Spain.

Evidence provided by the oral or traditional history of
Gao, as it has come down to us by way of the books of
seventeenth-century writers in Timbuktu, does not always
agree with the evidence of the tombstones. The actual
names of the kings on the tombstones are not the same as
the names remembered by oral traditions. Otherwise the
traditions greatly help to expand the three certain points
that are proved by the tombstones. They show that Gao
became a southern centre for the trans-Saharan trade in
early times, and that Gao, lying at the southern end of a
major trans-Saharan trade route, had long since become a
state on its own.

The traditions also suggest that Songhay established
themselves at Gao at the beginning of the seventh century,

pushing out the Sorko people who already lived there. But
Gao was not yet their capital; this was at Kukya, further
to the east, where their dias or kings ruled. These Songhay
were enterprising traders and welcomed Lemtuna (Berber)
travelling merchants from the Adrar oases to the north of
them. Through these Saharan merchants the caravan trade
with the Songhay market-centres prospered and grew.

At the beginning of the eleventh century—and this is
where the tombstones once again support the traditions—
the ruling Songhay king, whose title and name were Dia
Kossoi,* was converted to Islam. According to tradition,
this happened in 1010. Soon after this, the capital of Songhay was transferred from Kukya to Gao, and Gao entered
upon its period of growth. Just why Dia Kossoi accepted
Islam, and with how much sincerity, there is no means of
knowing. But probably he saw in his conversion a useful
way of gaining more influence with the Berber traders, who
were all Muslims, upon whose caravan skills he and his
people greatly relied for their trade. Like other Muslim
kings in the Western Sudan, then and later, Dia Kossoi and
his successors tried not to let their acceptance of Islam become offensive to their own people, who generally continued to believe in their own religions. Dia Kossoi was apparently careful to maintain court customs which were not
Muslim.

Many dias ruled after Kossoi. Gao began to expand its
power beyond the lands immediately round the city. One
reason for this was that the value and size of the trans-
Saharan trade were growing all this time. This growth increased the power and importance of Gao, whose position
was very favourable for trade.

Three hundred years after Dia Kossoi's reign, Gao became so wealthy and attractive that the great Mali ruler,

* The traditions, as recorded in the seventeenth-century *Tarikh
al-Sudan,* written in Timbuktu, claim that Dia Kossoi was the
fifteenth of the dia line.

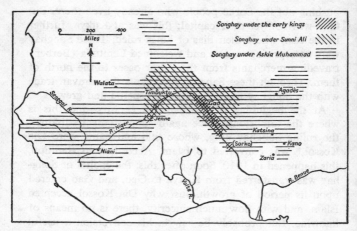

15   The expansion of the empire of Songhay

Mansa Musa, sent out his generals and armies to bring it
within the Mali empire. Apart from the wealth of Gao, it is
easy to understand why Mansa Musa should have done
this. He and his governors already commanded the southern
end of all the caravan routes across the western region of
the Sahara. By securing Gao as well as Timbuktu, they
could command the southern end of the routes across the
central region as well. In this way, as one may think, they
enormously strengthened the whole system of tax-collecting
on which the government of Mali depended for its revenues.

But this system, as we have noted, was too wide for
Mali's strength. It could not last. And Mali's overlordship
of Gao endured in fact only for some fifty years. In about
1335 the dia line came to an end and gave way to a new
line, whose title was sunni or shi. The second sunni, whose
name is given in the traditions as Suleiman-Mar, won back
Gao's independence from Mali in about 1375. Nearly a
century of varying fortunes then followed for the people of

Gao. After that they entered another period of expansion. Having defended themselves from their neighbours and rivals, they themselves began to push far outward on the path of conquest.

This expansion was especially the work of an outstanding military and political leader whose title and name were Sunni Ali. Like other great rulers before and after him in the Western Sudan, Sunni Ali came to power in a time of confusion and set out to build a large and unified system of law and order, central government, and peaceful trade.

It was Sunni Ali who was the true founder of the Songhay empire. He came to the throne in 1464. Before he died in about 1492, the narrow boundaries of the state of Gao were thrust boldly outward into a large and many-peopled community of states, and Songhay now rivalled the size and importance of Mali.

Even so the story of Songhay expansion had only begun. Sunni Ali was followed by Sunni Baru, who ruled for little more than a year and was then ousted by a man whose achievements were to overshadow those of Sunni Ali. This was the renowned Askia Muhammad, later known as Askia the Great, who began his triumphant career in 1493 and ruled for thirty-six momentous years.*

We shall come back to Askia Muhammad, and also to Sunni Ali, at a later point in this book. Now it is time to look at another aspect of this long period of growth in the Western Sudan: the rise of the great business cities of Timbuktu and Jenne.

Timbuktu and Jenne

Timbuktu today is a small and dusty town of no distinction. Certainly it was small and dusty when it was founded

* The title of *askia* derived from a military rank in the Songhay army.

about eight hundred years ago. But then its importance was very great, for Timbuktu became one of the wealthiest markets of West Africa, famous far and wide for its trade and for the learning of its scholars. Rising to importance a good deal later than its western sister-cities—Kumbi and Tekrur, Audaghost and others—Timbuktu long outlived and overtopped them. Here at the most northerly point of the Niger river there grew up a city that was deeply involved in commerce with both north and south.

By the fourteenth century, when Mansa Musa brought As-Saheli back from Mecca and ordered him to build new mosques and palaces, Timbuktu was well established as a trading city of key importance.

Yet it never became the centre of an important state, much less of an empire. In this it differed from Gao. One main reason for this difference probably lay in Timbuktu's geographical position. Well placed for the caravan trade, it was badly situated to defend itself from the Tuareg raiders of the Sahara. These restless nomads were repeatedly hammering at the gates of Timbuktu, and often enough they burst them open with disastrous results for the inhabitants. Life here was never quite safe enough to recommend it as the centre of a big state. Even in Mansa Musa's time, when peace and order spread widely across the Western Sudan, Timbuktu never became a central point of government within the empire.

The political record underlines this special geographical weakness of Timbuktu. From 1325 until 1433 it was part of the Mali empire. Then the Tuareg had it for a few years. In 1458 it was enclosed within the growing Songhay empire, where it remained until Moroccans invaded Songhay in 1591. These Moroccans, whose invasion we shall consider in its place, ruled over Timbuktu until about 1780, although for most of this time they were no more than a weak ruling class within the city, half-merged with the local population and often cut off from their original homeland. Then the Tuareg again had command of the city for a time, being followed in their overlordship by Fulani rulers in 1826, who in turn were followed by Tuculor chiefs (1862–63), again by the Tuareg (1863–93), finally by the French colonial invaders (1863–1960). Today, Timbuktu is a small city of the modern Republic of Mali.

But this political record would be misleading if it suggested that Timbuktu failed to enjoy long periods of peace and prosperous trade. On the contrary, the arts of peace and scholarship, of writing, theology, and the development of law, all flourished here and flourished greatly. These developments will be considered later.

Another of the great historical cities of the Western Sudan, Jenne, seems to have been founded, like Timbuktu, soon after the eleventh century, although there was probably a trading settlement here in still earlier times. But the history of Jenne is not the same as that of Timbuktu. An important difference lies between them.

Both were big trading centres. Timbuktu, like Gao and ancient Kumbi and Tekrur, was a middleman city between the traders of the Western Sudan and those of the Sahara and North Africa. But Jenne, by contrast, was a middleman city between the traders of the Western Sudan (especially of Timbuktu) and the traders of the forest lands to the south. It was through Jenne, at least after about 1400, that the gold and other goods of the forest lands passed increasingly to the caravan-traders who were waiting for these goods in Timbuktu and other southern "ports." And it was through Jenne that the goods of North Africa increasingly reached southward into the forest lands.

This special importance of Jenne was associated with the spread and activities of the Mandinka traders of Mali, the Dyula or Wangara trading companies, who pushed down into the forest lands and settled there as buying-and-selling agents, just as the Berber traders of the Sahara, further north, had settled in towns like Kumbi and Timbuktu and Gao.

These Dyula traders, each group or company united un-

der its Dyula-Mansa* by common language, Islam, and
experience, were a vital link between the gold-producing
forest lands and the whole great trading network of the
Western Sudan and North Africa. They dealt in many
things besides gold, notably in kola nuts. All their trade
passed back and forth through markets such as Jenne. The
long-established existence of this north-south trade within
West Africa is one important reason why it is entirely
wrong to think of the forest lands as being cut off, in ancient times, from the grassland plains to the north of them.
For the goods were carried by men, and were bought and
sold by men; and all these men met and talked, discussed
and exchanged ideas, and influenced one another through
many centuries.

Unlike Timbuktu and Gao, Jenne retained its independence until the end of the fifteenth century, though without
ever trying to become a large state or empire. One reason
for its safety from conquest lay in its powerful defensive
position. For much of every year, Jenne was encircled by
the flood waters of the Niger river, as indeed it still is today. Its inhabitants also built high protecting walls round
their city, somewhat like those that may still be seen at
Kano, and proved able to defend them. They were helped
by the fact that their southern neighbours were also independent of the big empires.

The Mossi states

These southern neighbours were peoples who lived in a
cluster of states between the great northward bend of the
Niger river—the region of Jenne and Timbuktu—and the
forest lands of Asante and Togo.

These states were never brought within the imperial systems of Mali or Songhay. They conducted a vigorous and

* Also known as Shehu-Wangara by Hausa-speaking people.

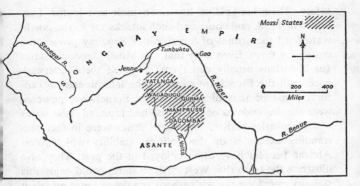

16   The Mossi states

independent life of their own. Often they were a danger to their prosperous northern neighbours, for they raided north-ward and north-westward with strong forces of cavalry. After about 1400, too, they began to act as intermediaries in the trade between the forest lands and the cities of the Niger.

Little is known of their origins. As in many other cases, the Mossi traditions speak of ancestors who came from the east, perhaps in the thirteenth century. There is some ground for believing that these incoming ancestors were re-lated to the Hausa peoples, and came originally from the region of Lake Chad. But they came a long time ago, if they came at all, and the Mossi of today are mainly the descendants of the Gur-speaking peoples who have lived in this country since very ancient times.

In the course of time, five principal states were to emerge. They were the states of Wagadugu, Yatenga, Fada-n-Gurma, Mamprussi, and Dagomba. All became strong before 1500. The territory of these states now lies within the modern republics of Upper Volta and Ghana.

The Mossi were never enclosed within the Mali empire, and were consequently a frequent peril to its wealth and

safety. Their hard-riding horsemen took and looted Timbuktu in 1338, and continued such attacks far to the northward until the armies of Sunni Ali of Songhay proved too
strong for them. Even after that, the Mossi-Dagomba states
(as historians usually call them) retained their independence until the French invasions of the late nineteenth century. Some of the rulers whom the French overpowered
were the descendants of those who had founded these states
many centuries earlier. The Mossi states were in fact outstanding examples of the political stability which West
African peoples have often enjoyed in the past. They also
illustrate the truth that West African states could enjoy this
stability over long periods without any dependence on Islam
or on Muslim ways of thought and government. For the
Mossi rejected all efforts to convert them to Islam, and remained staunchly true to their traditional religions.

Development of the central region of Guinea

We must now turn back for a moment from the details of
our story, and consider how the peoples of Guinea, of the
forest and coastal lands of West Africa, grew and developed in early times.

They evolved differently from their neighbours who lived
in the open plains of the north. Their country has dense
forests, much wider in those times than they are today, steep
hills, deep valleys, many rivers, heavy rainfall. These and
other contrasts raised different problems for everyday life,
politics and government.

The peoples of Guinea solved these problems with skill
and perseverance. They learned how to grow food in dense
forests. Even to this day their old farming methods have
scarcely been improved, although the coming of cocoa and
other new crops has greatly extended and developed these
methods. They discovered how to find where metals lay in

the earth, and how to mine and work these metals. They built up their own systems of community life and government, sometimes very different from the systems of the grassland plains, occasionally very much the same.

Some time around the twelfth century, central Guinea entered a new stage of development. New patterns began to be woven into what we have called the cloth of history. They were the product of interplay between the peoples who already lived in Guinea and new ideas and influences moving in from the Western Sudan.

New states were formed. New alliances of states came into being. There occurred a vast and complicated movement of peoples; although, as we have seen, the actual number of migrating groups may never have been large. It is to this obscure shifting round of populations that one may trace the traditional beliefs of so many peoples in Guinea that their ancestors came from somewhere else.

At some point around the twelfth or thirteenth century, it seems, the incoming ancestors of the Akan peoples of modern Ghana and the Ivory Coast began moving into their present homelands. They appear to have come from the north, from the grassland plains of the Western Sudan. Perhaps they moved in order to escape the chaos and confusion which had followed on the collapse of Ancient Ghana, perhaps they were discontented with their treatment in the rising empire of Mali.

These incoming ancestors intermarried and merged with the peoples whom they found. By about 1200, if not before, the Akan were already beginning to settle in the lands to the north of the forest, in northern Asante* and the grassland country beyond, while others had pushed further south. These others moved towards the coast along the banks of the Volta river, or, later on, directly through the tall forest. They were formed in different clans and groups and peoples, and were the founders of the later

* Ashanti in English usage.

states of Denkyira, Adansi, Fante, Akwamu, and many others.

Much the same movement and settlement brought Ivory Coast peoples like the Senufu to their present homelands.

Bono-Manso

Among early states, there was Bono in the Takyiman area. A little more is known about it than about the others, for it was through Bono that the principal trade with the states and empires of the Western Sudan—and thence, through many hands, with North Africa and Europe—became important. Here in Bono the Mandinka traders of Mali, the Dyula, made their base in central Guinea.

Bono traditions indicate that it was founded by a strong chief or king called Asaman, who is said to have reigned between about 1295 and 1325, and by his queen-mother Amayaa, who is said to have reigned between about 1297 and 1329. But the present view of scholars is that these traditional dates are too early and that this new political system in the Takyiman region was really founded in about 1400.

Asaman and Amayaa built their first capital at Tutena,* not far from the present town of Nkoranza, but soon moved to a new capital a few miles further west. This they called Bono-Manso, the town of the land of Bono; and it was here that they settled. Other Akan states emerged in this region. Some of them came under the sway of Bono-Manso. Thus the king of Bono became a king of kings. He became, even if in a small way, an emperor. Bono traditions celebrate this achievement. Those who recite them still sing: "Ahene mu ahene owura, daseansa!" King of Kings, to you above all, everlasting thanks!

It is important to note why these early Akan states were

* In Akan, Tutena means "a new settlement."

small. They were formed in dense forest country. There was no chance of building big states or empires which could be controlled by fast-moving bands of cavalry. Movement was difficult. Political authority could not stretch very far, at least in those early days. Later on, with the expansion of political ideas and trade, this would change. In the eighteenth century, the Asante empire would include nearly all of modern Ghana, together with some of the Ivory Coast and Togo as well. But this kind of development was still in the future.

The traditions of early Bono also tell us something else of key interest. They say that gold was discovered in the Twi river and around Perembomase during Asaman's reign, and that this discovery led to a new prosperity and to social progress. The truth behind this particular tradition is no doubt rather different. Gold was almost certainly discovered in this area long before Asaman's reign, but it was probably not much worked. Now, soon after 1400, there came a stronger demand for gold from the Western Sudan, itself responding to a bigger demand from North Africa and Europe. This led the Dyula traders to travel south in search of gold, and it was offered to them in Bono. So the founding of Bono was partly the result of a growth in the gold trade. Once again, new ways of earning a livelihood went hand-in-hand with new methods of political organisation.

Bono continued to be an important state until much later times.

Along the coast of modern Ghana

The earliest peoples whom we can identify near and along the coast of central Guinea are those who formed their states, and their traditions, in the fifteenth and sixteenth centuries. These are the early states of the Fante and other Akan peoples, of the Nzima to their west and of the Ga-Adangme and Ewe to their east.

Although the coastal peoples of this early period were probably few in number, they were not without resources. They lived at what was then the backdoor of Guinea, faced with the empty ocean, but they evolved a stable way of life, and they also developed good relations with their inland neighbours. When Portuguese sailors first arrived on the coast of Guinea in the 1470s, they found people who were quite ready to trade with them. What is more, they also found Mandinka traders who had come from the inland empire of Mali. We have records of how the Portuguese were first received at Elmina. There, in 1482, they asked for permission to build a castle, and this permission they eventually received from the chief of the Elmina district, whose name is given in the Portuguese records as Caramansa. Some scholars have also seen in this word Caramansa a sign of Mandinka-Dyula presence on the coast of modern Ghana in the fifteenth century. They point out that the second part of the word is the same as the Mandinka word mansa, king or chief. It seems more likely, however, that Caramansa may only be a mistaken way of writing Kwamina Ansah, a name borne by several later rulers of Elmina.

Here is how the Portuguese of 1482 described their meeting with Caramansa at Elmina. "He was seated on a high chair dressed in a jacket of brocade, with a golden collar of precious stones, and his chiefs were all dressed in silk . . . These noblemen wore rings and golden jewels on their heads and beards. Their king, Caramansa, came [towards the Portuguese] in their midst, his legs and arms covered with golden bracelets and rings, a collar round his neck, from which hung some small bells, and in his plaited beard golden bars, which weighed down its untrimmed hair, so that instead of being twisted it was smooth. To impress his dignity, he walked with very slow and light steps, never turning his face to either side.

"While he was approaching with this solemnity, Diogo de Azambuja [the Portuguese captain] remained very quietly

on his little platform until, when Caramansa was among
the Portuguese, he went to meet him. Caramansa took the
hand of Diogo de Azambuja, and letting it go again,
snapped his fingers saying 'bere bere,' which means 'peace,
peace.' This snapping of the fingers is a sign among them
of the greatest courtesy that can be offered . . ."

The Portuguese went on to describe Kwamina Ansah as
a man "of good understanding, both by nature and by his
dealing with the crews of the trading ships, and he possessed
a clear judgment. And as one who greatly desired to understand what was proposed to him, he not only listened to the
translation of the interpreter, but watched each gesture
made by Diogo de Azambuja; and while this continued,
both he and his men were completely silent; no one as
much as spat, so perfectly disciplined were they . . ."

These words imply much about the organisation of the
small states along the coast of central Guinea in the fifteenth century. They had chiefs and counsellors, orderly
government, firm rules of public behaviour, trade with their
neighbours and trade with the interior. Though distant from
the great centres of political and economic development
of those days, they must be seen as an integral part of West
Africa's developing civilisation.

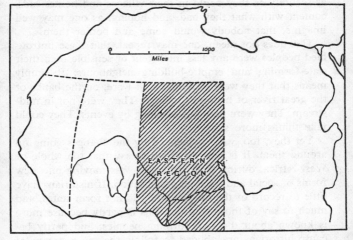

17　The eastern region

7 THE EASTERN REGION I

The socio-political development of the eastern region between A D 1000 and 1500 reflects that of its western neighbours, especially in relation to the more important structures, those of Kanem-Bornu and the Hausa states. Here, too, we find a steady crystallisation of systematic power at the centre, and the emergence of new forms.

Not all the populations of West Africa, however, were drawn to the same extent into new forms of social life and government. Many peoples of the grassland country, like many people of the forest lands, went on living much as they had lived before, knowing and caring little of the world beyond the reach of their pastures or farms, living as securely as they could in their villages and homesteads, content with what they had, and hoping, as one may well imagine, that nobody would come and bother them.

This does not mean, one may repeat, that these untroubled peoples were any less intelligent or sensible than their state-forming and empire-building neighbours. It simply means that they were standing, as it were, on the banks of the great river of historical change. They were not in midstream. They were not whirled along by events. They could take things more slowly.

Yet they, too, were influenced by the changes going on around them. It is not too much to say that the whole of West Africa, during these centuries, was moving into new forms of social and political organisation. If historians have little to record of the peoples who did not form states, and much to say of those who did, this is partly because more is known about the state-forming peoples, and partly because historians are obliged to follow the main stream of political and social change.

The empire of Kanem-Bornu

The ancient and powerful empire of Kanem-Bornu was as important for the eastern region of the Western Sudan as were the empires of Ghana and Mali for the western and central regions.

Its earliest beginnings, like those of Ghana, are veiled in the shadows of a distant past. Probably they may be placed soon after A D 800. Then it was that four or five early states, including those of the Kanuri and Zaghawa peoples, appeared in the neighbourhood of Lake Chad.

Here, as elsewhere, the trade between West Africa and North Africa proved important for political as well as for commercial reasons. For economics and politics always go hand in hand; and here, to the east and west of the great lake, there lay a vital crossroads of trade.

In these lands around Lake Chad were situated the southern market-centres of the trans-Saharan trade not only with Libya and Tunisia in the far north, but also with Nubia on the middle Nile and Egypt to the far north-east. These markets were likewise valuable for all goods going north from the lands of eastern Guinea which lie in southern Nigeria today.

So the little states of the Chad region, like the large empire into which they grew, faced southward towards eastern Guinea, north-eastward through the hills of Darfur to the distant Nile, and northward by way of the Bilma oasis and the settlements of Aïr to Libya, Tunisia, and Egypt. This key position did much to shape the fortunes of Kanem-Bornu. Its rulers were nearly always in touch with North Africa, with the peoples of the Nile, and with their neighbours in the south and west.

The royal traditions of Kanem-Bornu have a good deal to say about early times. Like other royal traditions, they

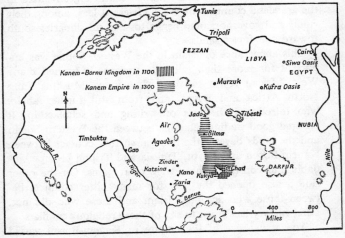

18 The early expansion of the Kanem-Bornu empire

have two disadvantages. They are not exact. And they tell little or nothing of how ordinary folk lived and worked. All the same, they form a broad and useful guide to the main political events.

The early empire of Kanem, reaching some way to the east as well as to the west of Lake Chad, came into being under a line of kings belonging to the Sefuwa family. This dynasty held power from about A D 850. Two centuries later, in 1086, there came an important change. A Sefuwa king called Hume, later known as Ibn 'Abd al-Jelil, accepted Islam as his own religion and that of his court. From this time onwards the Sefuwa kings and emperors of Kanem-Bornu, who continued to rule for another eight hundred years, were always Muslims.

This happened, we may recall, at about the same time as the Almoravid Muslims were battering at the cities of non-Muslim Ghana, and not long after Dia Kossoi of Gao had likewise accepted Islam.* It was indeed during the eleventh century that Islam made its first big advances in the grassland countries of West Africa, at least among their rulers and governors, and began to send missionaries south toward the forest lands.

This appearance of Islam in the Western Sudan was important for more than religious reasons. It opened many West African states to the influence of Muslims from North Africa and Egypt, and from still further afield, who introduced the arts of writing and scholarship. It ensured good trading relations between the Western Sudan and the lands beyond the Sahara, so that contact between Kanem-Bornu and Egypt, Tunisia and Tripoli became valuable and constant. These were clear gains. On the other side it also opened the way for many bitter conflicts between those who accepted Islam and those who did not. Later history has much to say of these religious conflicts.

The actual size of the empire of Kanem-Bornu varied

* See page 66.

with time and fortune, as did all these systems. Its central
or metropolitan people were the Kanuri, just as the Mandinka were the metropolitan people of Mali and the Songhay the metropolitan people of the empire of that name.
The Kanuri lived then, as later, around Lake Chad. But
they had, of course, no frontiers in the modern sense of
the word. Their kings made alliances with neighbouring
rulers. When the kings were strong enough to do so, they
forced these neighbouring rulers to pay tax and obey their
orders. But like other kings of those times, the rulers of
Kanem were not dictators. They were not all-powerful.
They had to listen to the advice and opinions of their
lesser kings, chiefs, and counsellors. Within Kanem itself,
they generally drew their power from a great council of
leaders of the Sefuwa family. This council consisted of
about a dozen principal governors who reigned over different parts of the empire. These ruling men had titles
which were in use for many centuries. Some of the titles,
like *galadima* and *chiroma,* are still used today in northern
Nigeria.

Firmly based in Bornu and around Lake Chad, sometimes at war and sometimes at peace with the Hausa kingdoms to the west of them, the lords of Kanem usually
faced their greatest difficulties in the east. Here they met
with energetic peoples, notably the Bulala, who resisted
their rule; and the extent of the Kanem empire shrank or
expanded according to their failure or success in mastering
these easterly peoples by means of diplomacy or war.

But whether large or small, according to the stress and
shift of events, the success of the empire of Kanem can be
compared to that of Ancient Ghana, while it was perhaps
even greater than the empires of Mali or Songhay, if only
because it lasted longer. What the Kanuri and their allies
and subjects were able to do, over a very long period and
in a region of great importance, was to bring the advantages of a single system of law and order to a great many
different peoples. And it was through this large empire that

West Africa kept in regular touch with vital centres of
civilisation beyond the Sahara, especially Egypt. It was
through Kanem that the goods of Egypt and other northern
lands, horses and fine metalware, salt and copper, came
into West Africa by way of the eastern Sahara; and it was
often through Kanem that the goods of West Africa, notably
kola and ivory, were taken in exchange to those northern
lands. In this respect the markets of Bornu and Kanem
were sometimes as important as the markets of Hausaland,
or as those of the central and western regions of the Western Sudan.

The picture is an erratic and often puzzling one. Not seldom the Kanem rulers and their allies achieved their suc-
cesses by conquest or invasion, rapine and the plunder of
their neighbours, being in their habits and appetites no
different from other conquerors of their time. No doubt
there were many peoples who altogether failed to see in
Kanem any kind of helpful development. Is it then reasonable to speak of "progress" in this connexion? A satisfactory answer would take us into the realms of historical
philosophy, and might not even then be very helpful. Perhaps there is a loose general rule that may be applied. All
progress in those days brought benefit to some at the
necessary expense of others. But wherever states and empires in the past may repeatedly be seen to have helped
the expansion of production and trade, opened new ways
of livelihood, found wealth for the enlargement of the arts
of peace, and sometimes brought a wide security from
everyday perils and fears to large masses of ordinary people, then the balance of development against that of persecution will generally appear as positive. Only much later,
in the different circumstances of our own times, does persecution become the absolute badge of failure.

Kanem, like its great contemporaries, may be said to
have achieved a balance of progress, and even of considerable progress. There were periods of disaster, times of
hopeless misrule, moments of appalling misery for many

constituent peoples. Generally, though, this great imperial
system must be seen as one of the fundamental builders of
traditional civilisation in western Africa.

The Hausa states

The traditions of the Hausa states, situated in the lands of
northern Nigeria, go back to their kings of the eleventh
century A D.

Perhaps these kings were related to the men who would
later help to build the Mossi states further to the west.*
Their history is in any case an ancient one. According to
the Kano Chronicle, a collection of Hausa traditions written down many centuries later, and whose dates, of course,
are not exact, the first sarki, or king of Kano, was Bogoda,
who came to power as early as A D 999. We can probably

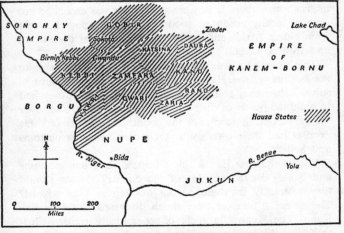

19   The Hausa states and their neighbours

* See pages 72–73.

conclude that a number of Hausa settlements, each dependent on its main city, began to appear on the political scene some eight or nine hundred years ago.

These Hausa states had three main reasons for existence. These reasons were to be found in their cities. Each main Hausa city or town (for these settlements were at first quite small) was a place for government and military defence. Neighbouring farmers could take refuge there when threatened by invaders or raiders. In exchange for this protection, they paid taxes to the men who ruled the city, who in turn paid the soldiers and kept law and order. These men were in turn ruled by a sarki or king, a member of one or other leading family.

Secondly, each Hausa city was a market place for the nearby countryside. Here farmers could exchange their products for the goods that craftsmen made in leather and other materials.

Thirdly, each Hausa city became gradually a centre of international trade. It became a place for the exchange not only of locally produced goods but also of goods brought from North Africa and Egypt, from the rest of the Sudan, and from Guinea.

This prosperity was the result of long development. In the beginning, the Hausa states had difficult problems to solve. Before they could grow strong and wealthy, they had to build the power of their cities and extend this power over the neighbouring peoples of the countryside. Many of these peoples had their own ways, their own religious customs and beliefs.

Should the new Hausa rulers impose their own customs and beliefs on the peoples of the countryside, or should they tolerantly let these people worship as they wished? The question was certainly much discussed in towns like Kano. The Kano Chronicle offers a nicely framed illustration of this kind of problem. According to this tradition, the sarki in A D 1290 was a certain Shekkarau. One day Shekkarau's counsellors came to him and complained of the disloyal talk they had heard among country people coming into town. Shekkarau replied that such discontent could be settled, he thought, without fighting. But Shekkarau's counsellors were not sure that he was right. "If you try to make peace with these people," the counsellors argued with him, "they will only say that you are afraid of them." And they advised the sarki not to listen to the delegates of these discontented folk.

But when the delegates came to Shekkarau, and entered his palace, and stood before him, they begged him to let them keep their customs and beliefs. For "if the lands of a ruler are wide," they argued, "then he should be patient. But if his lands are not wide, he will certainly not be able to gain possession of the whole countryside by impatience." And the sarki agreed with them. As the Kano Chronicle explains, "he left them their power and their own religious customs."

Behind this little story, nearly seven hundred years old, one may see how hard it was for the chiefs of the towns and the chiefs of the countryside to reach agreement and settle down together for their common benefit. One may also see that while there was warfare among these states, there was also diplomacy—the effort to end disputes by compromise and peaceful give-and-take.

Islam came to Hausaland somewhat later than elsewhere in the Western Sudan, perhaps because of the strength and self-sufficiency of the Hausa cities. For the same reason, no doubt, Islam failed to acquire the same degree of popularity and success in Hausaland, at any rate until much later times. But the Hausa cities were often visited by Muslim scholars, and the Hausa traders and governments took over the script of the Arabs, using it to write their own language. Unfortunately, very few old Hausa documents have come down to us. Many are said to have been destroyed by the Fulani conquerors of Hausaland after 1800.

There were many Hausa cities and therefore many

Hausa states. Daura and Gobir, Katsina, Kano and Zaria
—these are only five of the better-known names. Sometimes
these states banded themselves together for their common
good. Often they quarrelled. They never had a single central government. They did not form a Hausa empire. Yet
the Hausa states, generally more friendly with each other
than with their non-Hausa neighbours, had great influence
and commercial power over a wide area of the eastern
region.

By the end of the period we are considering here, A D
1000 to 1500, Katsina and Kano had emerged as the
strongest commercial centres of Hausaland. After 1400
most of the Hausa kings accepted Islam, and methods of
government accordingly changed. Rulers like Muhammad
Rumfa, who ruled Kano 1465–99, introduced many new
methods from nearby Kanem and Songhay. They formed
troops of soldiers, built palaces and demanded free labour
from their countrymen. By these means they grew strong
and rich. In later times, Kano's importance as a place of
work and business eclipsed even that of Gao and Timbuktu. Kano became a centre not only of trade but, even
more important, of a thriving handicraft industry. It made
cotton goods for the whole of the Western Sudan. By the
nineteenth century it might have been the Manchester of
old West Africa.

One important point about these states was that they
were in close and constant touch, sometimes by war but
more often by peaceful trade, with the peoples of the forest lands of eastern Guinea, notably with the Yoruba and
their neighbours. It was largely through Hausaland that
goods from the Yoruba country went northward into the
Western Sudan and across the Sahara to North Africa; and
it was largely through Hausaland that the peoples of
eastern Guinea could import the North African goods they
needed.

The Hausa states, then, were a necessary and therefore
prosperous link between Guinea and the far north. Partly

it was for this reason that the Songhay rulers, as we shall see in the next chapter, wished to gain control of Hausaland, and succeeded for a short time in doing so. Some of the Kanem rulers also tried to control the Hausa states. Kano became a vassal state of Kanem for part of the fifteenth century. But most of the Hausa states remained independent until 1800.

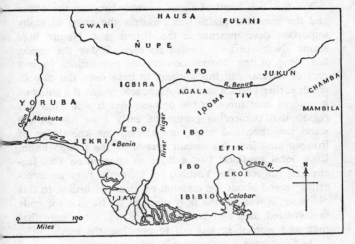

20 The peoples of eastern Guinea

8 THE EASTERN REGION II

In eastern Guinea, the broad and fertile region of southern Nigeria and its immediately neighbouring lands to west and east, the earliest political events which are known with any certainty were the work of the peoples whose descendants still live in that region today: the Ibo, Ibibio, Efik and their neighbours, the Edo-speaking peoples, and the Yoruba and their neighbours. These events can to some extent be traced back, through European records, to the fifteenth century; but before that, because these people did not use the art of writing, historical knowledge can derive only from archaeology, the study of languages, and oral tradition.

Yet this rich band of forest country between the ocean and the grassland plains was certainly the scene of many important developments in the distant past. Nature here seems always to have smiled on men. Today the region has some of the densest countryside populations in any part of Africa, and this appears to have been the case in much earlier periods as well. Archaeology and the study of languages lend force to the opinion that it was from this region that pioneering groups of early Iron Age people some two thousand years ago carried the knowledge of iron-working into the distant forests of the Congo basin. Even local tradition has a little to suggest on this fascinating subject. The Yoruba, for example, have an interesting legend about the creation of man. According to this old story, it was at their holy place of Ile-Ife that the gods first created men and women, and it was from here that men and women spread out to populate the earth.

As time went by, the peoples of eastern Guinea, as of other parts of Guinea, changed their ways. They too were swept along on the river of history. They found new and more effective methods of earning a living. They evolved new systems of keeping law and order. Some of them built states and empires.

The Ibo and their neighbours

The political systems of Africa, as we have already noted, did not always develop into forms of centralized and bureaucratic rule. Quite a number of peoples found it possible to do without any regular apparatus of government. They continued to live peacefully together, to defend themselves and enlarge their wealth, with the help of very little central authority. Among these peoples were the Ibo who live now, as they have lived since times beyond memory, in the fertile lands to the east of the lower reaches of the Niger river.

Does this mean that the Ibo and other peoples without chiefs or kings were any less successful than the peoples who elected chiefs and formed themselves into states with central governments? Far from it. Some of these peoples without chiefs repeatedly showed themselves, on the contrary, to be among the most go-ahead of all the peoples of Africa; very active in trade, very skilful in politics, very shrewd in dealing with their neighbours. The Ibo themselves are such a people; the Ga of eastern Ghana, who acquired kings only at a relatively late point in their history, are another.

The truth is that these peoples without chiefs, or without clearly formed central authorities, also evolved their own types of state-system. The Ibo, for example, have clearly had their own methods of political organisation for a very long time. This organisation was undoubtedly the result of many political developments in the past. But the Ibo traditional system is harder to analyse, and so harder to define, than the kind of social systems which unite upwards to a king or supreme chief. For it rested on a very complicated arrangement and distribution of political power. It lay somewhat nearer to traditional African forms of social organisation by separate families, by separate groups of kin, and by separate lines of descent from one generation to another.

When we say, too, that people have lived without chiefs, we are in danger of getting the wrong idea. Peoples like the Ibo and the Ga (in the time before the latter had kings) undoubtedly recognised that their communities needed law and order. They understood that the making and the enforcing of law and order required that political power should be given to this or that kind of man or woman. They made sure that such men and women, who wielded political power, should enjoy a special place of honour and authority.

Unfortunately, little is known about the distant past of the Ibo and their neighbours. This is partly because, lack-

ing supreme chiefs or kings and central governments, they
tended to compose and remember far less spoken history
about what happened to them. Most kings and supreme
chiefs, on the other hand, had experts whose job it was to
remember and pass on to their children the dates and main
facts about every reign. These royal traditions are obviously helpful to historians. Where they are missing, it is
more difficult to build a detailed picture of the past.

What we can say about the Ibo and their neighbours is
that they have lived in their present homeland for a very
long time; that they have worked out their own methods
of self-government; and that these methods generally
helped them, after the beginning of trade with Europeans
in the Niger delta, to make good use of new contacts.

There is also a small number of peoples in eastern
Guinea, as in other parts of the forestland, who have remained on the banks of the river of history. Tucked away
in corners of the forest or in steep valleys or distant hills,
they have stayed outside the sweep and movement of events,
and have changed their political and social systems far less
than most other peoples.

The Yoruba and Ife

Political development west of the lower Niger took other
forms. Here was the home of the Yoruba people, who
appear to have founded a number of small states, under
powerful chiefs, as much as nine hundred years ago.

The Yoruba have several traditions about how their people began life. One of them says that it was at Ile-Ife, which
the Yoruba regard as the cradle of their nation, that mankind was first created. Another tradition tells the story of a
great ancestor and hero called Oduduwa. He is said to have
come from far in the east and settled at Ile-Ife, and it was
from here that his descendants went out to rule the various
branches of the Yoruba. One of his sons, for example, is

said to have become the first alafin of Oyo, as well as
being the father of the first oba of Benin, while another
was the first onisabe of Sabe; his eldest daughter is remembered as the mother of the first alaketu of Ketu (in modern
Dahomey), while another daughter gave birth to the first
olowu of Owu.

What historical truth lies behind these legends and beliefs? They point, like other legends of the same kind, to
the early arrival of newcomers who settled in Yorubaland
and merged with the more numerous people whom they
found there. These people who were already living in
Yorubaland had certainly been there since distant Stone
Age times. Archaeological evidence suggests that they were
pioneering metal-workers and fine artists in terra cotta, and
that they were possibly related to the people of the Nok
Culture.* Experts in language explain that the Yoruba
language (like other languages nearby) probably came into
existence in remote times, and possibly as much as three
thousand years before the present day.

Then who were the ancestors, personified by Oduduwa
in the traditions, who joined these people and built the
Yoruba civilisation of historical times? Here again, modern experts in the study of language have something useful
to say. They think that there were two main movements
of incoming ancestors, one towards Ekiti, Ife, and Ijebu
inside the forest belt, and another towards Oyo on the
northern edge of the forest. The earliest of these migrations
may have occurred in about A D 1000.

Where did these incoming ancestors come from? Some
Yoruba legends say that they came from Arabia and quite
a few Yoruba customs seem to reflect the ideas of ancient
peoples who lived along the middle Nile, notably the people
of the ancient empire of Kush. No doubt the truth about
where the incoming ancestors came from, however, is that
they came from the Western Sudan, where they, like other

* See pages 16–18.

peoples of the Chad region, had felt the influence of those old Nile civilisations which had sent traders and travellers across Africa in ancient times. Entering Yorubaland, they brought new political ideas and methods with them. They introduced or evolved new types of government. We may see the legendary reflection of this in the story of how Oduduwa produced children who ruled the various branches of the Yoruba in new ways.

Yorubaland in any case embarked on a new stage of development at a time that was not long after (and may even have been a little before) A D 1000. This was a period, one may note, of great change in many parts of West Africa. Then it was that the states of Hausa first took shape, and that the state of Kanem underwent a big expansion. In Yorubaland a number of towns and settlements were founded in the forests to the west of the Niger. Each possessed its own network of family and clan loyalties and duties, its recognised elders, its appointed chiefs and supreme chief. They varied in size and power according to the skill of their rulers and the wealth of the countryside in which they were founded. But all of them regarded Ile-Ife as their traditional home.

On the remarkable nature of old Yoruba civilisation, at least after about 1300, there is some very striking evidence in terra cotta and brass. At Ife, for instance, Yoruba artists were called on to celebrate the Oni of Ife and his kinsmen, and evolved one of the finest schools of sculpture that the world has known. They modelled works in clay and brass that are of undying power and beauty. Here, too, we find an interesting thing. For a study of these sculptures shows that some of their features are reminiscent of those of the terra cotta sculptures of the Nok Culture people in earlier times. On the other hand, the Ife brass sculptures were made by a special method, using wax, which was certainly used by the sculptors of the ancient civilisations of the Nile. Yoruba civilisation may thus be seen as a creative combination of many ideas, customs and beliefs that were born in Guinea as well as in other parts of Africa.

Like other peoples of the period before the discovery of science, the Yoruba explained their political ideas in terms of religion. They found religious explanations for their world and the way men lived and should live, since they had not yet learned to find scientific explanations. But Yoruba religious loyalty to the oni of Ife could not prevent troubles among the various states. Although the oni was the senior religious figure among all the Yoruba chiefs, these never accepted his authority in political matters. On the contrary, they quarrelled a great deal with each other, competed with each other, and contested each other's rights. Only in much later times did one of the Yoruba states grow powerful enough to dominate many of the others. This was Oyo, about whose empire more will be said in Chapter 11. Before the rise of Oyo, however, another strong power appeared in southern Nigeria, that of Benin.

The empire of Benin

It seems that the first rulers of Benin, a trading settlement and afterwards a city, of the Niger delta, acquired their power soon after the forming of the first Yoruba states, or perhaps at about the same period. Tradition knows them as the Ogiso dynasty.

There is no doubt that the Edo people of Benin took some of their political ideas from their Yoruba neighbours. Tradition says that hundreds of years ago (probably about AD 1400) the Edo of Benin became dissatisfied with their rulers. They accordingly sent to Ife and asked Oduduwa for one of his sons to rule over them. He sent them Prince Oranmiyan (or Oronyon); and Oranmiyan started a new period in the political life of the Benin state. This does not mean, of course, that the Edo took over Yoruba ideas wholesale. Even if a close connexion existed for a time between some of the rulers of Benin and their contemporaries of the Yoruba states, the Edo were very much a people with ideas of their own. We can see this in many ways. Their artists, whether at Benin itself or in other Edo towns, were especially brilliant in the skills of working metal, and evolved many styles of great distinction.

Edo expansion at Benin dates back to a period long before the first European written reports were made in the second half of the fifteenth century, and was possibly linked to Benin's strong trading position on the Niger delta, although the details here are far from clear. Tradition suggests that the political system and customs of Benin were already well established by the fifteenth century. By the sixteenth century Benin had become an important power in the land. Now it was that the artists of Benin, like those of Ife before them, were required to celebrate the power and authority of their rulers. In doing so, they developed a special style of royal sculpture that was different from the more popular (and often more beautiful) styles which were liked by ordinary folk. As well as producing many fine heads and figures, the royal artists also designed and made many hundred brass plaques, or large rectangular pictures in metal, which were used to decorate the oba's palace. Many of these fine old sculptures, whether in the royal style or in other styles, have survived and become famous throughout the world.

Here again we come across an interesting point. The sculpture of Benin was mainly in brass. Yet brass cannot be made without copper, and there is no copper in southern Nigeria. So the copper must have come from somewhere else, and it must have come in exchange for goods produced or sold by the Edo of Benin. Benin, in other words, was deeply concerned with foreign trade. This trade seems to have consisted in buying copper and other goods from the Western Sudan in exchange for Edo cotton stuffs and other goods. Once again one perceives, even if here in a shadowy way, how the rise of states and empires could be intimately linked with the production of goods and the exchange of goods. Much of the power of the empire of Benin, like that of other big states and empires, may be thought to have been built on economic foundations of this kind.

By the middle of the sixteenth century, perhaps earlier, the oba of Benin ruled over an area which spread from the region of modern Lagos to the Niger delta. Even when the Portuguese first came into touch with Benin in 1486, they were impressed by the great size of empire and the authority of its ruler. Benin had in fact become the largest of the political systems of Guinea. It traded far and wide, received ambassadors from Portugal and sent ambassadors to Europe.

Those were the days when Portugal was glad to find friends among the strong rulers of Africa. A Portuguese report of the early sixteenth century relates how the oba of Benin wished to learn more about Europe than his Portuguese visitors could tell him and, with the good will of the king of Portugal, sent one of his chiefs to find out. "This ambassador was a man of good speech and natural wisdom. Great feasts were held in Portugal in his honour. He was shown many of the good things of Portugal. He returned to his own land [as he had come] in a Portuguese ship. When he left, the king of Portugal made him a gift of rich clothes for himself and his wife, and also sent a rich present to the king of Benin . . ."

Oba Ewuare

Written down not long ago by Chief Jacob Egharevba, the royal traditions of Benin speak vividly of this period. One of the most famous obas of this time of expansion was Ewuare, who came to the throne in about 1440. He is said to have travelled widely in Guinea and even to have visited the Congo.

Ewuare was "powerful, courageous and wise," say the traditions. "He fought against and captured 201 towns and villages in Ekiti, Ikare, Kukuruku, Eka, and Ibo country. He took their rulers captive, and he caused the people to pay tribute to him.

"He made good roads in Benin City . . . In fact the town rose to importance and gained the name of city during his reign . . . It was he who had the innermost and greatest of the walls and ditches made round the city, and he also made powerful charms and had them buried at each of the nine gateways of the city, so as to ward against any evil charms which might be brought by people of other countries in order to injure his subjects."

It was under Ewuare, too, that the empire of Benin had its first sight of Europeans, for in 1472 the Portuguese captain Ruy de Siqueira brought a sailing ship as far as the Bight of Benin.

But Ewuare is remembered as an outstanding ruler not only for his conquests and breadth of contact with his neighbours. He also presided over important political developments. For it was under Ewuare, according to tradition, that the State Council of Benin was formed, together with other new political institutions; and it was from this time that the political system of Benin acquired not only a powerful central ruler but also a central government, with officials and departments and regular means of administering the empire.

Nupe and Jukun

The pressures of change that were felt and activated by the Edo and the Yoruba after about A D 1000 were also potent in eastern as in other parts of Guinea. If we knew more about them we might be able to place the apparently rather isolated achievements of the Yoruba and Edo into a wider and more meaningful perspective. We might also

find that the traditions which relate Yoruba state-forma-
tion to immigrants from the north or east, and Edo traditions of the same kind to influence from the Yoruba,
should more properly be traced to political and social
developments of a much more purely local and complex
kind.

What seems clear, at all events, is that other states were
founded in this period, some of which afterwards became
famous and endured for many years. The Jukun state was
one of these. Nupe was another. Little is known of the
circumstances of their emergence. In later years the Jukun
kingdom, lying to the north of the river Benue, which is a
major tributary of the Niger, became strong enough to
threaten the independence of some of the southern Hausa
states, notably Zaria. Yet little is heard of it in early traditions. It must have been fairly strong by the late fourteenth
century, however, for the Kano Chronicle tells of a Hausa
king who made war on the Jukun at about that time, and
died in doing so.

The creation of Nupe, lying astride the lower course of
the Benue, is traditionally attributed to a founding hero
called Tsoede or Esigi, who, learning from the example
of prestigious Benin, succeeded in binding a number of
Nupe communities into a single political unit. Certainly
there is some ground in Benin traditions for thinking that
this, or something like it, is what really happened. Yet
there are aspects of Nupe culture which suggest that this
imposingly rounded polity was a good deal more than a
mere offshoot of Benin. There may well be a case for
thinking that Nupe had an earlier foundation, and was in
fact, like Benin, one of that string of early polities which
emerged in this region before A D 1400, whether by the
subtle pressures of local change or by the gradual stimulus
of example from the Western Sudan.

However that may be, Nupe flourished. Enjoying a useful commercial and political position between the lower
Niger country to the south and Hausaland in the north,

its people won renown for their craftsmanship in many materials. Though often prosperous, Nupe was not always fortunate in war. It offered a prize that was often worth a big effort for the taking. There were times when it was obliged to pay tribute to the energetic Yoruba states to the south-west, especially Oyo after 1700; and other times when the Hausa or Fulani of the north had the upper hand.

In selecting the Jukun and Nupe states to end this section, I am conscious of the many others that have not been mentioned. Yet these few examples will perhaps be enough to indicate the richness and complexity of the West African scene by the opening years of the sixteenth century.

PART TWO

THE CIVILISATION OF THE SIXTEENTH CENTURY

AD 1500–1600

INTRODUCTION

To isolate the years A D 1500–1600 and identify them as a separate and distinctive period on their own may be little more than a mere historiographical convenience. Not many people in West Africa will have been conscious of any such concept. Muslim scholars, true enough, worked by a centennial chronology, and this for them was the tenth century. But the retrospective isolating of this hundred years has a more solid justification than that. For this was a period which, with its innovations, its ever burgeoning variety, its now brilliant and now sombre measure of achievement or disaster, may be seen as a central part in the picture of West Africa's past.

There was much development. Craftsmen worked in a wider range of skills. Farmers cultivated new crops for food, trade, and manufacture. Traders extended their business: scarcely any fragment of western Africa, from the waters of the far Atlantic to the hills of Cameroon, now lay beyond the reach of their middleman skills and trading trails. Outstanding men ruled and judged, made war or pursued the arts of peace, wrote books and spoke poetry, composed music or carved in wood and ivory and clay.

But now it was, too, that new ideas, inventions, and invaders came in from elsewhere. If this was a time of development it was also one of great change, or, more accurately, of an immediate prelude to great change. In a profound sense one may think of this "central period" as the ending of a major epoch and the outset of another.

Through nearly five centuries, ever since the invasion of Almoravid Berbers from the north-west in the middle of the eleventh century, the peoples of West Africa had remained free from outside interference, though not of course from trans-Saharan influence. They had exploited this freedom; and, within the limits that were open to them, they had built many vigorous polities and cultures.

But they had paid a price for this immunity from interference. They had missed the urge and pressure of all those currents of scientific thought and mechanical invention that were already flowing, for reasons which lie beyond the scope of these pages, among the European inheritors of the high civilisations of Antiquity. Africans might be no less happy in their lives for this absence at the birth of mechanical industry. It would indeed be hard to argue that the knotted skein of European growth during these years, with its dreadful wars of religion, the squalor of its medieval towns, the bondage of its servile peasantry, was capable of yielding a better life, or even as good a life, as most West Africans then knew. Yet from now onwards, and increasingly, these peoples fell into a relative inferiority of military, commercial, and above all mechanical power. And this growing imbalance between Africa and Europe was to become of paramount significance later on.

Now, at all events, the old isolation began to be ended. During this century the ships of several European nations sailed frequently to the coasts of Africa and India, opened European conquest and plunder of the islands of the Caribbean and its surrounding mainland, and, with all this, discovered a new range of violent ambition and adventure. Much of this helped in western Europe to shape new patterns of power whose influence was felt increasingly along the Guinea seaboard.

At the same time there were large changes in Egypt and much of the rest of North Africa. These likewise fashioned new trends of power and pressure. Little by little, West Africa began to be drawn within the tide and pull of world affairs, sometimes with constructive results and at other times with the reverse. Most of the coastal peoples gained from the new maritime trade; but already the overseas slave trade, small as yet though ominous, had edged its way upon the scene. And in 1591, sounding their trumpets of disaster, the soldiers of the Moroccan sultan marched down across the wastes of the Sahara and wrecked the Songhay empire. There opened a long and often difficult period of transition.

The sixteenth century may be said to mark the end of old West African history, and the beginning of modern times.

9 THE WESTERN REGION IN THE SIXTEENTH CENTURY

Senegal, the Woloff and Futa Toro

The main themes which should concern us in the far west of the Sudan, near the Atlantic coast, are two in number: the activities of the Woloff empire, and the rise of a new state in old Tekrur, the region of Futa Toro along the south bank of the Senegal river.

As to the first, the Woloff political system continued to consist of three provinces, Walo, Cayor, and Baol. These now became stronger and wealthier, thanks partly to growing trade with European sea-merchants who now brought their ships to the Woloff coast and the Senegal river. A Portuguese report of 1506* says that Portuguese merchants brought horses, cotton goods and other manufactures for sale here and took slaves and a little gold in exchange. The king of the Woloff was so strong at this time that his armies were reputed to number as many as 10,000 horsemen and 100,000 foot-soldiers.

It was in this region of the Senegal coast that the Portuguese trade in African slaves first became important. This trade had begun in the 1440s. At the start it had been simple piracy. Portuguese sailors and soldiers had fortified the little island of Arguin (on the north coast of the modern Republic of Mauretania). From there they raided the mainland right down to the mouth of the Senegal river and beyond, seizing prisoners whom they enslaved, and ravaging the coastal country.

Towards the end of the fifteenth century, however, piracy had given way to an often peaceful trading partnership

* That of Duarte Pacheco Pereira: *Esmeraldo de Situ Orbis*.

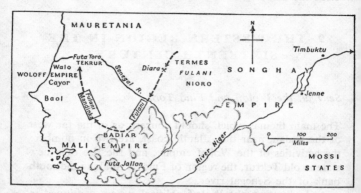

21 Some important Fulani and Mandinka movements in the sixteenth century

between Portuguese sea-merchants and the kings and chiefs of the mainland of Senegal. Slavery and the slave trade were not condemned in those days. Both flourished here as elsewhere in the world.

The new state in Futa Toro is interesting for several reasons. One is that the Fulani people and their near-relations, the Tucolor,* now made their decisive entry on the stage.

We have come across the Fulani in earlier times. They were concerned in the fall of Ancient Ghana and the rise of its successor states. But by this time they had spread far across the grasslands of West Africa from their original home near the upper Senegal river and the upper Niger. They had sent out nomad groups of cattle-breeders both eastward and westward. These groups were certainly small to begin with, but they built up their numbers. Some of them settled down and formed states of their own, so that, in the course of time, there came to be two kinds of Fulani: "cattle Fulani" who lived the old nomad life of the coun-

* Tucolor means "people from Tekrur." They were, in fact, for the most part Fulani.

tryside, and "town Fulani" who preferred to dwell in towns. Because of this, and because of their wandering habits, the Fulani have played an unusual and at times a leading part in the history of the Western Sudan.

What some of these Fulani did at the beginning of the sixteenth century is told by traditions which may be accepted as truthful in outline, though not in detail. A group of Fulani cattle-breeders, ruled by a prince called Tengella, was living at this time in the broad plains between Termes and Nioro, lands that were once the homeland of Ancient Ghana in the country between the upper Niger and the Sahara. This area had passed from the control of Ghana to the control of Mali, and was now under the authority of the emperor of Songhay whose capital lay at Gao. This emperor, as we shall see in due course, was the vigorous and efficient Askia Muhammad, afterwards called Askia the Great.

Tengella Koli and the Denianke

Tengella, the Fulani leader, revolted against the overlordship of Askia Muhammad. No doubt he and his people wanted freedom of movement for their cattle. Perhaps they also objected to the taxes which they were supposed to pay to the officials of their Songhay overlord. Tengella led his warriors across the plains against Diara, one of the old successor-states of Ghana whose king was now a vassal (in this case, that is, a tax-paying under-king) of the Songhay emperor. There is reason to think that Tengella was encouraged by the reigning emperor of Mali, who was now a declining rival of Askia Muhammad of Songhay and no doubt glad of any allies he could find.

Askia Muhammad's brother Amar led an army against this Fulani raider. The two armies met near Diara in 1512. Amar won, and Tengella was killed. Yet this proved only the beginning of the Fulani adventure.

Tengella had a son named Koli by a wife who belonged to the ruling family of Mali. Tengella Koli led his dead father's warriors south-westward, crossed the upper Senegal river and arrived in Badiar, a region which lies to the north-west of the Futa Jallon mountains.* Here he was joined by many Mandinka soldiers, who saw in him a bold leader as well as a relation of their own overlord, the emperor of Mali.

Seeking a new home, these Fulani and Mandinka allies marched north-westward into Senegal, passed round the fringe of the Woloff states, and fell upon the ancient state of Tekrur in Futa Toro. This state was then ruled by a family of Soninke chiefs who owed loyalty to the king of Diara, and had done so, with some interruptions, ever since the old days of upheaval after the fall of Ghana. Tengella Koli and his Fulani-Mandinka army overthrew these Soninke chiefs in 1559 and set up a new line of kings.

These new rulers in Futa Toro were called the Denianke. They proved strong and capable enough to remain in control of Futa Toro until 1776, more than two centuries.

Notice, here, three developments.

First, these Fulani had changed their way of life. Those who had set out to invade Diara at the beginning of the century were little more than a raiding band of cattle nomads. They were after revenge for real or fancied hurts; even more, they were after loot in the settled lands of Diara. They behaved no differently from the nomad Tuareg of the southern Sahara, who often attacked the settled lands and cities of the Western Sudan. But the Fulani who conquered and settled in Futa Toro, some fifty years later, were a people ready to abandon their wandering ways and build a state of their own. It may be that this change was largely due to their long contact with Mandinka people who were not nomads.

* In the modern Republic of Guinea, and not to be confused with Futa Toro.

The second development, flowing from the first, was that these Fulani had adopted new ways of living together. They had accepted the political authority of chiefs and ruling families settled in one place. They had adopted city manners, and acquired an interest in trade.

Thirdly, these Fulani-Mandinka state-builders in Futa Toro held fast to their own religions. They resisted Islam. And because they resisted Islam, the Muslim traders of Futa Toro (of old Tekrur) began to quit the trading towns which had long existed here. This kind of thing, we may recall, had occurred before, when the non-Muslim rulers of old Tekrur had attacked and taken Kumbi, Ghana's ancient capital. Then the Muslim traders of Kumbi had retreated northward and founded a new trading centre in the southern Sahara at Walata, a market that was still important in the sixteenth century.

There followed from this clash of religions a real decline in the commercial importance of Futa Toro, and one that was to last for some time. It was in this period, it seems, that ancient and even famous markets like Tekrur itself, Sila, and Berissa began to vanish from the map. The writers of North Africa had often mentioned these markets in the past. Today we do not even know exactly where they lay.

Further decline of Mali

The imperial system of Mali largely collapsed in this period. This is not to say that the peoples of Mali also entered a time of cultural or even commercial decline. Some of them, on the contrary, embarked upon new initiatives of their own. But the emperors themselves had less and less power. Their governments wielded less and less authority. Their armies went from defeat to defeat.

Yet the grand old system, now more than two hundred years old if we reckon its life from the time of Sundiata

Keita, still enjoyed widespread respect. Many peoples had grown accustomed to thinking of the Mali mansa, the Mali koy, as their rightful overlord. The habit of thinking this was slow to die. And so it came about that the fame and reputation of this once wide system of imperial rule lived on in memory and even to some extent in a loose customary allegiance, after its real power had become weak and defenceless.

Even in the days of Askia Muhammad (1493–1528), the traditional frontier of Songhay and Mali was still recognized as running through the region of Sibiridugu—astride the upper Niger, that is, in the neighbourhood of the river-city of Segu. And Niani, the capital of the old empire, was still a large and prosperous city. Commercially, too, the traders of Mali, the famous Dyula companies, were the most enterprising and successful merchants of all the western and central regions of West Africa. They travelled far and wide, across the plains and through the forests, trading even on the distant coast of central Guinea.

But the political power was mostly gone. Even as early as 1400 the Songhay ruler of Gao is said to have pillaged Niani itself. In 1431 the Tuareg rushed into Timbuktu. By the end of the century Mali had no power to the east of Segu. Even within his homeland, as the story of Tengella Koli shows, the Mali emperor could seldom do more than stand aside and let things happen. He could not prevent Tengella Koli from entering his lands without permission, nor from raising an army among the Mandinka of Badiar, nor from taking this army northward to the conquest of Futa Toro. Yet he certainly tried. In 1534 he sent an ambassador to the coast for help from the Portuguese, with whom he and his predecessors had enjoyed good diplomatic and trading relations. But the king of Portugal was unable to help, and did nothing except send messengers and gifts to his ally Mansa Mahmud II. The time was still far ahead when Europeans would be strong enough to have any direct influence on the affairs of West Africa.

Western Guinea, Gambia, Sierra Leone

Southward of the Woloff states, and along the coast of lower Senegal and Gambia to the shores of modern Liberia, new influences were also at work. The ocean was no longer empty. Trade increased. With this there came the gradual shaping of the countries which we know today.

European pioneers had now begun to make reports about these lands, and Pereira's report of 1506, already mentioned,* has something to say about the markets of the Gambia river. Far up this river "there is a country called Cantor [probably between Basse and Yarbutenda]. It has four villages of which the biggest is called Sutucoo and has 4,000 inhabitants. The others are Jalancoo, Dobancoo, and Jamnan Sura. They are surrounded by palisades of timber . . . At Sutucoo there is held a big market. Mandinka traders come there with many donkeys. And when times are peaceful, these traders visit our ships [in the river], and we sell them red, blue, and green cloth of cheap manufacture, linen and coloured silks, brass rings, hats and beads and other goods. Here in peaceful times we can buy five to six thousand *dobras'* worth of good quality gold. These lands of Sutucoo and their neighbours are part of the Woloff kingdom, but the people speak the Mandinka language . . ."

In this one may see how the peoples who lived along the coast and near by, having long known the influence of strong powers from the inland country, now began to find new partners from the sea. Comparable reports were made by Portuguese and other European sea-merchants for much of the seaboard of Guinea.

Pereira also speaks of the Bulom people of Sierra Leone, describing them as warlike folk who dealt in gold, which

* See page 111.

they bought from the inland country in exchange for salt. This gold the Portuguese in their turn obtained for brass rings, large basins, and cotton goods. "And in this country you can buy ivory necklaces that are carved better than anywhere else." So greatly did the Portuguese admire the skills of West African ivory-carvers, indeed, that wealthy traders and noblemen commissioned many beautiful objects, such as salt-cellars, for their own use at home. Pereira explains how Sierra Leone, the Mountain of the Lion, got its name.

"Many people," he wrote, "think that the name was given to this country because there are lions here, but this is not true. It was Pero de Sintra, a knight of Prince Henry of Portugal, who first came to this mountain. And when he saw a country so steep and wild he named it the land of the Lion, and not for any other reason. There is no reason to doubt this, for he told me so himself."

Behind the Bulom (or Sherbro, as they are sometimes called) was the kingdom of Loko, speaking a related language. To the north of them were the Temne; and behind these again, over the modern frontier of Sierra Leone with the Republic of Guinea, were the Susu and the Fulani of the Futa Jallon, as well as other Mande-speaking peoples, and the Kisi, whose language is related to that of the Bulom.

It was at this time, too, that the little group of islands off the shore of modern Conakry, capital of the Republic of Guinea, were first used by European sea-merchants as a base for trading expeditions, and were named the Ilhos dos Idolos (Islands of the Idols) from which they have their present name, the Islands of Los. Eastward again were the Kru and other coastal peoples, and the Mende and their neighbours who live in the lands behind the coast. All were influenced both by political events in the forest lands and by the arrival of new opportunities for trade with sea-merchants.

10 THE CENTRAL REGION IN THE SIXTEENTH CENTURY

Greatness of the empire of Songhay

Nowadays the Songhay people number about 600,000. Most of them are fishermen and farmers who live along the banks of the middle Niger between the region of Timbuktu and the western borders of northern Nigeria. They play their part in the political life of the Republics of Mali and Niger, but they have long since ceased to have a state of their own.

Yet their state in the sixteenth century was the largest in West Africa with the exception of Kanem-Bornu. They enclosed many peoples within their empire, both to the south and to the north of the great river; and their exploits hold a brilliant place in the record. These came partly from their very favourable position along the Niger; partly from the wealth and power of their trading cities; and partly from the vigour and intelligence of their political ideas and methods.

For a long time, under Mali, the Songhay had warred with the famous rulers of that western empire. Gradually they had worn down the power of Mali. In 1375, as already noted,* they recovered their old independence and freedom of action. They used this to promote their trading power, as well as to raid and plunder their neighbours, pushing squads of fast-moving cavalry even as far away as Niani, the Mali capital, in 1400. All this was the prelude to expansion. The Songhay now embarked on the same great enterprise as their distant forerunners of Ancient Ghana and their one-time overlords of Mali. They brought

* In Chapter 6.

an enormous area of the Western Sudan into a single system of trade and imperial government. This was above all the work of two outstanding rulers, Sunni Ali and Askia Muhammad.

Sunni Ali

Anyone who travels in the Songhay country today will find the name of Sunni Ali, better known as Ali Ber, or simply as the Shi, remembered still with honour and respect, although he died nearly five centuries ago. He is thought of as a famous wizard, a man who understood a great deal about magic, but also as a ruler of irresistible foresight, power, and courage.

He became king of Gao and of its nearby Songhay lands in about 1464. Mali was by then becoming weak, and its countries were in confusion. The Tuareg were raiding from the north, the Mossi from the south. Other peoples were claiming their independence along the banks of the Niger. The trade of great cities, Gao among them, was threatened by the insecurity of the times.

Sunni Ali was one of those great military captains of the old days whose energy and ambition kept him always in the saddle, always fighting, always at the head of one army or another. Knowing no other means of uniting the Western Sudan except by war, he made war often and with a ruthless skill. The early years of his reign read like little more than a list of battles. He moved on swift horses from one campaign to the next, shifting his place of residence, reorganising his armies, refashioning his plans, restless, invincible. In his long reign of thirty-five years he was never once defeated.*

He began by fighting off the Mossi, who were making raiding ventures against Timbuktu, the second city of the Songhay lands. He pursued these raiders far into the west,

* See Map 15 on page 68.

then turned swiftly on the Dogon and the Fulani, who had
the same ambitions for plunder, in the neighbourhood of
the hills of Bandiagara. By 1468, four years after becoming
emperor, he had cleared the country of immediate danger
and at once attacked the Tuareg, who had held Timbuktu
since 1433. Unbeatable, he drove the Tuareg out of Timbuktu. Their chief, Akil, fled to distant Walata, while Sunni
Ali set about punishing the leaders of a city who had done
little to defend themselves against the enemies of their su-
zerain lord.

Religious disputes were at work in this. The leading
men of Timbuktu had been strictly Muslim for a long time
now, and generally followed the beliefs of their trading
partners from North Africa and the Saharan oases. Their
leading *qadi,* or chief religious figure, tended to regard
himself as the independent ruler of a Muslim city within
the largely non-Muslim empire of Songhay. Here, as elsewhere, the coming of Islam to the Western Sudan had
given rise to conflicts not only of religious belief, but even
more of custom, laws, and political loyalties. Faced with
Tuareg occupation of their city, the leading men of Timbuktu seem not to have fought very hard against it: both
they and the Tuareg, after all, were Muslims interested in
the trans-Saharan trade. They did not want to be occupied
by the Tuareg, but they may have tried to use this occupation as a means to reassert their independence against their
Songhay overlord.* Sunni Ali, at any rate, thought they
had. He accused them of having acted disloyally to him,
and treated them harshly. Herein lies the reason why the
author of the *Tarikh al-Sudan,* himself a man of Timbuktu, afterwards described Sunni Ali as a tyrant and op-
pressor, reflecting in this the general opinion of all his
learned colleagues.†

* Later on, as we shall see, much the same thing happened
when Timbuktu was occupied by Muslims from Morocco.
† See "Law and order" and "Clash of beliefs" in Chapter 14
for more on this interesting subject.

With the recapture of Timbuktu, Ali had only begun his bold career. He now laid siege to Jenne, a vital market-centre for the trade in gold and kola and other goods from the southern forest lands. Jenne had never yet been taken by an invader, and even Ali's success was doubtful after a bitter siege of seven years. Yet by 1476 he had the whole lake region of the middle Niger, west of Timbuktu, largely in his hands.

Through all these years of struggle, and through later years, Ali found means to fight back against a host of raiders. In 1480 the Mossi of Yatenga daringly sent cavalry to raid as far as Walata on the verge of the Sahara. Ali launched his own cavalry after them, drove them back, pinned them down again in their own country of the south. He did the same with others of their raiding kind, Gurmanche, Dogon, Koromba, Fulani of Gurma: with all those peoples, in short, who lived along the southern margins of the Niger Valley and envied the wealth of its towns and markets. Yet it would be wrong to see Ali as no more than a skilful soldier. His achievements in peaceful government were by no means insignificant.

Askia the Great

Sunni Ali died in November 1492 while returning from an expedition against the Gurma, and his son, Sunni Baru, was named ruler of Songhay two months later. Sunni Baru reigned for only fourteen months, being then defeated in battle and deposed by a powerful rebel. This rebel was Muhammad Turé, who became Askia the Great.

Here, once again, religious disputes were mingled with personal ambitions. In Songhay at this time the market cities were of growing wealth and importance. The leaders of these towns were mostly Muslims, and, because of this, Islam was now extending its influence and customs among the townspeople of the empire, as indeed in other parts of the Western Sudan as well. While largely loyal to the traditional beliefs of the countryside, Sunni Ali had found it wise to make a number of concessions to Islam, although, as we have just seen in the case of Timbuktu, he did not hesitate to oppress Muslim leaders who failed in political loyalty. Sunni Ali, in other words, set out to protect both the interests of the people of the towns and the interests of the people of the countryside. Always a skilful politician, he had considerable success in holding the balance between these often opposed sets of interests.

Unlike his father, Sunni Baru refused to declare himself a Muslim and at once made it clear that he was going to side entirely with the non-Muslim people of the countryside. Between the townsfolk and the countryfolk—the traders and the farmers of Songhay—he chose the latter. But the people of the towns were too powerful to be treated in this way. They feared they would lose power and influence. They believed their trade would suffer. They found a rebellious leader in Muhammad Turé.

The consequences were far-reaching. With Askia Muhammad, the empire of Songhay entered on a new stage in its impressive political life. Becoming emperor at the age of fifty, he reigned from 1493 until 1528, and carried the political and commercial power of the empire of Songhay to its greatest point of expansion. Three aspects of his reign deserve emphasis.

In the first place, Askia Muhammad made a sharp break with the religious and family traditions of the sunni line. He based his power firmly on the towns, and, in line with this, ruled as a strict Muslim. Although many traditional customs and practices were still observed at his court, his laws and methods were increasingly in accord with Islamic ideas. In this, clearly, he measured well the trend of power in Songhay. This is shown, among other things, by the fact that he could be absent on a pilgrimage to Mecca for two years (1495–97) without causing himself any trouble at home. During this pilgrimage the sharif of Mecca, spiritual leader of the Muslims, named him as his deputy or caliph for the Western Sudan. Returning from Mecca, Muhammad set himself to remodel the laws and customs of his empire along more strictly Muslim lines.

Secondly, a point we shall come back to in Chapter 14, Muhammad took over the administrative changes made by Sunni Ali, and developed them still further. He built up a machinery of central government that was stronger and more detailed in its work than any other known in the Western Sudan.

Thirdly, he used his talents as a political and military leader to continue with the imperial plans of Sunni Ali, and to carry them to a point where he successfully united the whole central region of the Western Sudan and even pushed his power, as Kankan Musa of Mali had done two centuries earlier, far northward among the markets of the Sahara.

No people of the Western Sudan were free from the pressure of Songhay power. Their disciplined cavalry were a force to be feared. Like Sunni Ali, Askia Muhammad fought the Mossi of Yatenga and their raiding neighbours. In 1505 he even tackled Borgu (in what is north-western Nigeria today), though not with much success. In 1512 he mounted a big expedition against Diara. Successful there, he sent his troops still further westward, and attacked in the name of Islam the Denianke king of Futa Toro in distant Senegal.

Then he turned his attention eastward again. His generals invaded the Hausa states, carrying all before them and meeting with serious resistance only at Kano. His distant frontiers now extended, at least in theory, as far as the borders of Bornu. Yet the addition of Katsina and other Hausa states to the countries which paid tax and loyalty to Songhay was worth little, unless Songhay could also gain possession of the principal caravan-markets to the north. There, too, lay the Tuareg, ancient enemies of Songhay and of the cities of the Niger. So Muhammad sent out his generals once more. He ordered them to march north-eastward into the hot and thirsty lands of Aïr, far north of Hausaland.

Faced with the armies of Songhay, perhaps the best-organised troops that the Western Sudan had ever seen, the Tuareg could do nothing but turn about and flee into their native desert, making for wells where no large army could hope to follow them. Muhammad ordered his generals to found a colony in Aïr, and many Songhay were settled in and around the ancient market of Agadès. Some of their descendants may be found there to this day.

In 1528, by now more than eighty years old, Muhammad became blind. He was deposed by his eldest son, Musa, and died after much misery ten years later.

Invasion of Songhay

Askia Musa reigned for only three years, being killed by his subjects in 1531. Like Sunni Baru before him, he turned against Islam and was considered a tyrant by his Muslim subjects. He was followed by Bengan Korei, who took the title of Askia Muhammad II and ruled until about 1537. Then came askias Ismail (1537–39), Issihak I (1539–49), and Dawud (1549–82). With the long reign of Dawud, the empire again enjoyed peace and prosperity, being rivalled in size and power only by Kanem-Bornu to the eastward. The old conflict between Islam and traditional religion was still at work, but Askia Dawud seems to have proved unusually successful in satisfying both sides. Though himself a devout Muslim, he was careful not to suppress traditional religious customs, and even maintained many of these in the ceremonial of his court.

After Dawud, harsh times lay ahead. They began under Askia Muhammad III (1582–86), and led to disaster during the rule of his successors Muhammad Bani (1586–88) and Issihak II (1588–91).

Troubles broke out at home. The old enemies along the southern fringe of the empire—the Mossi and their neighbours—were far from crushed. The Hausa states revolted against Songhay overlordship during the reign of Muhammad III. And in 1582, the year that Muhammad III succeeded Dawud, a new note was struck, full of menace for the future. The sultan of Morocco sent a force of two hundred soldiers to seize the vital salt-deposits of Taghaza, far in the north of Songhay but claimed as part of its domains. These soldiers were armed with a weapon not seen before on the battlefields of the Western Sudan. This was the arquebus, an early form of musket. Firearms had now appeared for the first time on any scale. They were to have a profound and sometimes terrible effect on the fortunes of West Africa.

This little skirmish in a remote part of the Sahara was to open a war between Morocco and Songhay which proved disastrous for the men of Gao. Why did it happen? It will be helpful to turn aside for a moment to consider this question.

Briefly, there were two reasons, one military and the other commercial. In 1578, invaded by the Portuguese, the Moroccans had won a resounding victory at the battle of Al-Ksar al-Kabir. Historians have called it one of the decisive battles of the world. For many years it ended any idea of European conquest in North Africa. But it also encouraged the Moroccans to turn southward.

The Portuguese had invaded Morocco with an army of 25,000 men. At Al-Ksar al-Kabir they met with total defeat. It is said that only a few hundred Portuguese escaped to tell the tale of that day. The reigning prince of Fez died in the hour of victory and was succeeded by his younger brother, Mulay Ahmad, then aged twenty-nine. Mulay Ahmad was at once named Mansur, the Victorious. Skilfully, he welded Morocco into a strong state again, and ended wars and rivalries both by the power of his armies and by generous gifts. But his purse was far from bottomless, and soon he began to look round for new ways of filling it. Not surprisingly, he looked to the south, to the Western Sudan, as the Almoravids had done in earlier times. Under Askia Dawud, the riches of Songhay had acquired a glittering reputation throughout North Africa. Even the kings and merchants of distant Europe had begun to hear tempting tales of the wonders of the Western Sudan.

Sultan Mulay the Victorious began by nibbling at Songhay power. He raided Taghaza. But it brought him no good. He could seize the salt-deposits, but he could not keep an army in that thirsty place. He thought again. He decided to launch an army right across the Sahara and attack the men of Songhay in their own homeland. By this means, he believed, he could plunder the wealth of Songhay and vastly enrich himself with West African gold.

This army set forth in 1591. It was led by a soldier named Judar, by origin a Spanish Christian who had accepted Islam, and was composed of 4,000 picked men. Half of these were infantry armed with arquebuses, a primitive kind of gun and yet the most up-to-date weapon in the world of that time. Half of these arquebus-carriers were Spanish Muslims and the other half Christian renegades—Portuguese and Spanish prisoners who had agreed to serve in the Moroccan armies, and accept Islam, rather than suffer death or long imprisonment. There was also a force of 500 horsemen armed with the arquebus, and 1,500 light cavalry equipped with long spears such as can be used from a horse. The army even took half a dozen small cannon with them across the desert.

This force of mercenaries and ex-prisoners crossed the Sahara, taking many weeks from Marrakesh to the Niger, and fell upon the lands of Songhay with the fury of men who knew there could be no retreat. Gathering his troops, Askia Issihak tried to resist, but the powerful armies of Songhay now met soldiers at Tondibi even better armed and disciplined than they were. They retired before the

firearms of Judar's men. Weakened by trouble and revolts
at home, the Songhay ruler lost battle after battle, often
with heavy casualties. The Moroccans pushed into Timbuktu and then into Gao, hoping to find large stores of
wealth ready to their hand. In this they were at first not
altogether disappointed, though the profits of this war were
never as high as Sultan Mulay had hoped.

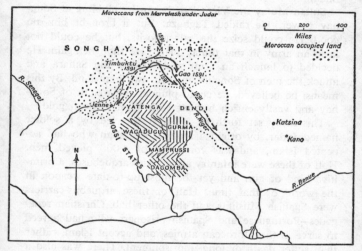

22   The Moroccan invasion of Songhay

Routed in battle and driven from their trading cities, the
Songhay did not give in. The towns were lost, but the
country folk fell back on guerrilla tactics. Unable to meet
the Moroccans in pitched battle, they built up small raiding
parties, attacked Moroccan posts and garrisons, harassed
the invaders in every way they could, fighting to recover
their land. They were never more than partially successful. Having lost the towns, Songhay proved unable to recover. Its great edifice of central authority was undermined

from within and without. Nothing could make it strong again, and with this collapse the power of Islam likewise dwindled or was lost for many years ahead. There began another stage in the history of the Western Sudan, a stage in which the non-Muslim peoples of the countryside were once more to assert their power to rule.

The states to the south of Songhay

We noticed in a previous section a number of peoples, the Mossi of Yatenga, the Dogon, the Gurmanche, and others, living along the southern frontiers of Songhay. These little polities were of old formation. In the fifteenth and sixteenth centuries others began to be formed in their neighbourhood—in the wide lands between the forests of modern Ghana and the northern curve of the Niger river. Among these were the Mole-Dagbane states of Mamprussi and Dagomba. Towards 1600, Dagomba chiefs also formed the little kingdoms of Wa and Buna.

Another such state, still small and obscure in the sixteenth century, was Gonja, lying in the lands between the Black and White Volta rivers of northern Ghana today. Gonja became powerful only at the beginning of the seventeenth century, but requires a mention here. Like its neighbours, Gonja lay on some of the trade routes between the gold-producing lands of the Akan, in the central part of modern Ghana, and the markets of the middle Niger region, including Jenne. At some time between 1550 and 1575 the emperor of Mali, accustomed to have gold from the Akan flowing northward into his empire, found that the supply was seriously falling off.* He accordingly despatched a force of Mandinka cavalry to see what could be done

* What had happened, in fact, was that the Akan had begun selling part of their gold production to Portuguese traders along the coast to the south of them, the Gold Coast as it now came to be called by Europeans. See page 132 below.

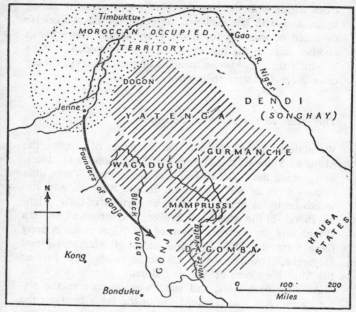

23   The founding of Gonja

about this. These were the armoured warriors, the bull-
dozing tanks of those days, who founded Gonja. Having
got themselves into the lands of the White Volta, they
started by founding seven little states and set out on a commercial and political career of their own. Later again, in
the eighteenth century, these would come within the overlordship of the Asante empire.

The Akan and their neighbours

Control and exploitation of gold mines in the heart of
their forest lands brought the Akan fresh strength from the

expansion of trade with the Western Sudan (and, through the Western Sudan, with North Africa). Of potentially even greater help was their position near the coast, which brought them new opportunities of profitable trade with sea-merchants. This is the period in which the states of the Akan and their neighbours, whether in the forest or near the coast or along the coast itself, begin to emerge from the mist of legend and take fully historical shape.

Bono continued in Takyiman as before. But now it had important rivals. Further south, about fifty miles from the coast in the country of the Kwisa and Moinsi hills, Adansi was established some time before 1550 under a ruler whom tradition remembers as Opon Enim. Westward of them, along the valley of the Oda, there were the Denkyira. At first under Adansi overlordship, Denkyira became independent during the reign of Adansi's Ewurade Basa. The Adansi then had to pay tribute to Denkyira. Objecting to this, they moved eastward into Akim, where they made a new home. South-east of Denkyira, meanwhile, the Akwamu began to nurse new political ambitions, although the rise of their empire came only after 1640. On the eastern Gold Coast, meanwhile, the Ga took the lead among the various branches of their people, shifting their capital from about eight miles inland to the present site of Accra.

All these and similar movements must be seen against the background of the special problems, political and economic, which these peoples now faced. What was really happening, beneath the confusing surface of events, was an underlying effort to organise these forest and coastal lands into political systems which could take full advantage of their commercial opportunities. Here, in fact, was the same onward-moving process of development as in the Western Sudan; but here, because of dense forest and broken nature of the country, divided by hills and rivers, the emergent political systems were on a smaller scale.

Throughout this century the trade with the north remained more valuable than the newly growing trade with

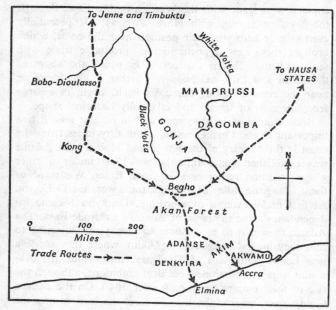

24　Trade-routes to and from Akan country

sea-merchants along the coast. Now, as before, the Dyula traders conducted their commerce from a main base at Begho on the northern outskirts of the Akan forests where the gold was mined. From Begho the main trading route went north-westward through Dyula towns and little states, such as Kong and Bobo-Dioulasso ("the house of the Dyula traders of Bobo"), that lay in the northern part of the modern Ivory Coast, and thence on to Jenne. Another main route went north-eastward from the Akan forests to Hausaland. Both were used for the export of gold, kola, and other items, and for the import of salt, copper, and manufactured products from the north.

Coastal trade grew important during the sixteenth century. The gold trade began to move southward as well as northward; not much at first, yet in steadily growing volume. In 1554, for example, three English ships bought on the Gold Coast no less than 400 pounds of gold of fine quality, as well as thirty-six barrels of peppercorns and about 250 elephants' tusks. This shift in the movement of gold exports began to have political consequences: in the north, as we have just noticed in the case of the foundation of Gonja, but also in the south, where previously weak coastal peoples began to develop a new strength. As the coastal trade grew, so also did the little states along the coast. We shall see in Chapter 19 what became of them.

11 THE EASTERN REGION IN THE SIXTEENTH CENTURY

Expansion of the empire of Kanem-Bornu

The empire of Kanem-Bornu, situated in the plains to the west and east of Lake Chad, entered on a period of growth that was the work of the ruling Sefuwa and their governors, generals, and counsellors, drawing on the support of the Kanuri people and some of their near neighbours.

Mai Idris Katakarmabe (whose traditional reigning dates are 1507–29) took over a state that seems to have been peaceful within itself, but was limited to most of Bornu and the region round Lake Chad. This ruler set out to re-establish control over the lands of the Bulala in old Kanem, east of the lake. He won a famous battle at Garni-Kiyala, north of the lake, after which his Bulala opponent, Dunama ben Salma, accepted the mai's overlordship. The latter then led an army back to Njimi, the old Kanem capital near the lake, more than a century after his predecessors had been obliged to flee from it. The Bulala kings were left to rule in old Kanem, but were supposed to pay loyalty and tribute to the new Kanem, west of the lake in Bornu. This indirect rule of old Kanem by kings living in Bornu was to continue for more than a century, though it was never easily maintained.

The next king, Mai Muhammad (1529–44), at once faced a Bulala attack. This failed at the cost of the Bulala leader's life. Mai Muhammad followed this success by marching north into Aïr, then under Songhay rule; and it appears that from this time onward the country of Aïr, vital for the northward caravan trade from Bornu and Hausaland, came under the general overlordship of Bornu.

Under Mai Ali (1544–48), Bornu clashed with Kebbi in the west of Hausaland. The reason appears to have been that Kebbi, perhaps eager for a bigger share in the wealth of the northern caravan route, had begun raiding the Tuareg and Songhay settlers in the oases of Aïr. These appealed for help to Mai Ali, who marched a Bornu army northward round the Hausa kingdoms (passing south of Zinder) and attacked the kanta or king of Kebbi in his fortress town of Surame, west of Katsina. The Kebbi king

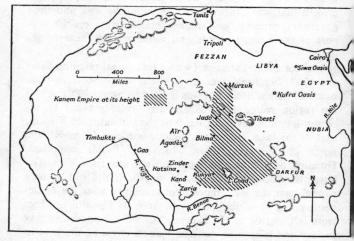

25   The empire of Kanem-Bornu at its height

evacuated Surame, but Ali, for reasons which are not clear, turned in his tracks and made for home. The Kebbi army set out to chase him and his soldiers. They caught up with Mai Ali's army near N'guru and fought several battles. But the king of Kebbi and his men were ambushed on their homeward journey by the men of Katsina, and the king was slain. From now onward, Katsina increasingly took the lead among a number of flourishing but disputatious city-states in western Hausaland.

We must follow the detailed story of the rulers of Kanem-Bornu a little further, for an outstanding leader was soon to appear. When Mai Ali died in 1548, his son was still a minor (royal descent here being from father to son). So his nephew Dunama took power and reigned from 1548–66, and was followed by a son of Mai Muhammad whose name was Dala (Abdullah). Mai Dala reigned from 1566–73. At this point the Bulala revolted again and were once more defeated. Yet the homeland of Bornu was by now badly shaken. Dunama had even taken the step of fortifying his capital, Gasreggono, a sign of weakness never shown in earlier times; and raiders threatened from every side.

Mai Idris Alooma

Meanwhile the little son of Mai Ali was growing to manhood. This young prince, whose name was Idris, lived far away from Bornu in old Kanem east of the lake, where the Bulala kings still ruled. No doubt he lived there because his mother was the daughter of a Bulala king, and had returned home on the death of Mai Ali. This woman, Queen Amsa, is said by the traditions to have shown great courage in protecting the life of Idris against efforts by Mai Dunama and Mai Dala to slay him, the rightful heir to the throne of Bornu.

But Idris could not win his rights when Mai Dala died in 1573. The throne was seized by Dala's sister, the formidable Queen Aissa Kili, and it was only after seven years of civil war that Idris could at last overcome his rivals and clear his path to power. He reigned from 1580 until 1617, and became one of the strongest and most successful of the kings of Kanem-Bornu. In hard-riding and hard-fighting wars he revived the old empire and built a new one. He died in 1617, still at the head of his troops, was buried in a marsh at Aloo, and has been ever since remembered as Mai Idris Alooma.

His reign, like that of other forceful monarchs of his day, is notable both for military innovation and political success. Better than his predecessors, it would seem, Idris Alooma was able to reap the advantage of administrative and social developments which had now been maturing for more than a century. These, notably the emergence of long-service armies composed of semi-professional warriors of servile status, had long since made it possible to strengthen the executive, in the person of the king or his immediate nominees, over against rivals, lesser kings, and the common folk alike.

Here again one sees how far-ranging were the political consequences of Islam. Solvent of traditional loyalties, of pagan loyalties, the new religion repeatedly helped to underpin the power of men who ruled in new ways. More and more, the kings of the Western Sudan were now disposed to look for their authority not to the old ties and customs of past allegiance—although these they were often careful to observe and at least partially satisfy—but to the service of personally appointed officials and dependents, palace guards, eunuchs, and others who owed their standing in society to the king's will alone and not to any bond of kinship.

There followed a deepening in social stratification, and, inevitably, a turning-away from the "traditional democracy" of old. In a broad sense, the politics of the "extended family," the politics of kinship, were gradually displaced by the politics of personal rule, élite rule, even to some extent class rule. This undoubtedly denoted considerable progress towards political effectiveness at the centre: the same progress, however different in context, as occurred with the vast extension of vassalage in the feudal Europe of the eleventh and twelfth centuries. But this progress, here as in feudal Europe, was achieved at a heavy cost in the practices of tolerance and social equality.

With all the new paraphernalia of courts and palaces, retinues and professional soldiers, the costs of royal maintenance went steadily up; as they rose, so also did the forced contributions of ordinary people. Taxes multiplied: here, for instance, may be traced the remote origins of those social discontents in Hausaland which were eventually to promote the Fulani-led revolution of 1804. Slavery became institutionalised in new and wider forms. A greater distance than ever before separated the king from his subjects. Interposed between them, now, stood a host of officials entirely dependent on the king. Unpopular policies became ever more possible.

Warfare, by the same token, grew more absolute. Quilted armour, chain mail, iron helmets: all these had appeared among the royal armies of Bornu and Hausaland soon after the beginning of the fifteenth century. Now muskets followed; and it was not the least of Mai Idris Alooma's innovations to import muskets and Turkish instructors from Tripoli, and train a corps of musketeers of his own. They were probably capable of doing very little damage, given their small numbers and the wild unpredictability of their weapons; but they must certainly have enhanced the mai's prestige.

Ibn Fartua, a Kanemi writer of those days who served at the court of Idris Alooma, has left a description that affords a vivid glimpse of royal pomp. It tells of the coming of ambassadors from the mighty sultan of the Ottoman empire, then the most prestigious ruler in the western world, and of how they were received.

Mai Idris went out to receive the ambassadors at the head of companies of his quilt-armoured cavalry. "On the next day, all the soldiers mounted their horses after equipping themselves and their horses with armour, with breastplates, shields, and their best clothing. When we had all ridden a short distance we met the messengers of the lord of Stambul . . . The troops of our lord were drawn up on the west in rank after rank, leaving enough space between their ranks for the wheeling of any restive horse. Then our troops charged [towards the Turkish messengers and their escort], and they galloped their horses towards us. This continued for a long time until the infantry were tired of standing still. After that our lord continued on his journey . . ."

"O, my wise friends and companions!" continues Ibn Fartua. "Have you ever seen a king who is equal to our lord at such a moment, when the lord of Stambul, the great sultan of Turkey, sends messengers to him with favourable proposals?"

As in times past, Kanem-Bornu once more stood firmly at the crossroads of trade and travel between West Africa and the Fezzan, Tripoli and Egypt. Reunified by Idris Alooma, who also thrust his imperial army far eastward into Darfur, it linked the peoples of West Africa to the wide world beyond the desert; in this it played the same part as Songhay and Mali had done before it. Kanem was never called on to face invasion from Morocco or the north, and the reconstructed empire remained within the frontiers that Idris had traced for more than a hundred years.

Rise of the Hausa states

Built in a fertile land, rich in craftsmen and determined traders, the Hausa cities were now far stronger than before. By 1350 the more important of them had pushed out their power across the neighbouring countryside until they had begun to form state-frontiers with each other. Many wars followed, not of long endurance or attrition but designed to win this or that local advantage or to bring home plunder. Here too the methods of Islam reinforced the strength of individual rulers and the cities whose merchant interests these rulers served.

Kings increasingly stepped out of their old rank of *primus inter pares*. Taxes and tolls grew heavier. The needs of courts and armies weighed down on tax-paying citizens. Armouries glinted with the metal of expensive coats of mail and helmets. By the 1440s there were even a few muskets, brought in from the north by way of Bornu. Slave-labour began to be used on an imposing scale. In 1450, for instance, the then ruler of Kano, Abdullahi Burja, a tributary vassal of the Kanem-Bornu empire, sent out men on raids for slaves which are said to have yielded a thousand a month; traditions say that he established no fewer than twenty-one settlements of royal slaves with a thousand men in each. To all this, Islam provided the ideological guide and justification, most notably, perhaps, when the Kano ruler Mohamed Rumfa (1465–99) commissioned a scholar of North Africa, Al-Maghili, to write his afterwards famous *Obligations of Princes*.

These changes were the price of centralised rule by a strong executive, very much the stimulus of Islam in these regions; and, while some communities could find the price a heavy one, others saw it as exceedingly worth paying. For the Hausa cities and their surrounding countryside grew fat with trade and farming production. New techniques of long-distance commerce by the facility of currency and credit went hand-in-hand with an extension of scholarship in the cities, and with considerable technological advance at the level of craftsmanship. Travellers from distant lands were impressed by the prosperity they found here. One such visitor, a North African called Hassan ibn Muhammad al-Wazzan az-Zayyati (Leo Africanus),* has

* Captured by Christian pirates during a voyage in the Mediterranean, Hassan ibn Muhammad was taken to Rome. There he took the name of Leo Africanus, and wrote, in rather poor Italian that was improved by his editor, Giovanni-Battista Ramusio, his famous book about the Western Sudan.

left us some colourful descriptions of Hausaland as he and fellow-travellers saw it at the beginning of the sixteenth century.

Gobir in the west was rich in people and in cattle. "The people are in general very civilised. They have very many weavers and shoe-makers who make shoes like those that the Romans used to wear; and these they export to Timbuktu and Gao." Probably Leo Africanus was thinking of sandals of the Tuareg fashion. The Gobir town of Madawa made such sandals for long afterwards.

Of the state of Guangara, later absorbed by Katsina, he wrote that it was "inhabited by a great number of people who are governed by a king with more than 7,000 infantry armed with bows, and 500 foreign cavalry on call. He draws a great revenue from dealing in goods and from commercial taxes . . ."

Kano, he found, was "encircled by a wall made of beams of wood and baked clay; and its houses are constructed of the same materials. Its inhabitants are civilised handi-craft-workers and rich merchants . . ."

But all this prosperity, whether from trade or taxation, had its disadvantage. It attracted raiders. Thus Guangara, whose king had such great revenue from trade and taxes, was menaced by both Songhay on the west and Bornu on the east. After a long siege Kano had already fallen to the armies of the Songhay emperor, Askia Muhammad, who obliged its ruler to pay him one-third of all the annual revenues of Kano; and Kano, as we have seen, had also fallen for a time under the overlordship of Bornu. Other Hausa states suffered in the same way. Gobir and Katsina, for instance, were attacked by Kebbi as soon as the latter had regained its independence from Songhay in 1517.

In the south, Zaria or Zaz-zau flourished. For much of the sixteenth century this was the strongest state in Hausa-land, making vassals both in east and west, and even for a while having control of Nupe and the Jukun kingdom in the south.* This brief though brilliant rise to supremacy is said to have been the work of a remarkable queen called Barkwa Turunda and even more of her forceful daughter, Queen Amina, who reigned for thirty-four years, subduing both Nupe and the Jukun.

Little is certain about these events in Zaria. Yet two points may help to explain them. The first is that Zaria, like Kano, held a key position in the trade between the lands of what is now southern Nigeria and the caravan markets of Hausaland and Bornu. Further to the south, so did Nupe and the Jukun, which is no doubt why these two states were often at war with Zaria. Each will have wanted to secure a greater control of the north-south trade. The second point is that Zaria, in having female rulers, had made a compromise between Islam and West African religion, and was therefore able, at least for a while, to make the best of both worlds—to appeal for loyalty, that is, from both Muslims and non-Muslims.

Towards the end of the century the Jukun turned the tables on Zaria. They began pushing northward. By 1600, according to tradition, they had mastered Bauchi and Gombe, and had possibly brought Zaria itself under their temporary control. Even Kano felt the shock of their raids. This interesting Jukun state continued its vigorous if eruptive life until finally defeated, and reduced to subjection, by the Fulani generals of Uthman dan Fodio at the beginning of the nineteenth century.

Here as elsewhere the bare record speaks much of raids and wars, quarrels and miseries. Rulers strove with one another for power and wealth, competing for the taxes without which they could maintain neither governments nor armies, battling for the trade routes that guaranteed the taxes, struggling for the cities where the craftsmen lived and the treasuries lay.

How, one may ask, did the common folk fare in all

* The Hausa name for Jukun was Kwororafa.

this? Badly enough, no doubt: with deepening social stratification, it was necessarily they who met the price of progress in technical and political efficiency. This was not European feudalism; yet some of the effects, as already suggested, were not much different. At the same time it needs to be remembered that the tightened rule of the Hausa kings, though less and less constrained by traditional ties, was itself subject to a whole array of checks and balances. If later evidence is anything to go by, these polities may even be said to have developed something in the nature of a limited constitutional government. The kings were not absolute rulers, nor were their subjects without means of redress.

Court officials owing allegiance only to the king might be harsh and irresponsible in their use of power. They were counterposed by traditional officials who retained some of the old representative quality, and who could and often did employ their authority against the "court party." It might be possible to plunder some of the people some of the time and, by all the evidence we have, a few of them all of the time. Yet anything more extensive or prolonged than this would have tended to overturn the careful balance at the top. For a majority of Hausa—or at any rate for the *talakawa*, the freemen, as distinct from the *cucenawa*, the slaves—the executive and its nominees could seldom have been more than an occasional nuisance. There were many raids, but these were brief; many wars, but these were small. Meanwhile, as already noted, there is evidence of a growing prosperity in which large numbers, bond or free, will have shared in some degree or other. And this was a steady expansion that continued for many years.

The Niger delta

The history of the peoples of the Niger delta, of all those southern Nigerian lands that are watered and divided by the many outflow-rivers of the great parent stream, may be said to have begun after about A D 1500.

Groups of Ijaw fisherfolk and salt-makers had lived here since early times. Little is known of them, although their ancestors had probably come from the region of Benin and Iboland. Pressures of population in Iboland, always fertile in people, now combined with the new attraction of coastal trade with European sea-merchants to carry more people into the delta lands. These newcomers were of many origins, Ijaw, Ibo, Edo, Jekri, Ibibio, Efik, and even some Tiv and Fulani from the distant north. As time went by, the Ibo became more numerous than any other people in the delta, and Ibo became the language most often spoken.

These delta peoples lived on islands in the swamps and along the banks of their creeks and rivers, and relied greatly on canoe-transport. Facing special problems of their own, they became a population with notably different ideas and ways of life from their neighbours of the inland country. They were called Ndu Mili Nnu, the People of the Salt Water, by the inland Ibo; and it was they who dominated and drove the trade of the whole Niger delta from the Cross river to the river of Benin, along a coastline of more than three hundred miles from east to west. They it was, too, who opened the channels of sea trade to the energetic Ibo of the inland country.

The People of the Salt Water developed many political and social institutions of their own. They found special and often very ingenious solutions to the problems of living together in the delta, a land of creeks and islands, dense vegetation and many difficulties. These delta institutions began to be developed in the sixteenth century.

Oyo and Benin

West of the lower Niger the Yoruba continued to organise their lands, as before, in a large number of small states. All of them used the same language, and were further linked together by common customs and beliefs, while all their chiefs recognised a common ancestry. But they were not united into a single state or even into a system of states. Each acted for itself. They had good trading relations through Nupe, which they sometimes dominated, with the Hausa states to the north of them; and so, by way of the Hausa markets, with the whole trade of the Western Sudan.

Prominent among them was Oyo in the north of Yorubaland. This was because the Yoruba of Oyo did not live in forest country and were able to build up strong forces of cavalry, buying their horses from their Hausa neighbours. After about 1550, Oyo began to extend its authority, not only over Nupe but also over some of its Yoruba neighbours, including those of Egba, Egbado, and Dahomey, who lived in fairly open country free of forest; and later again, after 1600, Oyo became a strong empire. Yet with its power resting mainly on cavalry, Oyo was never able to win any firm control over the forest areas.*

Meanwhile the rulers and people of Benin now reached the greatest extent of their political and military power. Several notable rulers are mentioned in the royal traditions for this period.

Oba Esigie, who came to power in about 1504, brought Idah, a state lying between Benin and the river Benue, under his authority. He also entered into good relations with envoys of Portugal who were now arriving more frequently on his coasts. Missionaries came from Lisbon and

* More information on politics in Oyo and Benin will be found in Chapter 14 under "Methods of government."

were well received. One of them, Duarte Pires, wrote to the Portuguese king in 1516, telling how generously the oba had shown them hospitality, and how he had "sat them at table to dine with his son." This oba is remembered as a man of learning, and as having practised astrology (*Iwe-Uki*). He could speak and read Portuguese, and is said to have reigned for nearly half a century. Benin itself had by this time become a city of great size, wealth, and distinction.

Orhogbua followed Esigie in about 1550, Ehengbuda in about 1578, and Ahuan in about 1606. All three are praised in the royal traditions as sensible and forward-looking rulers, the memory of Oba Ahuan being especially honoured because he was a herbalist and skilful maker of charms.

The first Englishmen to reach the present land of Nigeria arrived at Gwato, the port of Benin, in 1553 during Oba Orhogbua's reign. A Portuguese who was with them wrote afterwards that the oba (like Esigie before him) could speak, read, and write Portuguese. These Englishmen bought a cargo of peppercorns in exchange for metal pots and pans and other goods.

Westward of Nigeria, in what is modern Dahomey, the states of the Yoruba, notably Ketu, and the empire of Benin shared control over much of the inland country and over a number of petty states along the coast. The Fon people had yet to make their successful bid for independence. The Ewe were already well established in the southern country of what is modern Togo.

12 THE CULTURE AND
CIVILISATION OF WEST AFRICA
IN THE SIXTEENTH CENTURY I

Unity and continuity

The towering rise and crash of states and empires, the reigns of kings and queens, conquest and invasions, victories and defeats: these are the skeleton of history, and this is by itself a lifeless thing. To support the living reality of the past, these dry bones need the flesh of everyday experience. By the sixteenth century there is fortunately enough evidence available for West Africa to enable one to grasp at least a little of this reality.

It is of course an extremely varied scene, rich in local idiosyncrasy and contrast. This was a civilisation of an often acute diversity, a clamour of many different languages and prayers and interknotted interests. Some populations prospered; others barely survived. Some exploited their wealth and opportunities; others lost or let slide those they had. If there was much progress, this cut both ways; in those years the advantage of one population was almost necessarily the handicap of another.

Yet for all its diversity it was also a civilisation of great underlying unity. This underlying unity came from the common origins and formation of nearly all these peoples. They were all or nearly all shaped and influenced by the same general options and conditions, by the same kinds of gain and loss, by the same West African land and life.

There is a third preliminary point to be made. This was a civilisation which enjoyed, and which continued to enjoy even in the tumultuous times that now lay ahead, a similarly great continuity. It enshrined a process of profoundly indigenous development and growth. It was to a large extent self-propulsive; and it is easy to see why. For many centuries, because of the northern wasteland of the Sahara and the southern walls of Central Africa's massive rain-forest, these populations were left to work out their own problems in their own way. Of major invasions from outside we can count only three: the Almoravid incursions of the eleventh century, aimed at the markets of Ancient Ghana; the Moroccan expedition of the late sixteenth century, aimed at the wealth of Songhay; and the nineteenth-century onslaught of the Europeans, aimed at the whole continent.

The first two of these invasions were soon over. They were painful, even disastrous, to the lands they touched; but these lands were few. Safe behind their seas of sand and water, most West Africans were unaware of these events or barely disturbed by them. Trans-Saharan influence was another thing. It had great consequences in the Western Sudan and to some extent in Guinea as well. It introduced new techniques of trade, government, and religion. It brought in the arts of writing. It promoted scholarship. But this was a many-sided influence which could be and was absorbed and locally adapted by a civilisation whose cultures had long since become strong in their own right.

How people lived

West Africa has about eighty-five million people today. In the sixteenth century there were certainly far fewer. There were also fewer kinds of food. But more were now added. Valuable plants and fruits such as maize and pineapples were brought from Central and South America in the ships of Portugal. These new crops were eagerly accepted, and spread rapidly. Though without any knowledge of modern science, West Africans had already solved many of the essential problems of living in their vast and difficult region.

They had developed a degree of immunity against dangerous fevers. They had learnt the secret of many medicinal herbs and how to use them to cure sickness. They had discovered how to look after cattle in conditions of great heat. They had become experts at growing food in the forest. They had found out how to recognise minerals in rocks, how to sink mines, how to get the ore and smelt and work it. They had developed a wide range of hand-manufacture in many materials. They had worked out religions of their own. They had evolved effective methods of government, though mostly without the use of writing.

These skills understandably impressed foreign visitors. A Portuguese report of 1506, that of Duarte Pacheco Pereira, tells how high-quality cotton goods could be purchased at many points along the Guinea coast. An English captain called William Towerson wrote in 1556 of the "fine iron goods" that were hand-made in Guinea: "spears, fish-hooks, farming tools, and swords that are exceedingly sharp on both edges."

Of all their material skills, tropical farming and mining deserve a leading place in the record. In both these fields, West Africans were far advanced among the peoples of the sixteenth century—so far advanced, indeed, that it was Africans, even though working as slaves, who later pioneered the development of tropical farming and mining in the Americas.

But these advances were made within the framework of a subsistence economy, and this subsistence production, as distinct from production for exchange in money, placed clear economic and social barriers around further development. A farmer, then, would see little or no point in producing more food than was needed for his family. A blacksmith would make enough hoes or spears to be sure of getting the food his family needed, but he would not sell them for money, since money had little or no part in his economy; he would take them to market and barter them for what he needed.

Of course the detailed picture was not quite so simple. There was a growing quantity of internal and external trade; and this trade was carried on in foods that were grown, and goods that were manufactured, with the idea of exchanging them for other goods or for various kinds of money. The beginnings of a money economy did indeed develop wherever traders gathered in markets and began to deal in goods for sale. This development will need some further discussion.

The fact remains that nearly all West Africans still lived outside the centres of this small though steadily expanding money economy of the towns and big markets. Even inside these centres, the idea of employing men and women in exchange for wages or salaries was still in the future. The only form of regular employment that was known was a kind of servitude, domestic or household slavery, in which wages played no part. Employment outside the towns and market-centres was likewise in the same form of slavery, or else, as in the forest areas, in work provided by customary duties and age-grade organisations. Once again money and wages played no part.

This is not the place to speculate on the full effects of this absence of money and of the habit of working for money. One main effect, though, was to keep the production of goods at the same general level as before. People were content to live as they had always lived. They felt no need for the invention or adoption of machinery that would enable them to produce more goods, as well as more kinds of goods. In short, all the goods that were required for a subsistence way of life could be well enough grown or made by the simple tools that were already known.

Within the limits of their subsistence way of life, West Africans in the sixteenth century worked in many skills and produced many different kinds of goods. But these limits made it hard, even impossible, for West Africans to move towards a scientific view of life, or to invent and use machines. For it has always been the need for new methods of production that has led to the invention and use of such methods; and here the need was scarcely felt. In this respect West Africa now fell rapidly behind Europe.

These points go some way to explain many of the setbacks, as well as many of the achievements, of the populations of the sixteenth century.

Production, trade, and money

Yet even within the limits of a largely subsistence economy, forms of production and trade were already many and valuable.

West Africa exported a wide range of goods to the outside world. These included gold, ivory, cotton stuffs, animal hides and leather, kola, peppercorn, and mutton. Some of these goods, such as mutton, went only as far as the oasis peoples of the Sahara. Others, such as gold, went as far as northern Europe and Asia.

How large was this production? It was often surprisingly great. So far as cotton goods are concerned,* some idea of its size may be had from the writings of the outstanding nineteenth-century German traveller Heinrich Barth. He wrote about cotton production in the busy Hausa city of Kano during the 1850s, but what he said of Kano then will have been largely true of other cotton-weaving towns in earlier times.

"The great advantage of Kano," Barth wrote, "is that commerce and manufactures go hand in hand, and that almost every family has its share in them. There is really something grand in this kind of industry, which spreads to the north as far as Murzuk, Ghat, and even Tripoli; to the west, not only to Timbuktu, but in some degree even as

* First brought to West Africa across the Sahara, long before the sixteenth century, cotton was grown in many West African countries, and was much used for clothing.

far as the shores of the Atlantic, the very inhabitants of
Arguin [on the coast of Mauretania] dressing in the cloth
woven and dyed in Kano; to the east, all over Bornu, although there it comes in contact with the native industry
of the country; and to the south it maintains a rivalry with
the native industry of the Igbira and Igbo, while towards
the south-east it invades the whole of Adamawa, and is
only limited by the nakedness of pagan peoples who wear
no clothing."

The hand-manufacture of cotton stuffs, in short, was
valuable to many West African peoples.

And what about gold? It is no exaggeration to say that
the prosperity of many states and empires was founded on
the mining and export of gold from very early times.

There are many thousands of old mine-workings in West
Africa, especially in the regions of Asante and upper
Guinea. Nobody will ever know exactly how much they
produced in pre-colonial times, but it was certainly a great
deal. Professor Raymond Mauny, who has made the most
careful estimates so far available, believes that West African
gold production during the sixteenth century amounted to
about nine tons a year. He also considers that about the
same amount of gold was produced for a long time both
before and after that time.

Of these nine tons of gold produced every year, about
four probably came from the goldfields of central Guinea
(Asante and its neighbourhood), and about four from
western Guinea (the Buré region of the modern Republic
of Guinea). "The total amount of gold extracted in West
Africa from ancient times until 1500," Mauny estimates,
"may be placed at several thousand tons; with an amount
of about the same size, perhaps 3,500 tons, for the period
between 1500 and 1900."*

These large figures speak eloquently of the skill and

* R. Mauny, *Tableau Géographique de l'Ouest Africain,* Dakar
1961, pages 300–1.

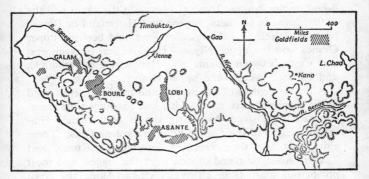

26   Gold-producing areas of West Africa

determination of West Africa's miners. They were obliged to find and mine the gold-bearing ore, crush it, and extract the gold by primitive hand-methods. Yet they produced every year a total that was nearly half as much as the amount produced by modern methods in the colonial period. As late as 1938, for example, the production of West African gold stood at only twenty-one and a half tons.

Growing production led to more trade, more markets, and more trading routes. The trans-Saharan trade had first set in motion this process of expansion. People had come south across the Sahara and bargained for gold and other goods. They brought their own goods in exchange—fine metalware, silks and woollens, beads and horses—and West Africans were glad to have them. New appetites were created. New trading systems were opened, and new sources of production were tapped.

All this expansion, in trade and production for trade, was well advanced by the beginning of the sixteenth century. It still affected only a minority of West Africans; but this minority was much larger than in earlier times. Nearly all main regions were now linked together by well-established trading routes. These ran between the south and the north: between southern Nigeria and Hausaland or Bornu, between Asante and the middle Niger, and between upper Guinea and the upper Niger. They also ran between east and west: between Asante and Hausaland, for example, and between Asante and upper Guinea.

All these centres of production and markets were linked to the great northern cities which had conducted the trans-Saharan trade since very early times: with Jenne, Timbuktu, Gao, and their sister-cities to west and east. These cities, just like their vanished forerunners, Kumbi and Tekrur, Audaghost and others, were the biggest and most prosperous markets in all West Africa. Along the coast of Guinea, meanwhile, a new system of trade with sea-merchants was beginning to grow in size and value. Small as yet, this now rapidly expanded.

With the growth of trade, there came increasing modifications of the subsistence economy by the spreading use of a wide variety of forms of money. These forms were seldom or never coins. The main types of money were cowrie-shells, various weights of brass, various sizes of iron bars, various lengths of cotton cloth. Europeans discovered in this century something that North African traders had found out much earlier: West Africans were careful traders. "These people," reported an English captain, John Lok, after a voyage to Guinea in 1553, "are very clever in their bargaining. They will not overlook a single bit of the gold they offer for sale. They use their own weights and measures, and they are very careful how they use them. Anyone who wants to deal with them must do so decently, for they will not trade if they are badly treated."

Who were the merchants? Along the trade routes they were mostly Hausa and Mandinka, often established in small towns they had founded or enlarged along these routes. In the big cities of the north they were also Kanuri and Songhay, Soninke, Fulani, Woloff, and many others. Along the coast they were Ibo, Ga, Akan, Nzima, and their neighbours. In many markets the biggest merchants were the most important men of the country: chiefs and kings, elders and counsellors. These were all men who needed wealth to pay for government and soldiers, to maintain their courts, to make gifts to visitors.

Long before, King Tenkaminen of Ancient Ghana had monopolised the gold and salt trade.* Many of the sixteenth-century kings and chiefs now did the same with new items of production and new means of trade. When European ships sailed up the Benin river, for example, and dropped their anchors off Gwato, the river-port of Benin, they entered into trade not with anyone they might meet but only with agents and merchants selected by the king. "Nobody is allowed to buy anything from Europeans on this coast," observed a Dutch report of the seventeenth century,† "except the agents and merchants whom the king has named for this purpose. As soon as one of our ships drops anchor, the people inform the king, and the king appoints two or three agents and twenty or thirty merchants whom he empowers to deal with the Europeans."

It was much the same in the Western Sudan. Passing through Bornu at the beginning of the sixteenth century, Leo Africanus reported that the king of that empire was especially interested in buying horses from North Africa and Egypt. He paid for these horses in various ways, but notably in war-captives who were used as slaves in North Africa and the Mediterranean countries. Yet the merchants who brought the horses, and took away the slaves, were allowed to deal only with the agents of the king himself. If the king happened to be away when they arrived at his capital, custom obliged them to sit and wait until he came back again.

In return for its exports, West Africa bought a wide

* See "Revenue and wealth of Ghana" in Chapter 4.
† The same had certainly been true here in earlier times.

range of goods from many parts of the world: cheap cottons and expensive silks from Asia, swords and knives and kitchenware from the dark little workshops of early industrial Europe, hand-written books and thoroughbred horses from the Muslim north, jewellery and trinkets, early types of firearms, gunpowder and shot, bars of iron and rings of copper in great quantity, and much else besides. All these had their accumulating influence on West African ways of life.

When considering what these kings and merchants did with their wealth one has again to bear in mind that this was not yet an economy of investment. Wealth brought a new measure of personal comfort to those who could obtain it: luxury tableware and clothing were often high on the list of African imports. The power to trade for firearms, gunpowder and ammunition often became of critical military and political importance at least in the eighteenth century, though scarcely in the sixteenth. Wealth also supported royal prestige. But above all it supported royal expenses, not indeed by allowing the payment of wages, for the concept of wage-labour still lay ahead, but in making possible the feeding and equipment of dependents and the bestowing of gifts by means of which the political system was largely motored and made to work. Taking their wealth with one hand, and giving it away with the other, the kings and chiefs were able to keep it circulating among a large number of their subjects.

Cities

A Dutchman has described the city of Benin as he saw it in 1602. It greatly impressed him. "When you go into it," he wrote, "you enter a great broad street, which is not paved, and seems to be seven or eight times broader than the Warmoes street in Amsterdam. This street is straight, and does not bend at any point. It is thought to be four miles long.

"At the gate where I went in on horseback, I saw a very big wall, very thick and made of earth, with a very deep and broad ditch outside it . . . And outside this gate there is also a big suburb. Inside the gate, and along the great street just mentioned, you see many other great streets on either side, and these also are straight and do not bend . . .

"The houses in this town stand in good order, one close and evenly placed with its neighbour, just as the houses in Holland stand . . . They have square rooms, sheltered by a roof that is open in the middle, where the rain, wind, and light come in. The people sleep and eat in these rooms, but they have other rooms for cooking and different purposes . . .

"The king's court is very great. It is built around many square-shaped yards. These yards have surrounding galleries where sentries are always placed. I myself went into the court far enough to pass through four great yards like this, and yet wherever I looked I could still see gate after gate which opened into other yards . . ."*

Little or no stone was used in building these cities, for it was easier and cheaper to build in wood and clay, one reason why the archaeologists have found West Africa so exasperatingly short of satisfactory ruins. The wealthy market centre of Jenne, for example, was built entirely of short-lived materials. Leo Africanus tells us that "the king, the men of religion, the doctors of learning, the merchants and those of wealth and authority" lived in "houses made like huts, of clay and thatched straw." Yet absence of stone was not a sign of absence of civilisation. This same

---

* Recorded in O. Dapper's *Description of Africa,* first published in Amsterdam in 1668. Dapper did not himself visit Africa but collected reports from other Dutchmen who did. Most of these reports, at any rate as regards West Africa, referred to the early decades of the seventeenth century; and Dapper's book was in some respects out of date by the time he published it.

traveller found that the people of Jenne were "very well dressed." They had reason to be. They enjoyed a lucrative trade with the Akan peoples in the south and those of the Western Sudan in the north. "It is because of this blessed city of Jenne," wrote the author of the *Tarikh al-Sudan,* Abd al-Rahman as-Sadi, in the seventeenth century, "that caravans come to Timbuktu from every side," for Jenne, standing where it did, had become "one of the great markets of the Muslim world."

The architecture of Timbuktu was much the same, though it had a few buildings in brick as well. Leo Africanus found "many handicraft workers, merchants and cotton-weavers" there. European goods were much in use. There was also an abundance of grain and other foods, while milk and butter were in good supply. The king possessed a huge treasure in gold. "The royal court," Leo wrote, "is very well organised and splendid. When the king goes from one town to another with his train of courtiers, he rides a camel; but horses are walked behind him by his servants. Should there be any need for fighting, the servants take charge of the camels and all the soldiers mount horses." He estimated that the king had about 3,000 horsemen and a much larger number of infantry. The best of these horses were brought across the Sahara from North Africa.

Gao, capital on the rising Songhay empire, was described by the same observer as "a very large town without any defensive wall." He thought that most of its houses were poor and ugly, but reported that there were "several fine ones where the king and his courtiers live." Gao's inhabitants were mostly rich traders who spent their time in travelling on business. "Bread and meat are very abundant, but they have no wine or fruit. Yet their melons and cucumbers are excellent, and they have enormous quantities of rice. Fresh-water wells are numerous there."

Leo considered that the revenues of Songhay were great, but so were its expenses. Luxury goods brought across the Sahara for the king, nobility, and rich merchants were very dear. Imported horses, woollens, swords, cavalry harness, medicines, and jewellery all cost far more than in the countries where they were made.

Yet the cities grew. They too were a fruitful part of West African civilisation.

Education and learning

Outside the towns of the Western Sudan, teaching was restricted to popular instruction in the skills and customs that were needed and observed in everyday life; to training in traditional law; and to the preparation, similarly by example and by word of mouth, of priests, practitioners in herbal medicine, and other specialists.

All West African religions possessed a body of beliefs, more or less many and complex, which "trainee priests" had to learn and know how to use. They acquired this experience either from the priests of shrines in their home or nearby villages, or sometimes in regular "academies" established at a regional centre. Similarly, all who wished to practise as doctors, whether in the use of herbs or magic, had to be taught their art from men and women who possessed the necessary qualifications and reputation. Metalworkers, weavers, boat-makers, drummers, warriors and others had to learn not only the material techniques of their respective crafts, but also the spells, rituals, and other magic which were believed to be essential to success in their work.

Apart from these requirements in rules of behaviour, religion, and craftsman skills, there were also the needs of government. Many peoples had organised themselves in communities which gave much authority, for the taking of community decisions and the keeping of law and order, to special associations or groups. Entry into these societies was generally by rites that were secret. These rites had to be taught to would-be members. All the members of such associations also had to know about the history of their own people or branch of a people. They were further expected to know about their law, their methods of enforcing the law, and their punishments for those who broke the law. Where peoples had organised themselves in states with central governments and kings, there likewise had to be teaching in the skills and methods of administration by civil service. Many states also had groups of elders whose task was to learn the traditions of their country, recite these on proper occasions, and teach them to younger men.

There was altogether a great deal of formal education in sixteenth-century civilisation. But with some exceptions, important though few, it was a matter of word-of-mouth teaching of skills, customs, laws, traditions, and the like. It was done for the most part without the aid of writing and reading: the culture was non-literate.

This was a stage of society, moreover, in which education was generally thought of as being a part of religion. It was therefore not based on science, and so could do little to promote technical progress. Skilled craftsmen were trained in the methods of the past, and were content to follow the old methods. They felt no need to experiment. Having a religious attitude toward their methods of production, they were even discouraged from experiment.

One has to think of this civilisation, accordingly, as both moving forward and standing still. It was moving forward because of its unfolding energy and growth and wealth. And yet it was also standing still because of its non-scientific attitude to methods and technology.

This aspect of standing still should not lead to a depreciation of the achievements of sixteenth-century civilisation. The farmers, the miners who found metals and the smiths who worked so skilfully in these metals, the weavers and woodcarvers, the artists and musicians, the chiefs and counsellors, the traders and tellers of tales: all these and their fellow-specialists were successful because they had discovered and evolved new techniques. All this discovery and evolution was the product of steady development.

Religion and learning

There was also the impact of two universal religions, Islam and Christianity. One may call them universal religions, open to all, in that they differed in this important respect from religions created in West Africa. Muslims and Christians believed that it was their duty to send out missionaries and convert others to their faith. Those who adhered to West African religions had another view of the matter. They conceived of their faith as being intimately their own possession, a charter as it were of their own separate identity, and thus not capable of being shared by neighbours near or far.

So far as Islam is concerned, this difference was already of great significance. Even by the fifteenth century, Muslim missionaries were pushing across the Western Sudan and down into the southern forest lands. Yet Islam none the less remained a religion of the cities, towns, and larger market centres. Outside these its hold was weak and uncertain, and would remain so at least until the nineteenth century. Christian influence was far narrower, being restricted to a few missionary centres along the coastland whose power of conversion was minimal.

In the towns and cities where Islam was accepted, books and book-learning had taken an honourable place. While there is little good evidence for knowing when Islamic schools, founded for the teaching of the Koran and the *sharia,* the laws of Islam, first appeared in the Western Sudan, it is clear that they gradually spread. Muslim teaching of some kind certainly existed in the city of Gao as early as the beginning of the tenth century, and many Muslim missionaries were at work in the Western

Sudan during the eleventh century.* We hear of the growth of Islamic schools in the empire of Mali during the fourteenth century, as well as in the Songhay cities of the fifteenth century. By the sixteenth century, West African Muslim writers were at work on historical, legal, moral, and religious subjects.

Writing not long after 1520, Leo Africanus has much to say on this interesting point. Of the then capital of Mali, Niani on the upper Niger, he says that "they have many mosques, priests, and professors who teach in the mosques," and, as already noted, he considered the people of Niani "the most civilised, intelligent, and highly reputed" of all the peoples of the Western Sudan.

"In Timbuktu," he tells us, "there are numerous judges, professors, and holy men, all being handsomely maintained by the king, who holds scholars in much honour. Here, too, they sell many handwritten books from North Africa. More profit is made from selling books in Timbuktu than from any other branch of trade." Gao, on the other hand, could boast of no such brilliance. "The people here," Leo considered, "are absolutely ignorant. There is probably not one in a thousand who knows how to write. But the king of Gao," he adds with a touch of humour, "treats them as they deserve. For he taxes them so heavily that they are scarcely left with enough to live on."

In these cities, as in some others of the Western Sudan, learning drew not only on the talent and work of local people but also on those of Muslim scholars from other lands. "God has drawn to this fortunate city," wrote the author of the *Tarikh al-Sudan* about Jenne, "a certain number of learned and of pious men, strangers to the land, who have come to live here." As time went by the Islamic schools of Timbuktu and Jenne became famous throughout the Muslim world.

* See also pages 58 and 67 above.

The writers of Timbuktu

But Timbuktu and Jenne had well-known scholars of their own. The most renowned of the sixteenth century was probably Ahmad Baba. Born in Timbuktu in 1556, Ahmad Baba composed many works on Islamic law as well as a biographical dictionary of Muslim scholars. At least thirteen of his works are still in use by the *'ulama** of West Africa. His library was so good that it was held in high esteem for many years after his death. His bravery and independence of mind were also much respected, and it is not difficult to see why.

When the Moroccan invaders seized Timbuktu, Ahmad Baba refused to serve them. Fearing his influence and accusing him of fomenting a rebellion, the Moroccans took him in chains across the Sahara to Marrakesh. There they detained him for many years before allowing him to return home. There is thus a sense in which it may be said that Ahmad Baba, who never ceased to protest against the invasion of his native land, was not only an outstanding scholar but was also among the forerunners of West African nationalism.

Two important histories of the Western Sudan were written by scholars of Timbuktu. They are the *Tarikh al-Fattash,* the Chronicle of the Seeker after Knowledge, and the *Tarikh al-Sudan,* the Chronicle of the [Western] Sudan. Both were composed in Arabic, for this was the literary language of these learned men, just as Latin was the literary language of their contemporaries in Europe. Both were the work of West Africans born in Timbuktu. The first of these was Mahmud Kati, who was born in

* An Arabic word meaning "men of learning." Its singular is *mu'allim.* In West Africa this singular usually appears in its Hausa form, *mallam.*

about 1468 and is said to have lived to the age of 125; and the second was Abd al-Rahman as-Sadi, who was born in 1569 and lived until about 1655.

Both had fine careers. Kati was only twenty-five when the famous Songhay ruler, Askia Muhammad the Great, usurped the throne from Sunni Baru; Kati became a member of the askia's personal staff. He went to Mecca with the emperor and was thereby well placed to observe and understand the events of his time. He began his great book in about 1519, but his sons and grandsons, who were also scholars, continued to work on it and brought the story of Songhay and Timbuktu down to about 1665.

Abd al-Rahman as-Sadi was born only a few years before the Moroccan invasion, which he suffered as a child. He tells us in the *Tarikh al-Sudan* that it was because of all the sad events he had witnessed in his youth that he decided to write his book. In a moving preface he recalls how he saw "the ruin of learning and its utter collapse" under the hammer-blows of Moroccan onslaught. "And because learning is rich in beauty," he explains, "and fertile in its teaching, since it instructs men about their fatherland, their ancestors, their history, the names of their heroes and what lives they lived, I asked God's help and decided to set down all that I myself could learn on the subject of the Songhay princes of the Sudan, their adventures, their story, their achievements, and their wars. Then I added the history of Timbuktu from the time of its foundation, of the princes who ruled there and the scholars and saints who lived there, and of other things as well." For some of these "other things" we can be very thankful: they include, for example, many of the early traditions and legends of Ancient Ghana and Mali.

This capacious activity of Muslim scholarship and writing has never ceased in West Africa, but has grown and spread with the passing of the years. Today there are many *'ulama* with many pupils, whether in the northern country of the plains or the southern country of the forests. In the little town of Wa in northern Ghana, for example, the present writer was told in 1964 that its Koranic school was teaching a regular two-year course and producing about one hundred *talibe* or qualified students every two years. Often these *'ulama* have quite considerable libraries of their own with works ranging from manuscript books written many centuries ago, and since recopied, to books and lesser works composed only yesterday. It was from libraries such as these that Europeans first had knowledge of such works of historical learning as the *Tarikhs* of Timbuktu. Only in the last few years has there been any systematic effort at publishing the more interesting contents of these libraries, and much in this respect still remains to be done.

Religion and art

The origins of religion, in Africa as everywhere else, lie in the dawn of human society. They took shape in distant Stone Age times when mankind first multiplied and spread across the earth.

This means that some of the origins of West African religion should be sought in that wonderful "nursery" of primitive civilisations which grew up in the green and fertile Sahara during Stone Age times. Here, no doubt, is one large reason why African religions often resemble each other, at least in some of their ideas of worship. The sacred ram was a symbol of the supreme god of the pharaohs of ancient Egypt; but so it was for the Berbers of the Sahara and old North Africa; and so it still remains for some West African peoples. The python was honoured in ancient Meroe, capital of the African empire of Kush on the middle Nile more than two thousand years ago; and it is similarly honoured in other African lands.

But West African religions by the sixteenth century had long since grown into forms of their own. These were ex-

tremely varied, for they reflected the great variety of ways
in which men and women lived and worked. One may
think of them as having served a double purpose. In the
first place, they provided an explanation about how people
came to be what they were and the world what it was. And
apart from their spiritual motivation and value, they also
provided the social power by which people could make
laws and customs, and ensure that these were respected.

And so these faiths, no less than other faiths from which
they differed greatly in ritual, range, and manifestation,
were an indispensable means of helping people to live in
community, of expressing their higher hopes and aspira-
tions, and of linking the individual to the society in which
he lived. Their morality, in short, was ethical as well as
practical, their teaching mandatory as well as explanatory.
Many of them, not surprisingly, have retained their inner
sap and vigour even though traditional religion is now
declining rapidly in step with the dissolution of traditional
society.

Like all other religions before the age of science, they
embodied much magic and witchcraft; nor could they
have functioned otherwise. They also developed their own
body of thought about the origins and experience of mankind, and about the workings of the universe into which
mankind was born. These ontologies and metaphysical
systems seem often to have been remarkably complete in
themselves. In the case of one of the best-known of them a
Dogon sage, Ogotemmeli, took up thirty-three days in ex-
plaining Dogon cosmological ideas to the French ethnologist Griaule. Yet it goes without saying that they were
anything but logical outside their mythical terms of ref-
erence. Their service was to reflect the deeper moral truths
of everyday life, the difference between right and wrong,
between good and evil, and between the expectations of
the individual and his obligations to society. To this service
the proverbial wisdom of West Africa bears striking wit-

ness; the Akan, for example, have been said to possess more proverbs than are listed in the Bible or the Koran.

The characteristic arts of West Africa, dancing, singing, the playing of musical instruments, sculpture and the like, were also an important part of sixteenth-century civilisation. Sometimes they were only for amusement or the ornamentation of daily life, but often they were inspired by moral and religious beliefs, and were placed at the service of social and spiritual rites and ceremonies. In being thus linked to religion, West African arts were no different in *content*—in what they meant and did for people—from the arts of all other peoples who lived in the age before science. But they were very different in their *form,* in their shapes, fashions, and styles.

Surviving art forms in West Africa have a long pedigree. These masks and dances and sculptured figures have earned the label "primitive" from an outside world that has glimpsed them with a mixture of prurient shock and wistful admiration. The label is misleading. As evolved and practised over centuries, these forms were the product of an old and complex cultural sophistication. Like religions and proverbial wisdom, they helped men to express their beliefs, hopes, and feelings. If they spoke for energy and life, they also spoke for discipline, restraint, and right behaviour; and they spoke in many ways that echo back into a distant past. Here, for example, is the fragment of a song of praise to Tano, river god of the Asante, as recorded from the language of the talking drums some forty years ago:

The stream crosses the path,
And the path crosses the stream:
Which of them is the elder?
Did we not cut a path to go and meet the stream?
The stream had its beginning long long ago,
The stream had its beginning in the Creator:
He created things,
Pure, pure Tano . . .

Many of these old arts and songs have vanished from everyday life, together with the beliefs, ideas, and customs which gave them birth. The modern world has swept them away to museums. But the depth and value of the old life, so much a parent of the new, can be seen only when these arts of the past are given the place of honour they deserve.

14 THE ORGANISATION OF SOCIETY
IN THE SIXTEENTH CENTURY

Less effective representation, tighter control: this could be
one reasonably fair if crude way of stating the general
movement of society and government in this maturing
period of organisational forms which had come to birth
several centuries before. The road of popular fortune narrowed in West Africa, as it narrowed everywhere else,
and left a later world to face the problems of reinstalling
popular government in other and wider forms.

Early pressures of social change—the settlement of
nomad peoples and their multiplication in numbers and
diversity—the growth of trade, improvements in technology:
all these and their like had long since broken the relative
paralysis of Stone Age stability. Villagers had found they
needed chiefs. Chiefs had given birth to families of chiefs.
Families of chiefs had ruled together or fought together.
Increasingly, there had been the need for a strong hand
at the centre.

Out of this need there came states and empires, kings
and emperors. For a long time, even so, traditional forms
of democracy held their ground. The rulers could seldom
or never rule alone. They had to listen to their counsellors.
They were hedged about with age-old practice and prece-
dent. They were bound to give a hearing to the opinions
of ordinary folk. They could be removed from power if
they governed badly, and they often were. And this process did not occur everywhere, or at the same rate. People
who lived far from the main routes of trade, or in countries
with little natural wealth for exploitation, could and did
keep close to the old ways of rule by popular consent and
minimal organised control.

Many elements of these old ways remained vigorous,

though their real content might be less and less responsive
to their form. As late as half a century ago, for example,
the British ethnologist Rattray could collect in Asante the
following "public admonistions" addressed to a chief upon
his enthronement or, more properly in this case, his en-
stoolment:

Tell him that
We do not wish for greediness
We do not wish that he should curse us
We do not wish that his ears should be hard of hearing
We do not wish that he should call people fools
We do not wish that he should act on his own initiative
We do not wish things done as in Kumasi
We do not wish that it should ever be said
      "I have no time, I have no time"
We do not wish personal abuse
We do not wish personal violence.

The stratification of society

But wherever the process of centralisation went on, and
people formed themselves into states under elders, chiefs,
or kings, something very important happened to society.
Its old natural equality began to disappear. It became
stratified, as social position became determined by one's
degree of power and authority. Some men had the right to
become chiefs. Others could not become chiefs, but had
the right to elect them. Others again could not elect chiefs,
but only had the right to say how chiefs ought to behave.
Still others were pushed down into a lowly position where
they had to obey their masters without question.

Together with these horizontal divisions there remained,
however, older divisions of another kind, vertical divisions
which separated all the people of one clan from the people
of other clans, all the inhabitants of one village from their

neighbours, all the descendants of one set of ancestors from the descendants of other ancestors. These vertical divisions were in some ways even more important than the horizontal divisions, and they were already very ancient by the sixteenth century.

There also took place a third kind of stratification of society, caused by changing and expanding methods by which people worked and produced wealth. Craftsmen formed themselves into different groups, according to their skills: metalworkers, boat-builders, fishermen, farmers, diviners, priests, singers of songs, and many others. Some of these groups of craftsmen and specialists possessed much social power; others possessed little. How much social power each group possessed also varied from place to place. Among some peoples, for example, metalworkers were greatly honoured; among others, they were not.

Now these community divisions had already gone very far in West Africa by the early years of the sixteenth century, especially where the political consequences of Islam had taken their effect. Society had built, in other words, a ladder of social power. This marked an important if often painful stage in social growth; and it happened, as we know, in nearly every part of Africa as in nearly every part of the world.

Needless to say, men were seldom able or content to go on standing for long on the same rung of the ladder of social power. Slaves pushed upward into freedom. Kings were pulled downward. Poor men climbed to wealth, and rich men became poor. There was constant movement up and down. And this movement greatly influenced the events of political history, setting one people or state against another, and promoting wars and conquests. The progress of one people, as elsewhere in the world at this stage of society, had to be at the expense of some other people.

One further point. We have said that the dividing-up of society occurred nearly everywhere in the world. But it needs to be remembered that it went much further, and

became much more painful, in many of the countries of
Europe and Asia. There, because of much greater development in production and exchange of goods and wealth, society became divided into a class stratification of masters
and servants, with a few people having great social power,
and most people having little or none. There, too, movement up and down the ladder of social power became
difficult or rare, at least until after the French Revolution.

This far stiffer stratification had not happened in West
Africa. Indeed, it has still not happened. The horizontal
divisions have often remained of less influence than the
vertical divisions into different clans, descent-lines, and
communities. This is one reason why many of the old
equalities of life, much of the old democracy of the clan
and kinship system, are still alive and vivid in the West
African countryside today. This is also why most West
African governments during the sixteenth and seventeenth
centuries were much more democratic, much more respectful of the rights of individual men, than were most of
the governments of Europe.

By the sixteenth century, for example, much of the land
of Europe was in the private possession of a landowning
class. In West Africa, even today, most of the land is not
so divided. Yet the horizontal divisions in West African
society were, as we shall see, of growing importance.

Masters and servants

Old records and traditions reveal little of the way in which
ordinary folk lived, but much of the magnificence of kings.
Travellers from North Africa were greatly struck by the
power and wealth of West African rulers. Here, for example, is a North African description of the court of the
emperor of Mali. It is that of Ibn Batuta, who travelled
through Mali in 1352, but it was certainly true of later
times as well:

"The lord of this kingdom has a great balcony in his palace. It is called the Bembe. There he has a great seat of ebony that is like a throne fit for a large and tall person. It is flanked by elephants' tusks. The king's arms stand near him. They are all of gold; sword and lance, quiver of bow and arrows. He wears wide trousers made of twenty pieces of stuff, and they are of a kind which he alone may wear.

"Before him stand about twenty Turkish or other pages, who are brought from Cairo. One of these, standing on his left, holds a silk umbrella that is topped by a dome and bird of gold. The bird is like a hawk. The king's officers are seated in a circle near him, in two rows, one to the right and the other to the left. Beyond them sit the commanders of the cavalry.

"In front of him there is a person who never leaves him and who is his executioner; and another who is his official spokesman, and who is named the herald. In front of him there are also drummers. Others dance before their king and make him merry . . ."

There one catches a glimpse of some of those groups of men who had the right to serve the king and the state in special ways according to their training and position in society: counsellors, military officers, spokesmen, drummers, and others. But what about the mass of ordinary people?

They were generally divided into the "free" and the "unfree." We have to treat these words with care, because the actual amount of freedom and unfreedom greatly varied with time and place; and it was always possible for free men to become unfree, mainly by being captured in war, or for unfree men to become free by hard work, loyal service, or good luck. All the same, these major divisions existed.

They were clearly recognised. In Hausaland, for example, men very well understood the difference between the mass of ordinary folk who were free, the *talakawa,* and all those who were not free, the *cucenawa.* In Bornu, the nobles ruled over three big social groups known as the *kamba,* *kalia,* and *zusanna,* whose amount of freedom diminished from the first to the second, and again from the second to the third. Writing of the people of the seaboard of modern Ghana in 1700, a Dutchman called William Bosman observed five main divisions amongst the peoples whom he knew there. The first were kings and rulers. The second were chiefs whom "we should call civic fathers, their duty being to take care of their city or village, and to maintain law and order." The third division were those who had "acquired a great reputation by their riches, either got by inheritance or obtained by trade." The fourth were farmers and fishermen. The fifth were slaves.

Free men seldom lived or worked just as they liked. Their freedom usually rested on the protection of chiefs and lords, a protection that was given in exchange for taxes or regular tribute of one form or another. In this way, free men often became vassals or subjects of sub-chiefs, or of important chiefs, or of kings and emperors. These vassals owed service to their lords; but their lords owed them protection in return. It was upon this two-way system of service that many of the principal political systems of the sixteenth century were founded.

Unfree men were in much the same general position as the majority of free men, except that they had fewer rights and were often pushed down into very humble positions in society. They seldom or never had any political say in deciding how chiefs should behave. They were usually "tied" to a certain place and occupation, and were forbidden to move away or change their work. In the empire of Songhay, for example, unfree women were even forbidden to marry free men, a ban that was applied so as to ensure that the children of slaves should remain slaves even though one of the parents was not a slave. Askia Muhammad slightly changed this law, but the result was much the same. He laid it down that a slave woman might marry a free man, but that her children would still be slaves, to ensure that the king and his chiefs should continue to have a large source of cheap or "tied" labour.

Kinds of service

It is often difficult to draw a clear line between men who were counted as being free, and men who were considered as slaves. Since nobody worked for money, free men as well as slaves had duties they could not escape, and often these duties involved very much the same kind of work. One helpful way of seeing how things were is to read the *Tarikh al-Fattash*, which gives a detailed picture of everyday life in the Songhay empire.

The *Tarikh al-Fattash* remarks at one point that Askia Muhammad, who became emperor in 1493, acquired twenty-four special peoples as part of his estate. It describes who these peoples were, and what they did in return for the emperor's protection. We can regard them either as vassals or as slaves.

They served in different ways. Some of them had to cut fodder for the Songhay ruler's cavalry. Others were riverfolk and fishermen. These owed the ruler of Songhay a certain amount of dried fish every year. "It consisted," says the *Tarikh al-Fattash*, "of ten packets of dried fish to be paid by those who could afford as much . . . And every time the king was asked for river transport, he provided it from the canoes of this people, and they also supplied the crews."

Another of these vassal or slave peoples were called Arbi. Their job was to be bodyguards and house-servants of the king. As many as five subject peoples (groups whose exact numbers we do not know) were metalworkers. "They owed a duty to the king of one hundred spears and one hundred arrows every year for each family of them."

And so it went on, each vassal or subject group having to provide this or that service to their chief or king, and each chief or king, in his turn, having to protect them from enemies and to help them in times of trouble. Rulers who fully accepted this two-way system of service were thought of as good, while bad rulers were those who took what was due to them without giving help and protection in return.

There was, it should be emphasised, much movement up and down the ladder of power. Free men were taken prisoner in wartime, and were thrust down to the bottom rung; they could be used or sold as slaves. The Muslim rulers of the Western Sudan often raided their non-Muslim neighbours so as to secure supplies of free labour; and their non-Muslim neighbours did the same in reverse. Lawbreakers of some kinds were also reduced to slavery. Regular slave markets were held. In the city of Gao, for example, Leo Africanus observed "a market where many slaves, men and women, are sold every day. A girl of fifteen is worth about six ducats.* Little children are sold for about half the price of grown-ups." Many such slaves were sent northward across the Sahara.

At the same time we should remember, if only for the purposes of political and social analysis, that slavery in West Africa was seldom the harsh and pitiless bondage reserved for those who were taken across the Atlantic to the mines and plantations of the Americas. Rarely did this become chattel slavery. Traditional slavery in Africa—the term itself can be misleading—was usually a different institution, and a much milder one. Often it scarcely deserved the name of slavery in the sense that we have come to use it, being only a form of service which carried special duties and obligations. In strong contrast to trans-Atlantic customs and attitudes, slaves could easily work themselves into freedom. The very structures of society imposed upon owners the need to fit their slaves or bonded workers into the framework of family life. A slave could marry his

* A ducat was a coin in use among North African traders.

master's daughters, become a trader on his own account, acquire ranks of authority over free men, and, as several well-known cases prove, even rise to the eminence of kingship itself.*

Methods of government

Government through a highly trained and educated civil service is a modern development. But the states and empires of the sixteenth century had civil services of a less complicated sort. Their rulers governed through a system of governors and sub-governors; and each of these had his own bureaucracy. These office-holders or officials operated early forms of civil service.

This was a process which had begun long before, and certainly in the days of Ancient Ghana. Little is known of the ways in which the lords of Ghana organised their government, but they must clearly have had some form of civil service, rudimentary though it doubtless was, since they were able to secure law and order over wide regions and draw tribute from many peoples.

With the passing of the years, we learn more about these methods of government. A writer of the early fourteenth century, Al-Omari of Cairo, has described how Mansa Kankan Musa of Mali (1312–37) carried on his rule. It was one of this emperor's customs, we are told by Al-Omari, "that whenever someone who has been charged with a certain task or important affair reports to the king, the latter questions him on everything that has happened from the time of his departure to the time of his return, and in great detail. Legal cases and appeals also go up to the king who examines them himself. Generally, he writes

* This is untrue of areas such as Mauretania, where Berber peoples continued to treat their slaves with cruelty and contempt.

nothing himself, but gives his orders by word of mouth. For this, he has secretaries and offices." Already, in fourteenth-century Mali, there were the beginnings of a regular administration.

Yet early forms of civil service such as these tended to be easy-going and unreliable. The officials might be prompt and obedient when the king or governor was present, but when he was not they might also stop bothering about his orders. Or they might simply go on doing things as they had always done them, irrespective of what the king or governor might say. The governments of these early states, in short, were very loosely organised.

The sixteenth century brought developments in government, and not only in those areas where Islam had become important. The rulers of Benin, by no means Muslim, introduced a number of reforms that were aimed at tighter organisation and stronger central control. These were especially the work of Oba Esigie, who came to power at the beginning of the century and ruled for nearly fifty years. Esigie emerged as victor in an old power-struggle, which had been fought by many Benin kings before him, against Benin's most influential group of nobles, the Uzama. These Uzama nobles had previously enjoyed the right to choose, by election among themselves, who was going to be the king of Benin. Now they lost this right, and royal succession from this time onwards became inheritance by primogeniture.

Kings, nobles, governors

In this particular change one may see not only how the power of the king of Benin had grown, but also how the local traditions of the Edo people strongly influenced those political ideas which had come from Yorubaland or elsewhere. For the Uzama nobles of Benin had been in many ways like the Oyo Misi nobles of Oyo, whose power included the right to elect the alafin of Oyo. But while the Oyo Misi among the Yoruba continued to enjoy this right, the Uzama among the Edo did not.

At the same time that he deprived the Uzama of their political power, the king of Benin created two new kinds of noblemen: palace chiefs and town chiefs. In this he was no doubt seeking to balance two important influences in the state. While the palace chiefs were usually connected with the court, the town chiefs were often self-made men who had done well in trade or warfare, or in some other specialised way of life which did not depend on having court connexions.

With all this, the sixteenth-century kings of Benin became more powerful in their city. Yet they do not seem to have strengthened their hold over the Benin empire. Benin princes became rulers of different parts of the empire, even outside Edo-speaking areas, but they ran their own affairs very much as they pleased. Meanwhile, too, rebellious or defeated generals, exiled chiefs, and traders were setting up little Edo states of their own. They helped to spread Benin ideas and the Edo language, but not the power of the oba of Benin.

Other changes were taking place in Yorubaland, and especially in Oyo. Here, too, there was an extension of central government, but the position was different from that of Benin. The king or alafin of Oyo presided over a governing council which consisted mainly of the Oyo Misi nobles. These owed their position not to appointment by the alafin (as did the new palace and town chiefs of Benin) but to their membership of certain noble families. They continued, as in the past, to choose who should be the alafin out of a large number of princes. They decided whether Oyo should make war or stay at peace, and they carried out the day-to-day business of government both in the capital city and in the metropolitan or homeland provinces of the Oyo empire. Their leader was called the bashorun. His political duty was to head the civil administration. But he also had an important religious duty, one that showed just how powerful the Oyo Misi really were. This duty was to worship the orun or "spiritual double" of the alafin; and he could advise the Oyo Misi that the alafin was no longer acceptable to the "spiritual double." Whenever he did this, the Oyo Misi could depose the ruling alafin and elect another. The ceremonial act of deposition was the sending of parrot's eggs to the offending alafin.

Late in the sixteenth century, and during the seventeenth, Oyo expanded and developed its imperial system of rule. But the political powers of the Oyo Misi nobles were not extended directly to the non-Yoruba parts of the empire. The chiefs or obas of outlying provinces enjoyed some measure of self-government, and were bound to the alafin himself in a number of ways. Thus the alafin appointed resident officials in the different provinces, whose duties were to look after the collection of taxes, settle political quarrels, and stop the development of plots against the alafin's rule. These officials were usually men who had been slaves, and were called the Ilari. The alafin's authority was further strengthened by the spread of worship of Shango, a god who was regarded as the special protector of the alafin and his power. On top of this, all chiefs had to supply troops for the alafin's wars, attend the alafin's yearly festival at Oyo, and serve him in other regular ways.

Internally, whether subject to Oyo or not, the Yoruba states were politically organised in much the same way. All the Yoruba governing councils of the sixteenth century, for example, appear to have dealt with a wide range of everyday affairs—with questions of morals and religion, public health and security, justice and foreign relations. They controlled the public treasuries into which the taxes were paid. They supervised public building, trade, and national defence.

In the Western Sudan, too, there was a steady tightening-up in methods of government. Sunni Ali of Songhay

(1464–92) had divided Songhay into provinces and had appointed governors and commanders with staffs of their own.* As a convinced Muslim, Askia Muhammad (1493–1528) developed this system further still, improved its organisation, and brought in many ideas of his own. Songhay was thus divided into the provinces of Kurmina, Dendi, Baro, Dirma, and Bangu. Each had its own governor, called *fari* or *farma* or *koy;* the senior among them was the *kurminafari.*

At the seat of central government, the askia (like Sunni Ali before him) worked through an organised system of office-holders. There were a large number of war chiefs, as we shall see in a moment, and a still larger number of civil chiefs. The latter, for instance, included the *barey-koy,* who was in charge of all court arrangements, and was assisted by the *kukura-koy,* whose job it was to provide food and other necessary supplies, and by the *garei-farma,* master of the camp. There was also the *katisi-farma,* head of the "finance department," assisted by the *waney-farma,* responsible for questions of property, by the *bara-farma,* who was concerned with wages, and by the *dey-farma,* who looked after such buying and selling as had to be done on behalf of the royal government. Farming problems were likewise the business of the *fari-mundia;* forestry matters that of the *sao-farma;* while the *asari-mundia* was head of the "department of justice." Besides these, there were many other officials. Such systems were adopted in Kanem-Bornu and later borrowed to some extent by Hausa and other rulers.

Professional armies

Chiefs and kings and emperors of earlier times had relied on irregular and temporary conscription of their subjects,

* See also Chapter 10 above.

their vassals, or their allies. Some of them, like the lords
of Ghana in the eleventh century, could put enormous
armies into the field by this means of "call-up." These
were amateur armies. They served for a campaign or a
war, and then everyone went home again until the next
time.

The rulers of the sixteenth century found that amateur
or part-time soldiers could no longer meet their needs.
There were several reasons for this. As their executive
power grew, the ties of traditional loyalty weakened. Where
earlier rulers had been content to rely on the ties of lineage
obligation, ruling more or less as *primus inter pares,* these
new men found that such obligations were a restriction
on their centralised authority. Having adopted Muslim
techniques of trade and government as well as Muslim
beliefs, they were forced more and more to over-ride the
old lineage networks which rested on traditional religion.
But to do this, and survive, they needed soldiers who were
outside the lineage networks and who could be relied
upon to obey their masters, the Muslim kings, without
paying attention to the teachings of tradition. Full-time
armies, to some extent professional armies, therefore developed alongside the growing use of slave labour and of
slave officials. Into their service the kings took soldiers
whose status in society had become servile—generally
through capture in war—and whose obedience was therefore personal.

Another though lesser influence was that the weapons of
war were becoming more expensive and more difficult to
handle. Firearms, for example, were hard to buy, while
cavalry horses were expensive both to buy and to feed.
Men also needed special skills to use them, and only
regular training could provide these skills. Kings saw that
if they were going to lay out wealth for cavalry horses
and firearms, they would do better to give these to men
who were going to spend their life as soldiers, who would

be properly trained, and who would stay closely under the king's own command.

Mai Idris Alooma of Kanem-Bornu, as we have already noticed, was one of those rulers who took advantage of all this development in the means of making war. He imported muskets and instructors from Tripoli, and built up a little corps of musketeers. He found these useful for three reasons. First, they were professional soldiers, and so were always available for duty. Second, they trained regularly with their weapons, and so were good at using them. Third, they were war-prisoners who had become the king's slaves, and so were bound to his personal service.

Askia Muhammad of Songhay seems to have led the way in forming professional armies, his renowned predecessor, Sunni Ali, having relied on the old-fashioned draft. Muhammad, taking over a large empire and determined to make it larger, was not content with an amateur army: he wanted a full-time army, and he built one up.

How he did this may be seen in the *Tarikh al-Fattash*. Briefly, a full-time army was raised and placed under the command of a full-time general, the *dyini-koy* or *balama*. The askia also formed a full-time "navy" on the Niger. Sunni Ali had included Niger boatmen in his amateur military system. The askia turned these into professional sailors. This Songhay navy on the Niger he placed under the *hi-koy*, or admiral of the canoe-fleet. Another officer, the *tara-farma*, had command of a full-time force of cavalry.

Soldiers also began to become professional in the Guinea states. Some of the Yoruba governments raised full-time military units. Though perhaps a little later, special groups of professional warriors emerged in Iboland, men who were available to sell their war-making or defensive services to those peoples or rulers who might need them. Such warrior-mercenaries, or professional soldiers, were certainly busy along the great trade routes, providing escorts for the caravans, defending markets, chasing off raiders. Sometimes, as we have seen in the case of Gonja,* warriors like these helped to form new states.

It should be remembered that these long-service troops were only the core or nucleus of the army. Every state still depended on calling up amateur soldiers during time of war, for none of them had enough professionals. What sometimes happened now, however, in contrast with the past, was that the skill of the professionals was learned to some extent by the amateurs, especially in conquering states like Songhay where large armies fought many wars.

All this had mixed results. War became more frequent and more destructive. Ordinary folk suffered accordingly. But professional armies also reinforced the power of kings and governments, and, in doing so, made it easier to keep law and order over wide regions. Ordinary folk could gain from this.

These contradictory influences worked together during the sixteenth century. They led to political progress, but they also opened the way to unforeseen disasters.

Law and order

Some peoples had many laws, many social rules and regulations, and went to great trouble to enforce them. Other peoples got along with far fewer laws, and bothered far less about applying them. It depended on where they lived and how they lived. The sixteenth century also saw changes in this field.

There was a growth in the means of *enforcing* law, whether by specially appointed officials, by special associations elected or recognised for the purpose, or by the formation of soldier groups who took their orders from judges or kings (though judges and kings were often the same men). But there was also a growth in the means of *mak-*

* See pages 129 and 130 above.

ing law. This development of African law, of what is sometimes called customary law because it was not written down, formed an important aspect of the social scene.

It is an aspect that has been little studied; and we cannot follow it here. But an exceptional problem in the development of law does call for special comment. This was the clash between Muslim law and traditional African law. (Later on, a similar though more limited clash would occur between African law and European or Christian law.)

Muslim law rested on the *sharia,* a code of beliefs, observances, and rules laid down long ago, based on the teachings of the Koran. In its pure form, the *sharia* not only preaches that there is only one God, but frowns severely on all forms of sorcery and witchcraft. From its first introduction, accordingly, Islam clashed repeatedly with West African beliefs in many gods and in many forms of magic.

It clashed, of course, for various practical as well as religious reasons. We have mentioned in Chapter 10 how the rulers of Songhay tried to balance the interests of the Muslim people of the towns with those of the non-Muslim people of the countryside.* One reason for this opposition of interests lay in the very different rules which govern the inheritance of wealth among Muslims and non-Muslims. Another practical reason, especially important when it came to deciding on the choice of kings and chiefs, lay in the contrast between systems of primogeniture increasingly promoted by Islamic influence, and traditional systems of election from a more or less large number of possible candidates.

* See page 121.

Clash of beliefs

These and similar contrasts in custom and belief had results of great political influence. There was often an outright clash between those who continued to believe in their traditional religions, and those who accepted Islam. We have noticed some examples of this. When the non-Muslim followers of Sumanguru occupied the capital of Ancient Ghana, the Muslim merchants left the city and went to Walata, ruled by Muslims. Something of the same kind happened, later on, when the non-Muslim Fulani drove out the Muslim rulers of Tekrur.

The force of this clash varied with the times. Often there came a compromise. Some peoples accepted Islam, but none the less kept many of their old beliefs and customs. As well as the *sharia,* in other words, they also had the *'ada.* In the sixteenth century, however, the clash was often acute in the Western Sudan, because the late fifteenth century had seen a large expansion of Islam in the towns and cities. Later on, as we shall note, the cause of Islam suffered many reverses, only to assert itself once more in the eighteenth century.

Before leaving this subject, we may usefully return for a moment to the case of Songhay discussed in Chapter 10. By the time Sunni Ali came to the throne, in 1464, Islam was becoming strong among the merchants and leaders of the Songhay cities and market-centres. Sunni Ali accordingly made concessions to their beliefs and customs, and went out of his way to declare his respect for Muslim scholarship. "Without learned men," he is said to have remarked, "there would be no pleasure in life." But Sunni Ali based his political and military power on the support of the non-Muslim farmers and fishermen of the countryside; and his imposing record of success shows that in this he calculated wisely.

But Islam continued to gain converts and influence in the cities and market-centres, so that Askia Muhammad, coming to power at the end of the century, found himself in the opposite position to that of Sunni Ali. Although the askia was careful not to offend non-Muslim feelings, at least on matters of court ceremonial, he ruled as a strict Muslim and introduced many legal reforms. In order to devise these laws, and make certain that they were properly in line with Muslim thought, he applied for advice to a famous scholar of North Africa, Al-Maghili (d. 1504), whose advice was likewise sought by the ambitious Muhammad Rumfa of Kano.

This pro-Muslim policy served Askia Muhammad well. He built a still wider empire than Sunni Ali had done. But the conflicts between Muslims and non-Muslims, in Songhay as elsewhere, continued. Their full effects were felt with the Moroccan invasion of 1591, for the 'ulama of the Songhay towns then tended to accept the Moroccans as their natural Muslim allies against the non-Muslim people of the Songhay countryside. When Askia Issihak II faced the Moroccan army at the disastrous battle of Tondibi in 1591, his chief secretary and adviser, Alfa Askia Lanbar, even went so far as to persuade him to abandon the field. Later on, this Muslim official also betrayed some of the Songhay chiefs to the leader of the Moroccan invaders. In behaving like this, of course, the 'ulama of cities like Timbuktu could argue their own *raison d'état:* they were merely trying to recover their old independence. They backed the Moroccans against the Songhay rulers; once the latter were defeated, they turned round and became hostile to the Moroccans. But their attitude during the invasion tells a great deal about the political importance of the conflict between Islam and West African religion, both then and in later times.

15 NEW PRESSURES FROM OUTSIDE

If this many-sided civilisation of the sixteenth century remained the work of West Africans, it was often influenced as well, and sometimes with deep effect, by pressures and influences from outside. Important among these, now as in earlier times, were the opportunities and demands of long-distance trade.

For century after century, the gold and other products of West Africa were carried through the Sahara by the "ships of the desert," the slow but persevering camel caravans which brought to West Africa, in exchange, salt and other things that were valued by West Africans because they did not produce these goods themselves, or did not produce them in sufficient quantity. This interaction of West and North Africa had first become a central part of history in the early days of Ghana and Kanem.

In the sixteenth century these old and valued trading links were much disturbed by political troubles both in North Africa and in the Western Sudan. This had big consequences in the seventeenth and eighteenth centuries. To understand how and why they came about, we must leave West Africa for a while, and look at what was happening elsewhere.

Changes in North Africa: the Turkish empire

The old trade routes through the Sahara were composed of three main "groups": those in the west, in the centre, and in the east. The first set of routes, the westerly routes, linked West Africa by way of Mauretania to the rich Muslim states in Morocco and southern Spain, and, through

these, to the cities of western Europe. The second set, less
used than the first, linked the great markets of the middle
Niger by way of the Hoggar with Algeria and other markets of the central Maghreb.* The third set of routes, the
easterly routes, linked Hausaland and Kanem by way of
Agadès and Murzuk with the Fezzan (in southern Tunisia
today), Tripoli, and Egypt. Another important route went
eastward from Kanem-Bornu by way of Darfur to the
middle Nile, and so to Egypt.

There were cross-routes as well. Caravans from the middle Niger, for instance, could take the westerly routes to
the north; or they could go north-eastward to Aïr and then
to Murzuk by way of the great oasis of Tuat.

Events in the north now combined to disturb the trade
along nearly all these routes.

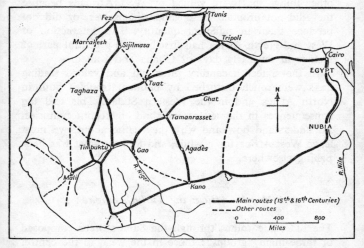

27 Caravan routes across the Sahara in the fifteenth and
sixteenth centuries

* Maghreb: Tunisia, Algeria, and Morocco.

So far as the westerly routes are concerned, this was largely the result of wars between Muslims and Christians in Spain and Morocco. Pushing the Muslims out of Spain, the Portuguese and Spanish came south across the Mediterranean. In 1471 the Portuguese captured some of Morocco's Atlantic ports, including Tangier; in 1505 they captured others. The Spanish, meanwhile, seized some of Morocco's Mediterranean ports. At the same time new conflicts broke out inside Morocco itself.

Later, in the second half of the sixteenth century, the Moroccans recovered most of their ports and began a slow recovery. But much had been destroyed. Sijilmasa, the ancient market city which lay at the northern end of the westerly caravan routes, had been ruined and never afterwards recovered. Even more serious for West African trade, there was now a frontier of warfare between Muslim Morocco and Christian Spain. Trade continued between the two; but it lost much of its former freedom of movement, and, in losing this, contracted in value.

Emerging from these costly wars, the Moroccan kings looked about for means of filling their empty treasuries. As we have seen, they picked on Songhay. They strove to capture the wealth of the Western Sudan. Their venture scarcely prospered, but it meant another big interruption in the peaceful flow of trade between West and North Africa.

At the same time a new power was rising in the eastern Mediterranean. This bore down on the central and easterly caravan routes, though with varying impact.

The empire of the Ottoman rulers of Turkey now began to expand westwards into Africa. Egypt became its target. Ruled since 1250 by a line of powerful soldier-kings, the Mamluks, Egypt had known prosperity and freedom from invasion, especially under Sultan Baybars (1260–77) and Sultan Kala'un (1279–90). But since then, military rule had weakened Egypt. It was now attacked from two directions.

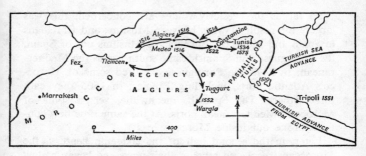

28   The Turkish advance on North Africa

In 1509 a Portuguese fleet under Francisco de Almeida fought and defeated an Egyptian fleet in the Indian Ocean. This gave Portugal control of the narrow straits which lead from the Indian Ocean into the Red Sea. By controlling these straits, the Portuguese hoped to capture the ancient and much valued trade which had long passed between Egypt and the western states of India, but in trying to capture this trade, the Portuguese largely destroyed and put an end to it.

This Portuguese intervention might not have mattered very much, since goods could still go overland between Egypt and the East, had it not been for another imperialist enterprise. This was the westward expansion of the Ottoman empire.

In 1517 the Turkish armies seized Egypt. In 1551 they occupied Tripoli. Irregular raiding companies* carried the power of their country still further westward through North Africa. They made themselves the masters of the coast of Tunisia and Algeria, founding new Turkish-dominated states along this seaboard.

There now developed a bitter Mediterranean rivalry between the Christians of southern Europe and the Muslim

---

* The Europeans of the Mediterranean, who often fought these companies, called them corsairs or pirates.

Turks advancing through North Africa from Egypt. Much of the sixteenth century passed in small harsh battles between the two sides, each seeking to win control of sections of the North African coastline and so acquire mastery of the trade with West Africa. In 1571 a partial decision was reached in a memorable sea fight between the Christians and the Muslims off Lepanto, on the western coast of Greece. The Christians had the victory but were unable to follow it up. They halted Ottoman maritime expansion but failed to win control of the Turkish province of Tunisia or the Turkish-ruled state of Algeria.

All these wars and upheavals damaged the trans-Saharan trade, especially on the western routes. After the ruin of Songhay and the establishment of Turkish power along much of the North African coast, trade was slow to recover. The movement of goods between West Africa and southern Europe by way of Tunis and Algiers, and between West Africa and western Asia by way of Egypt, was repeatedly barred by new frontiers of war or hindered by new imperial rivalries.

And when, finally, trade could again flow easily between West Africa and North Africa, the world had greatly changed. The "ships of the desert" were fast giving way to the ships of the ocean. Thanks to their progress in long-range sailing and ocean navigation, the mariners and merchants of Europe were firmly on the scene.

The coming of the Europeans to West Africa

Not many Europeans had sailed to West Africa before 1500, but then their numbers rapidly and regularly increased. They also sailed increasingly to India and other Far Eastern lands, as well as to the Americas.

This overseas enterprise was the product of important developments in Europe. One of these was the national growth of western and southern Europeans, notably the

Spanish, Portuguese, Dutch, English, and French, together with their expanding financial and military power. Another was the commercial interest which led these peoples, spearheaded by the Portuguese and Spanish, into trying to break the Muslim hold on international trade with Asia and West Africa. Faced with Muslim control of North Africa and Egypt, the Europeans now tried to "get round the back of the Muslims" by sailing far to the south and east. A third

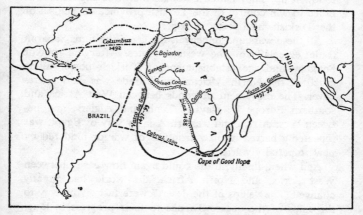

29   Some European voyages of exploration after 1433

and decisive development was Europe's new technical ability to build ocean-going ships and sail them out of sight of land.

Until the 1430s the seaboard nations of Europe possessed no ships that were good enough for long-range discovery.* Before that time, only the peoples of the East knew how to make great voyages at sea. Of these peoples the Chinese

* Scandinavian crews had sailed to North America several hundred years earlier. But these Viking voyages were not followed up, and the little colonies they established vanished at some unknown point in the Middle Ages.

were the most advanced. It was the Chinese who made the great naval and navigational inventions which first enabled the building of large ships that could withstand the tempests of the ocean. It was they who designed sails which could enable these ships to sail against the wind, "into the wind" as sailors say; and it was they who first used instruments such as the compass.

These Chinese inventions were taken over by other peoples who sailed the empty waters of the Indian Ocean and the eastern seas. Foremost among these were the Arabs. Through the Arabs and Asian peoples, inventions of this kind became known to the Europeans of the Mediterranean. Now moving into the age of science, these Europeans borrowed the new methods of sailing and navigating, improved on them, and began to build long-range ships of their own. In this the Italians, Spanish, and Portuguese took a leading part.

So far as West Africa was concerned, and for reasons that we need not discuss here, it was the Portuguese who mattered. Under an enterprising nobleman called Prince Henry (1394–1450) they forged ahead. The prince assembled a valuable library of charts and maps. He provided money for the building of ships and the recruiting of crews, and ordered these to sail down the western shores of Africa.

Until the 1430s the sailors of Portugal had never managed to go beyond southern Morocco. They had feared to voyage any further, because, apart from superstitious beliefs about the climate and conditions of sea and land beyond Cape Bojador, the winds along this part of the coast blow nearly always from the north to the south.* The Portuguese could sail southward with the wind behind their ships and sails, but these ships and sails were ill-equipped for returning northward against the wind. They had a saying which tells the story:

* See also "The sea-merchants" in Chapter 16.

> Who sails beyond the Cape Nun shore,
> Turns back then, or returns no more.

Now they built ships and sails which could master the winds, and in 1434 went for the first time far south beyond Cape Nun. Year by year, they sailed further. In 1446 their captains reached the mouth of the Senegal river. In 1472 they entered the Bight of Benin, having reached Elmina the year before. In 1482, they got as far as the mouth of the Congo. In 1488 Diaz rounded the Cape of Good Hope at the extreme southern point of Africa. Ten years later Vasco da Gama led three ships right round the Cape of Good Hope, up the eastern coast of Africa as far as Malindi (in modern Kenya), where he found an Arab pilot, Ibn Majid, who took him across the ocean to India. The Portuguese had passed through the ocean gates of the "Golden East."

Seamen of other European countries followed them, boldly risking long months at sea in small, slow, sailing ships and suffering many deaths and disasters, but drawn on always by the powerful hope of new discoveries. The Spanish were among them, but the main Spanish effort lay in the Caribbean, first reached by Christopher Columbus in 1492, and afterwards on the mainland of the Americas. Hard in the wake of the Portuguese and Spanish there came the French and English and then, towards the end of the sixteenth century and later, the Dutch and Danes, the Swedes and Germans of Brandenburg (as Prussia was then called). All these Europeans fought and quarrelled with each other, disputed their "rights" to this or that region of the sea and coast, and yet steadily added to European knowledge and experience.

Sometimes this work of exploration was violent and destructive, for early European captains often tried their hands at raiding and looting. For the most part, though, West African states were too strong to be attacked with much hope of success by soldiers from the sea. It was not many years before the raiding and looting gave way to peaceful trade and even, here and there, good friendship.

A new partnership

Coastal Africans now found that they could buy metal goods and other useful things from traders who came right to their beaches. This was highly convenient for these Africans of the coast, who had formerly had to rely on middlemen from the Western Sudan. Europeans, for their part, discovered that they could sell their goods for gold and ivory and pepper, all items of great value when resold in Europe, but which they too had formerly had to buy, through many middlemen, from the traders of North Africa. The records show that Africans and Europeans alike welcomed this new coastal trade, and did their best to make it grow.

In the sixteenth century these business dealings were useful only to peoples living along the Guinea coast itself. The main bulk of West African trade still went overland by the central and eastern routes across the Sahara. But the future of the coastal trade was to be of the highest possible importance; and now it was that the foundations for a big expansion were laid.

Throughout the century, it should be emphasised, the trade was largely one of partnership between Africans and Europeans. Both sides gained. They bargained keenly with each other, but they also respected each other. If this partnership could have continued into the future, history would have a very different tale to tell.

As the years slid by, the two-sided gain from this coastal trade became increasingly a one-sided gain, with Europeans benefiting more and more, and Africans less and less. The trade developed away from a peaceful exchange of raw materials and manufactured goods, and towards a massive trade in captives and in slaves. The beginnings of the over-

seas slave trade, a development of dark and terrible meaning for many African peoples, also lie in the sixteenth
century.

Here we shall examine only why this happened. For the
main growth of the overseas slave trade occurred in later
years.*

Beginning of the Atlantic slave trade

The slave trade grew big because of European activities in
the distant lands beyond the Atlantic.

In 1492, having boldly sailed across the Atlantic, Christopher Columbus and his men arrived at some islands in
the western Caribbean. Knowing nothing of the existence
of the American continent, although there are some who
think that he may have had knowledge of the Viking discoveries, Columbus believed that he had come near to
India. So he called these Caribbean islands the West Indies,
a name they still bear. Others followed Columbus, entering
the lands of North, Central, and South America.

These others, who were Spanish soldiers and adventurers,
ruined the American peoples whom they found. Their intention was not trade, but loot; not peace, but war; not
partnership, but enslavement. They fell upon these lands
with greed and the fury of destruction. And the American
peoples, unlike the Africans, were unable to defend themselves. Being at an earlier stage of social and technical
development than the Africans, they fell easy victims to
Spanish violence. Along the coast of Guinea, the Portuguese and other Europeans had begun by trying their hands
at violence. But they had given that up. The Africans they
met were too strong for them. In the Americas it was different.

* A summary of the results of the trade will be found in Chapter 24, pages 293–300.

There was terrible destruction of the "Indians," the name that was mistakenly given by these raiders to the native-born American peoples. A Spanish report of 1518, only twenty-six years after the first voyage of Columbus across the Atlantic, says that when the island of Cuba was discovered it was reckoned to contain more than a million "Indians," but "today their number does not exceed 11,000. And judging from what has happened, there will be none of them left in three or four years' time, unless some remedy is applied."

No remedy was applied, in Cuba or anywhere else; or none that made much difference. Whole populations of enslaved "Indians," forced to work for Spanish masters in mines and on plantations, withered and died, rebelled and were killed. Trying desperately to find new sources of free labour, the Spanish began sending out their own people under conditions that were no different from slavery. But they could not find enough of them. Where else to look for slaves? Africa provided the answer. Already the Portuguese and Spanish had imported a few West African slaves into their own countries. Now they began to export West Africans to the West Indies and the mainland of the Americas.

In this they faced enormous difficulties. They had first to seize or buy their African captives and bring them back to Spain and Portugal. They had then to get these men across the Atlantic without entirely ruining their health, no small problem in the foul old sailing ships of those days. Lastly, they had to turn these captives—or those who were still alive after the crossing of the seas—into slaves. But this, too, proved far from easy. For the Africans resisted enslavement by every means they could. Led by nameless heroes, they broke out in revolt after revolt. They spread fear and panic among the Spanish settlers. They went up into the mountains or deep into the forests, and founded free republics of their own. They made history in their fight for freedom.

But Spanish arms and organisation, together with the golden profits of the slave trade, proved too strong for them. In 1515 the Spanish shipped back to Europe their first cargo of West Indian sugar, then a luxury of great price. And in 1518, grim date in the history of Africa and the Americas, the Spanish carried their first cargo of captives directly from West Africa to the West Indies. After that, throughout the sixteenth century, the slave trade grew by leaps and bounds.

It continued to grow in later years. As the wealth and size of the American plantation-colonies became ever larger, so also did the demand for slave labour. There developed what was to become known as the *triangular trade*, a commercial system which greatly helped to build the con-

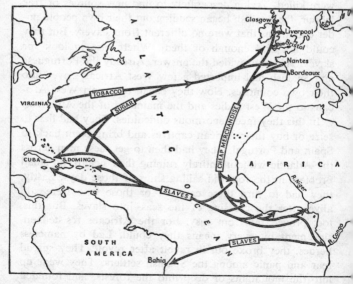

30   The triangular trade of the seventeenth to the nineteenth
centuries

tinued industrial and technical progress of western Europe
in the eighteenth and nineteenth centuries.

This new and potent trading system, starting in the late
sixteenth century, had three distinct stages or "sides," each
of which brought a profit to the merchants and manufacturers of western Europe. In the first stage, merchants in
the big ports of western Europe bought and shipped goods
for transport to West Africa. There these goods—cottons,
alcoholic spirits, metalware, and firearms—were sold to
African chiefs and kings in exchange for slaves. These
slaves were prisoners of war or condemned criminals. If
they had stayed in West Africa, they would have been
domestic or household slaves in the sense discussed already. African chiefs and kings often exchanged such
"slaves" among themselves. They saw no reason for not
selling them to Europeans. The Europeans accordingly
found it fairly easy to buy captives.

On the second "side" of the triangular trade, these captives were taken across the Atlantic, usually in irons, and
sold in exchange for sugar, tobacco, rum, and other products to plantation-owners, who turned them into real slaves.
The third "side" consisted in taking slave-grown American
products back to Europe and selling them at very high
prices.

On the Guinea coast the Europeans went on buying gold
and other goods. Increasingly, though, with the profits of
the "triangular trade" becoming ever greater, they con-
centrated on buying captives. The profits became so great
that in the eighteenth century the Europeans were even
carrying gold from Brazil to the Gold Coast in order to buy
captives they could not otherwise obtain.

Slaving and slave-produced wealth enormously enriched
some of the maritime nations of western Europe, especially
Britain and France. The capital thus accumulated in slaving
ports such as London and Liverpool, Bristol, Nantes and
Bordeaux made a contribution of probably crucial importance to the growth of the eighteenth-century factory

system and the industrial revolution which followed. But for Africa the case was reversed. Here the general consequences were ruin or impoverishment. Most of this still lay in the future. In the sixteenth century the cloud was no bigger than a man's hand; but soon it blew into a tempest, and the tempest roared and raged for years, even for centuries.

PART THREE

■

THE SEVENTEENTH
AND EIGHTEENTH CENTURIES

16 A PERIOD OF GREAT CHANGE

It is reasonable to think of the years around 1600 as a turning point, as the outset of a major epoch of transition that was to steer West Africa by many paths out of Iron Age civilisation into the very different civilisation of our own times.

Across the far plains and slow ascending hills of the Western Sudan the authority of the old empires was now at an end. By 1600 the imperial power of Mali had practically disappeared; only its ancient and imposing reputation lingered in the minds of men. The Songhay empire lay in ruins. Even Kanem-Bornu, though embarked on a new empire under Idris Alooma (c. 1580–1617) and his immediate successors, had begun to decline by 1700.

The end of the old empires brought trouble and confusion. Especially in the western and central regions, many peoples faced the need to build a new security. Power and initiative shifted back to the pagan peoples of the countryside. Muslim influence weakened for more than a hundred years, but then, as new leaders arose, took new political shape in a wide revival that was to cover much of the eighteenth and nineteenth centuries, and would be stopped only by the machine-gun fire of European invasion.

These events were accompanied by a gradual but important shift in trade from the western routes across the Sahara to the central routes; and from the central routes to the eastern routes. The western routes, for many years so vitally important, were employed less and less; during long periods they were barely used at all. By the end of the eighteenth century a French traveller called Venture de Paradis found there was only one caravan along the main western route every two or three years, while many other trails were barred or extremely hazardous. The nomads raided as they liked; the wells fell in and were not repaired.

The rare caravans travelled usually between Timbuktu and Wadan in the far west, thence passing northward by way of Wadi Nun to the cities of Morocco. One by one the market cities, which had relied on regular trade for their support, perished or declined. North of the desert, Sijilmasa, once so comfortable and prosperous, never recovered from its ruin during the conflicts and invasions of the Maghreb in the sixteenth century. South of Sijilmasa the old Saharan oasis towns of the westerly routes fell into decay or vanished altogether. The market cities of the central and western region of the Western Sudan suffered in the same way. They dwindled in wealth and power.

It was above all this decline of the cities that sent the cause of Islam into retreat, and gave the non-Muslim peoples of the villages their chance to take a lead once more, a chance that many of them seized eagerly. At the same time one should note that trade on the central routes was damaged less seriously and considerably recovered later on, while trade on the eastern routes, those going north from Hausaland and Bornu and Waday east of Lake Chad, almost certainly expanded after 1600. What had really happened, as we have noted, was that the bulk of the trans-Saharan trade had shifted eastward.

There were correspondingly large changes in Guinea, though in very different circumstances. Oyo rose to power among the Yoruba and became a strong empire. Benin city remained prosperous but the authority of its rulers seems to have steadily diminished outside its boundaries, especially after 1700.

New commercial opportunities with the sea-merchants, and notably a vast expansion of the Atlantic slave trade, deeply influenced many of the seaboard populations. In this respect, too, there came a marked shift in the weight of West African trade: increasingly, and with respect to the whole region, it shifted southward to the coast as the slow-plodding camel caravans of the north were rapidly supplanted by Atlantic sailing ships. These vessels might be very small when compared with later standards; they were none the less very large when compared in carrying capacity with a camel caravan.

These were years of tremendous expansion in the Guinea trade. Prosperous city-states were founded in the Niger delta. Others emerged along the coast of Dahomey. Almost all the populations of the Gold Coast and of what became known to Europeans as Sene-Gambia—reaching from the good harbours of Sierra Leone to those of Senegal—were active in this trade.

We shall therefore find the seventeenth and eighteenth centuries a period of great complexity and vivid interest. Many new departures make their vigorous mark upon the record. Many bold and remarkable leaders appear upon the scene, wrestling with the problems of a time of change. There are many disasters, but also many triumphs. In some ways the record of these centuries may be the most stimulating and dramatic of all West African history. In following this intricate story we shall find it helpful to modify the geographical order used in earlier chapters. Accordingly we begin with Guinea and work from east to west, taking Guinea to include the forest and part-forest country as well as the seaboard itself, and then go on to consider the Western Sudan.

The sea-merchants

A little has been said in these pages of the growing influence of sea-merchants from Europe and the Americas. But for a long time this influence was felt only along the coast, and even here it was often of small importance. To put all this in its perspective, it will be useful to consider just what this overseas influence was, and how it took shape.

By the early years of the seventeenth century, as we have

noted, sea-merchants from several European nations were arriving on the coasts of Guinea. But they were still few and far between. They had no political or military importance in West Africa. Their ships were weak and unreliable, their sea-maps and sailing instruments primitive. They knew little of Africa, while much of what they thought they knew was wrong.

To the perils of the ocean and the fevers of Guinea there were added other risks. These Europeans were not united. They fought each other fiercely and often. At first the Portuguese had the upper hand over the English and the French. Then the Dutch, being by now the foremost trading union of Europe, came into Guinea waters and took the lead. In 1637 they attacked and captured the Portuguese castle at Elmina with the help of local Africans. Five years later they threw the Portuguese out of the Gold Coast altogether.

European rivalries

Having broken Portuguese control of Europe's trade with Guinea, the Dutch now tried to set up their own control. They immediately found rivals in other European competitors, notably the English. There followed years of occasional battle and ambush between Europeans whose violent rivalries were watched with keen attention by coastal Africans. These sided now with one European group and now with another, according to their judgment of where their own best interests lay.

Yet the sea-merchants persevered, gradually working their way towards a peaceful partnership both with each other and with African merchants along the coast. Once again it is easy to see why. Behind these sea-merchants there were powerful political and commercial companies and interests who were now becoming strongly established in the West Indies and on the mainland of the Americas.

They needed the Guinea trade as part of their system of commerce; therefore they needed peace among themselves. So the coastal trade steadily became more extensive and less violent. Soon it was being carried on peacefully at dozens of regular markets along the seaboard. Of the forty-one trading castles that were eventually built by Europeans in modern Ghana, for example, no fewer than twenty-eight were constructed before 1700. All of them were built only after local African permission was given, and their owners continued until colonial times to pay rent to the peoples on whose land these castles stood.

While the seventeenth century was thus the period of the establishment of the European-American trade with Guinea, the eighteenth was the period of its large expansion. By the year 1800 there was scarcely a single coastal people without its close interest in the trade; and by this time, too, the influence of the trade had pushed inland to many peoples who lived some distance from the coast.

Yet the Africans, though deeply influenced by this maritime trade, always retained the upper hand. If the Europeans were masters on the water, the Africans were masters on the land; and they made sure that they remained so. Not until the middle of the nineteenth century would this balance of power be seriously altered to the European advantage.

Entrepreneurs in far-away Europe, now beginning to feel strong enough with their ships and their soldiers to go anywhere they wished and do anything they liked, fell into the mistake of thinking that the Guinea trade was run by Europeans from first to last. But the truth, as the traders on the coast well knew, was quite otherwise. "There is no small number of men in Europe," a Dutch official at Elmina Castle, William Bosman, was writing home to a friend in 1700, "who believe that the gold mines are in our power, and that we, like the Spanish in the West Indies, have nothing more to do than to work the mines with our slaves. But you should understand that we have no means of getting to these treasures, nor do I believe that any of our people have ever seen a single one of these mines."

Even in modern Ghana, where so many European castles were built, the sea-merchants landed and settled only with permission from the people of the seaboard. The Europeans might sit strongly in their forts, but they still had to pay rent for the land on which the forts were built. Beyond their walls, they could dominate the country only for the range of their musket-shots. Often these Europeans were attacked in their castles, and sometimes these castles were taken by African armies. In 1693, for instance, the Danish fort of Christiansborg in Accra was seized by the soldiers of Akwamu, held for a year under the flag of Akwamu,* and given back to the Danes only after the latter had paid a large ransom in gold.

Throughout this period, in short, the Africans were generally in complete control of their side of the trade. Often they were strong enough to punish European misbehaviour and insist on compensation for damages, or else simply to make use of the Europeans for their own political plans and strategies.

Growth of the Atlantic slave trade

Yet there was one thing that the Africans could not control, and this was to prove of decisive significance. For while they could decide to some extent what the Europeans wished to *sell* them, they could not control what the Europeans wished to *buy* from them. And what the Europeans wished to buy, more and more, and soon with a driving eagerness that overcame all opposition, was slaves.

We shall consider the results of the overseas slave trade at a later point.† Here we need notice only one or two leading aspects of it.

* The Akwamu flag depicted an African brandishing a sword.
† See Chapter 24, pages 293–300.

It began, as a large and regular system of trade, only in the second quarter of the seventeenth century. This was when the Portuguese were well established in Brazil; the Spanish on other parts of the mainland of South, Central, and North America; the English, French, Dutch, Danes, and Spanish on the islands of the Caribbean Sea. All these opened mines and plantations. They wanted more and more captive workers. They sent to Africa to find them, and there they obtained many millions.

Why did they succeed in this? The key to understanding why the slave trade began and grew lies in the master-servant organisation which operated in many states and societies. As in other countries of the world, then or at other times, West African chiefs and kings regularly turned war-captives and certain classes of law-breakers into slaves. These slaves, as we have seen, were not very different from most other men and women except that they had fewer rights. As often as not, they were little different from servants who had special duties and obligations.

And just as in other countries, then or at other times, African kings thought it perfectly legitimate to sell, barter, or simply give away their servants or slaves. Accordingly it was easy for European kings, when they found their own supplies of European or American-Indian slaves coming to an end, to obtain more from Africa. In 1562, for instance, the English captain Sir John Hawkins was presented with several hundred war-prisoners, whom he turned into slaves and sold across the Atlantic, in exchange for military help that he gave to two kings of Sierra Leone. Slave trading was a harsh and destructive aspect of the world of that time, and many nations had their part in it.

We have seen, too, that the slavery of Africa was a much less cruel servitude than the slavery which now developed in the Americas. Yet there is little reason to think that African kings, chiefs, and merchants would have stopped selling their servants and war-captives even if they had known the fate reserved for slaves in the Americas, for these kings, chiefs, and merchants were under powerful and growing pressures to continue selling men and women. In the first place, the Europeans now began to ask for slaves more than anything else, even more than gold and ivory. If refused slaves at one market along the coast, they simply went to the next market. If opposed by one chief, they applied to his neighbour. In the second place, kings and chiefs now began to need certain kinds of goods which they could obtain only from the Europeans. Of these, the most important were firearms.

Just as iron-pointed spears had proved better than clubs and stones a thousand years earlier, so now the musket became king of battles. A situation began to arise where chiefs and kings could feel safe only when they were sure of a supply of firearms. Yet these chiefs and kings, living in a society with almost no machine production, were unable to manufacture firearms for themselves. They had to buy them from abroad. Apart from a few that came south across the Sahara, all the firearms had to come from Europe, and the Europeans would seldom sell them except in part-exchange for slaves. Under pressures such as this the overseas slave trade rapidly developed into a massive export of captive labour to the Americas.

There were many cases where African kings, chiefs, or elders, seeing how destructive this trade had become to peace and prosperity at home, tried hard to bring it to a halt. We shall look at some of these cases later on.* But the pressures were too strong for them. Little by little, the overseas slave trade spread from the coastal countries to the lands behind the coast.

Firearms

This spreading influence was also linked to the changing organisation of African society. The rise of professional

* "Resistance to the slave trade" in Chapter 24.

armies came at about the same time as the arrival of the first firearms. This coincided, too, with the wars and troubles of the seventeenth century. Very large quantities of muskets now began to be imported. From England alone, at the height of the eighteenth-century Guinea trade, the gunsmiths of Birmingham were providing more than 100,-000 a year.

Here also there were gains as well as losses. By selling these guns, Europeans helped to spread war among Africans, since the buying of guns called for the capture of war-prisoners. But at the same time the guns strengthened Africans against European invasion or attack. The Europeans saw this latter point very clearly. Yet they on their side were as powerless to stop the sale of guns to Africans as the Africans were powerless to stop the sale of war-prisoners to Europeans, and for the same reason: they could never win agreement among themselves. The Dutchman William Bosman, then living at Elmina, explained this in a letter written home in 1700.

"The main military weapons [of the Gold Coast Africans]," he wrote, "are muskets or carbines, in the use of which these Africans are wonderfully skilful. It is a real pleasure to watch them train their armies. They handle their weapons so cleverly, shooting them off in several ways, one man sitting, another creeping along the ground or lying down, that it is surprising they do not hurt each other.

"Perhaps you will wonder how the Africans come to be furnished with these firearms. But you should know that we sell them very great quantities, and in doing this we offer them a knife with which to cut our own throats. But we are forced to do this. For if we [the Dutch] did not do it, they would easily get enough muskets from the English, or from the Danes, or from the Prussians. And even if we governors [of the official European trading corporations] could all agree to stop selling firearms, the private traders of the English or the Dutch would still go on selling them."

Cause and effect

Looking back today on all those confused events, one can
detect a clear chain of cause and effect running through
much of the story of the coastal lands of Guinea, and even
to some extent of the forest lands, during these centuries.

First, there is the slow beginning of coastal trade. New
markets and centres of African power appear along the
coast. New states emerge. These build themselves into a
controlling position, as middlemen, between the sea-
merchants on one side and the inland merchants on the
other.

In the second half of the seventeenth century there comes
an enormous expansion in the demand for slaves for the
mines and plantations of the Americas. Urged on by the
sea-merchants, the coastal rulers try to supply this demand.
They have to make wars in order to get hold of enough
captives.

These wars are increasingly made with guns brought
from Europe. But the European demand for slaves sharp-
ens the African need for guns; and this need for guns in
turn makes greater the need for captives with whom to pur-
chase the guns. By the eighteenth century the politics of
Guinea are deeply influenced by the exchange of African
captives for European manufactured goods, with guns high
on the list of these.

It seems worth while to have spent a little time on these
matters because, although they were only a small part of
the overall West African picture in the seventeenth and
even in the eighteenth century, they were a part of growing
importance. They set the scene for several very great developments. They show how it came about that large populations of African origin were settled in the Americas.
They explain why the influence of the sea-merchants, so
very small at first, should have grown so great as the years
went by. They help interpret much that happened.

17 BENIN, OYO, AND
THE DELTA STATES

Benin

The authority of the obas of Benin, at least outside their
city and its neighbourhood, appears to have contracted
gradually during the seventeenth century, but rapidly during the eighteenth. While the detailed reasons for this are
still far from clear, they arose in general from the changing
nature of politics and trade along the coastland of eastern
Guinea.

The sea-merchants were now offering many more opportunities for profitable trade. These, in turn, led to more
attempts by local people to win their independence from the
oba's authority. There were new wars, and, as the wars
multiplied, so also did the number of firearms that were
bought from the sea-merchants. Gone were the days when
the oba could hope to keep the control of expensive weapons in his own hands. Now they were available to rivals
and rebels.

With the rising quantity of firearms in many different
hands it became less and less easy for the oba of Benin, or
any other powerful chief in this region, to make sure that
his peoples remained obediently loyal. The traditions of
Benin speak of bad or harsh obas in this period; behind
such traditions one should no doubt understand the mount-
ing problems of government, as warfare and rebellion
spread across the land.

But these disturbing events did not necessarily mean a
decline in general prosperity. At least until the middle of
the eighteenth century, and perhaps later, Benin remained a
city of wealth and comfort. The chiefs and their families
continued to prosper. "The rich among them," wrote a
Dutch visitor, David van Nyendael, in the year 1700,

"wear a white calico [cotton] cloth about one yard long
and half as broad . . . Over that they wear a finer white
cotton dress that is often as much as sixteen or twenty yards
in length. This they pleat neatly in the middle, casting over
it a scarf about a yard long . . . Wives of great chiefs
wear calico cloths woven in this country. These cloths are
very fine, and very beautifully patterned in several colours.
The women wear necklaces of coral that are very nice to
look at. Their arms are decorated with bright copper or
iron bangles. Some of them wear bangles on their legs,
while their fingers are thickly crowded with copper
rings . . ."

This report indicates that local industries still flourished
in Benin, especially the crafts of weaving and metalwork-
ing, just as they had in the past. It affords as well a valuable
glimpse of the self-respect and dignity of the people of this
famous city. Van Nyendael found its inhabitants to be generally "good-natured and very civil," as well as generous in
their treatment of strangers. "But they certainly expect
that their good manners shall be repaid in the same way,
and not with arrogance or rudeness. And to think of forcing
anything out of them is to think of arguing with the moon.

"They are very prompt in business, and they will not al-
low any of their ancient customs to be set aside. But once
we [foreign merchants] comply with these customs, then
the people of Benin are very easy to deal with, and will
leave out nothing needed for a good agreement . . ."

History has many examples of great cities which continue to be comfortable while the states and empires around
them totter and fall. So it was with the great and ancient
city of Benin. Its dignified public manners, the fruit of centuries of social and political evolution, continued to surprise
and please the strangers who came here from beyond the
seas. They admired its government, its courtesy, its laws,
its tolerance. They praised its hospitality and care of visitors. They respected its sense of independence. Yet the
seeds of political decay were sprouting many weeds by the

end of the eighteenth century. Gradually, this old empire fell apart. And as it fell apart the security and comfort of Benin itself began to fail. The rulers and their priests, threatened by many perils, became more dictatorial. Their wisdom shrank. Their civilisation narrowed. One may see this even in the changing styles of Benin's wonderful art of sculpture in brass. These styles became less sensitive and delicate, more warlike and crude, closer to the spreading insecurity and confusion of the times.

Decline of the empire of Oyo

West of the lower Niger, in Yorubaland, events again took a different course. Under its supreme leader, the alafin, the empire of Oyo grew in strength and authority during the seventeenth century. It reached the peak of its strength in about 1650, and continued as a great power in this region for another hundred years, dominating the whole area between the Volta river in the west to Benin and the Niger in the east. It maintained during this time, through Egbado, a firm hold on the coastal trade; and it buttressed its authority over its subject peoples by a large and complicated military organisation, consisting of a full-time cavalry force together with part-time levies of troops from all its tributary states. This Oyo cavalry became famous and much feared.

After about 1750, however, Oyo began running into trouble. Disputes broke out between the ruling alafin and the powerful Oyo Misi nobles. The chiefs of subject Yoruba states now took a hand in these internal conflicts, siding with either the alafin or the nobles according to local interest or calculation; and the careful balance of political power within the empire became increasingly upset. By this time, too, the empire had grown so large that it must have been extremely difficult to govern through officials who made no use of writing, and had no written records.

The troubles of the alafin, like those of the oba of Benin, were undoubtedly increased by the growth of the coastal trade in slaves and firearms. This helped to spread warfare and raiding, and these in turn tended to promote revolt among the less loyal subject states of Oyo. There were ever-larger calls on the military and financial power of the ala-fin which led to stiffer demands on the subject states for soldiers and taxes. Such demands could not be popular.

Oyo's difficulties came in fact from three directions.

There was first of all a growing difficulty in keeping con-trol of the trade routes to the coast. These ran through forest lands where Oyo had never enjoyed much power, mainly because its cavalry could not operate in the forest. Growing strong in their middleman position between the sea-merchants and Oyo, and taking advantage of the trou-bles between the alafin and his nobles, the little states along and near the coast grew increasingly rebellious. They took advantage of the disputes at court between the Oyo Misi and the alafin.

After about 1750, the power of Oyo began to be chal-lenged from a new direction. For a long time the Fon peo-ple of Dahomey had paid tribute to Oyo.* Now they too entered the coastal trade in firearms, and, gathering their strength, made a bid for their independence. Oyo's armies were able to master the situation for many years but in the end, largely because of troubles at home, they failed. Dur-ing the nineteenth century, when the power of Oyo had dwindled to a mere shadow, the Fon were to turn the tables and themselves invade Yorubaland.

Thirdly, soon after 1800, there came a threat from the north. The rising strength of the Fulani rulers of Hausaland began to press down on the northern states which were subject to Oyo. The alafin of that time lost Ilorin in this way. Nupe threw off its loyalty. By the early years of the nineteenth century the empire of Oyo, for all these reasons,

* See Chapter 18.

had really ceased to exist outside the central region of Yorubaland; even there its power was on the wane.

As elsewhere in West Africa, the old systems in eastern Guinea were in crisis and collapse; and new political systems, shaped more closely to the needs of the new times, began to rise and take their place.

The delta states

The Niger delta is generally regarded as enclosing the low coastal plain and seaboard swamps between the Benin river on the west and the Cross river on the east. This measures roughly 270 miles along the coast and 120 miles into the interior, a vast and in some ways unique wedge of waterlogged country containing a maze of channels between the parent river and the sea. After about 1600 this unpromising delta became the home of thriving populations. As the ships from Europe and afterwards from the Americas nosed their way into creek after creek, active markets sprang into being.

Professor Onwuka Dike* has described this energetic and ingenious process. The places where these markets grew were widely separated from each other for there was plenty of room, and there were many serviceable creeks and river outlets. Usually, the points of settlement were "islands like Bonny dominating the mouth of a river which linked the hinterland to the sea. In time, each community developed the independence and individualism so typical of island dwellers. Every river mouth, every centre of trade, and, in some areas, every town had its overlord."

* *Trade and Politics in the Niger Delta, 1830–85,* Oxford 1956.

Government in the delta

These were highly specialised conditions, and they called
for correspondingly special forms of social organisation.
Although these forms were generally founded in the various
systems of kinship loyalty of the peoples concerned, they
evolved into new types of self-rule in response to the need
to bind together many groups of different ethnic origins,
some of whom had lived in the delta since remote times
but most of whom had lately arrived with the maritime
trade in mind.

The result was the characteristic city-state of the delta.
Shaped in the sixteenth century, this form ramified into a
diversity of related but different systems. By 1650 there
were many city-states, each of them, as Dike says, with
"all the apparatus of rule which enabled it to maintain law
and order, administer justice, make war and peace, organise and prosecute peaceful commerce."

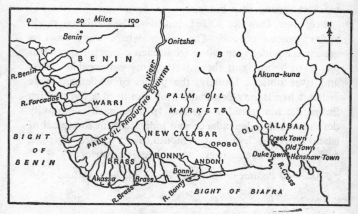

31   City-states of the Niger delta

Some, like ancient Athens, were republics. Others, like Sparta, were monarchies. Among the second were Bonny (a word corrupted by the sea-merchants from Ibani), New Calabar (Kalabari), and Warri: these were ruled by kings elected from members of their wealthiest and most prominent families. Among the republics were Brass and the market-towns of Old Calabar (Creek Town, Henshaw Town, Duke Town, and Obutong); these were ruled as republics by members of special political associations.

The Old Calabar towns, for example, were governed by Egbo, an Efik word for leopard. This Egbo or Leopard association proved remarkably effective. Its main object was to protect the interests of the merchants of the Cross river towns. Everyone who could afford to pay its entrance fees could join Egbo, but the merchants made sure that fees for entry to the top or ruling grades were high enough to keep power in the hands of the wealthiest among them. This "merchants' government" supervised all dealings with the Europeans, punished the latter when they misbehaved, and at the same time made and enforced the laws for lesser men and slaves. This was a mixture of limited democracy and rule by a commercial oligarchy.

Whether the central administration was monarchial or republican, however, the day-to-day life of these city-states was largely regulated by another characteristic institution, the "House system." This likewise went far to meet the needs of organising people of different origins, and, together with such societies as Egbo, took the place of the clan or extended-family grouping of previous times. The House may be seen as a kind of co-operative trading company based not so much on kinship as on commercial association between the head of a dominant family, his relatives and trading assistants, and all their followers and slaves.

There were many such Houses in the delta. Some of them, like those of the Pepples of Bonny, became famous throughout the western world. Often they were very large, for they might include not only the members of the House family itself, but also a sometimes large number of workers and servants or slaves. All these were employed not only in trading with the sea-merchants and with other Africans, but also in clearing and planting land, in founding new settlements, and in manning the trade-canoes and war-canoes on which the prosperity of each House depended. The House system is altogether a good example of the way in which new solutions were now invented for the new problems of the times.

The trade of the delta

All these city-states, like a number of others along the coast, grew prosperous on the Atlantic trade in slaves. One reason for this lay in their middleman position of monopoly. Because they occupied every river-mouth, and were skilful in politics, they obliged the ships from Europe and the Americas to deal with them, and only with them. Another reason for their success lay in the abundance of population that seems to have been present in the lands behind the delta.

This density of population helped to feed the supply of captives. As time went by, the trade became highly organised, being carried on by well-established rules and regulations for more than two centuries. Many Americans of African origin descend from ancestors who were shipped by the city-states of the Niger delta.

This long-standing export of people, this forced emigration to the Americas, may be compared with the similar export of people that was going on from Europe at the same time. Just as millions of people were taken out of West Africa, so also were millions of people taken out of Europe in these centuries: Italians, Germans, Irish, Scots, Poles, and many others. Few of the latter, it is true, were sent abroad by being captured and sold as slaves; they were none the less forced by hunger and unemployment to leave their homes and seek a new life across the seas. The real difference lay in the actual conditions of life in America for the Africans and the Europeans who were thus removed from their homelands. These conditions were far worse for the Africans, just as they would remain far worse for most of their descendants in later times.

How flourishing was this delta trade may be seen in many records of the time. An English captain* who wrote about Bonny, for long the biggest of the delta states, described it as "the wholesale market for slaves, since not fewer than 20,000 are sold here every year. Of these, 16,000 come from one nation, called the Ibos, so that this single nation has exported, over the past twenty years, not fewer than 320,000 of its people; while members of the same nation sold at New and Old Calabar, in the same period, probably amounted to 50,000 more." Like the slave-dealing merchants of the English ports of Bristol, Liverpool, and London or of the French ports of Nantes and La Rochelle, the chiefs and merchants of the delta states saw in this brutal trade the mainstay and guarantee of their own welfare.

The trade was no haphazard affair. Regular markets were held, governed by closely argued rules. "The preparation for these markets," wrote this same English captain, "generally occupy the Bonny people for some days. Large canoes, capable of carrying 120 persons, are launched and stored for the voyage. The traders add to their trade-goods by obtaining from their friends, the captains of the slave-ships, a considerable quantity of goods on credit . . . Evening is the period chosen for the time of their departure, when they proceed in a body, accompanied by the noise of drums, horns, and gongs. They generally come back at the end of the sixth day after their departure, bring-

* Captain John Adams, who was there between 1786 and 1800, and published his book in 1822.

ing with them, 1,500 to 2,000 slaves, who are sold to Europeans the evening after their arrival, and taken on board the ships."

Buying and selling with the European and American captains was a complicated business. There was much bargaining. The currency used was generally composed of trade goods like iron bars, rolls of cotton, or quantities of yams (needed by the slave-ships to feed their captives as well as their crews during the voyage across the Atlantic); cowrie-shells were also an important means of exchange. Any attempt by the European traders to bully or cheat their African partners was likely to be answered by a boycott. Operating through associations like Egbo, the House chiefs would simply close the river to European trade until the Europeans made good the damage they had caused. Here in the delta the Europeans had no castles and few shore stations but lived on old ships, called hulks, that were permanently anchored off the townships.

The complications of this trading system are very clear from the deals that were made. In 1676, for instance, the captain of the English ship *Bonaventure* bought a hundred men, women, and children, and had them duly branded by his crew with the special mark of the British Royal African Company: D Y, for Duke of York. To obtain these carefully selected captives he paid five muskets, twenty-one iron bars, seventy-two knives, half a barrel of gunpowder, and various lengths of cotton stuff.

Time and patience were needed for such bargains. Here is an extract from the records of another English ship, the *Albion-Frigate,* which arrived at New Calabar in 1699. First of all, as the customs prescribed, the captain sent messengers ashore to greet the king of New Calabar and ask him to open trade. "He gave us to understand that he expected one bar of iron for each slave more than Edwards [the captain of another English ship] had paid him. He also objected to our metal basins, mugs, beads, and other goods, and said they were of little value at the time." Bargaining continued. The next day "we had a conference with the king and principal natives of the country, about trade, and this lasted from three o'clock until night. But it had no result. They continued to insist on having thirteen bars of iron for a male, and ten for a female." The Europeans of the *Albion-Frigate* thought this too dear. They had supper with the king and went back to their ship. Agreement was reached only after another four days of argument.

Highly organised, this commerce was often conducted with a minimum of violence or confusion. The merchants on both sides gained from this, but their victims still suffered appallingly. Like their fellow-sufferers who were forced to leave Europe by hunger and unemployment, the Africans who were sent abroad faced terrible weeks at sea in foul old ships, got bad food, and met shipwreck and frequent death. But unlike the European emigrants, they were often chained during the dreaded "Middle Passage" from fear that they would revolt against their oppressors. This fear was well justified, for brave or desperate revolts at sea were numerous. And once the slaves were landed across the Atlantic, they were condemned to lifelong slavery under the most cruel conditions.

The story of these Africans is another one. Yet this story is also part of the history of Africa. In one way it was a very sorrowful part, in another way a triumphant one, for these Africans, shipped like cattle across the seas, none the less wrote a great epic in the annals of mankind.* Without them, the civilisation of the Americas could never have flourished as it did.

* See "Africans beyond the seas" in Chapter 24, pages 298–300.

18 DAHOMEY IN THE SEVENTEENTH AND EIGHTEENTH CENTURIES

General notes

The thinly wooded land of Dahomey is part of the open country which divides the forests of Nigeria from those of modern Ghana (see rainfall map on p. 8). This is one of the reasons why its history shows many contrasts with that of its neighbours.

Modern Dahomey, as a glance at Map 32 will show, includes the coastland between the frontiers of Nigeria and Togo as well as the inland country for some four hundred miles to the northward. These frontiers were established by French colonial invaders at the end of the nineteenth century.

In the seventeenth century there were two sets of political systems here. One of these was along the coast itself, the length of seaboard which European traders called the Slave Coast, and consisted of a string of small city-states. The other was in the hinterland behind the coast, and was composed of a number of more loosely organised polities, the most important of which was that of the Fon people based at Abomey.

Most of these populations, whether along the coast or in the interior, have traditions which point to a common origin in a region called Tado in what is central Dahomey today. By 1600, however, they were long since divided into different groups. Those along the coast now discovered the same chances of trade with sea-merchants as their neighbours in the Niger delta or the Gold Coast. The empty ocean became for them, too, a "frontier of opportunity." They grasped this opportunity with energy and courage.

Close to the ocean surf, the best-known of these seaside states were Jakin, Ouidah (also written Whydah or Fida), and Grand Popo. Immediately behind them lay Great Ardrah or Allada, the principal power along this coast for most of the seventeenth century and the one which generally controlled its weaker neighbours. All of these crystallised around the middle of the seventeenth century—at about the time, we may note, that increasing sugar production in the West Indies began to make increasing demands for African labour. Later, others were formed, including Badagry and Porto Novo.

Ardrah and Ouidah

These little states used the sea-merchants to their own advantage in the same way as did the cities of the Niger delta. Their kings fixed prices for the sale of goods, including captives, and sent their agents to bargain with the ships' captains. They likewise made the Europeans pay taxes. In order to trade with Great Ardrah, a merchant called John Barbot reported towards the end of the eight-

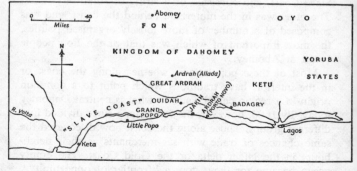

32   The Slave Coast

eenth century, "Europeans usually give the king the value of fifty slaves in goods, for his permission to carry on trade, as well as paying customs duties in respect of each ship. They also give the king's son the value of two slaves for the privilege of obtaining water for their crews, and the value of four slaves for permission to cut timber."

At first these kings found that the Europeans quarrelled so violently among themselves that they spoiled the trade. They took steps to stop this. As time went by, they came to terms with the Europeans, shared out the trading facilities among them, and reduced the amount of violent competition. The results were impressive. "Ouidah," wrote an English visitor, John Atkins, early in the eighteenth century, "is now the greatest trading place on the coast of Guinea, selling off as many slaves, I believe, as all the rest together —forty or fifty ships [French, English, Portuguese, and Dutch] loading their cargoes there every year."

Then came a new challenge from the inland country. This same visitor explained why. The king of Ouidah, he reported, was in the habit of buying captives from his neighbours, "but if he cannot obtain sufficient numbers of slaves in that way, he marches out with an army, and depopulates the country. He and the neighbouring king of Ardrah commit great depredations inland."

Now the Fon people of the inland country, who were raided in this way, already had problems of their own. They, like Ardrah and its neighbours, were officially subject to the Yoruba of Oyo. In the fairly open country where they lived, they found themselves at the mercy of cavalry raids by the armies of Oyo, who forced them to pay tribute. So the Fon of Dahomey came together in self-defence, and organised a strong state of their own.

The Fon expansion

They did this on new and revolutionary lines. Until now,
like other West African peoples, they had thought of their
king as being a father to them and ruling by the patriarchal
principle. On this conception the king's power is like a
strong pot, and the people are like the water in the pot: so
long as the pot is not damaged or upset, the water is safe.
But the Fon invented a different principle of government.
They likened the king's power to the water in the pot; the
life-giving water that was so scarce and precious to them.
The life of the nation was full of dangers and they compared it to a pot with many holes in it. Only if every citizen
placed his finger on a hole would the water—the king's
power—be kept from wasting.

This meant that the whole Fon people became directly
involved in support of their king, who was himself the
symbol and guarantee of their safety. Administration in this
new type of state was accordingly organised on army lines.
Chiefs acquired authority not by membership of this or
that family, as they generally did elsewhere, but by courage
and success in warfare; and they could be promoted, down-
graded, or transferred to other duties as the king thought
fit. Even women were called into this work of supporting
the king by direct service; and there appeared in Dahomey
regular units of women soldiers who fought for the king,
often with success.

Based on the town of Abomey, the Fon fully enter history with King Wegbaja in about 1650. Wegbaja was followed by Akaba in about 1685, and Akaba by Agaja in
1708. Under Agaja, an outstanding general and a skilful
ruler who reigned for thirty-two years, the state of Abomey
or Dahomey became strong enough to capture the coastal
states, though it was still forced to pay tribute to Oyo.
Agaja's warriors marched on Great Ardrah in 1725, and

took and sacked it. Three years later they pushed south again to the smaller states of Savi and Ouidah. In 1732 they took Jakin. After that, and for more than a hundred and fifty years, this coast was dominated by the kings of Dahomey.

Agaja seems to have had two motives in breaking through to the coast. In the first place, there is evidence that he wanted to call a halt to the slave raids of the coastal states, and even to stop the export of captives. It is certainly true that the number of captives exported from here greatly diminished after Agaja's conquest. Secondly, Agaja wanted to assure himself and his government and traders of better access to the sea-merchants: they were tired, in other words, of having to pay for their guns and gunpowder at the often exorbitant prices demanded by the "middlemen" traders of the seaside states.

Dahomey's hold on the coast was not kept easily. Ouidah and its neighbours tried to regain their earlier freedom of action; in this they were sometimes helped and encouraged by European captains and agents. Not until the 1740s did Dahomey win complete control. Then Ouidah became a Fon colony under the authority of officials sent from Abomey, the capital of Dahomey. Of these officials the most important was the *yavogun*. It was with him that the Europeans had to deal.

European influence was limited to the beach itself, and even there the Europeans were closely supervised by the *yavogun* and his staff. Only by special permission could Europeans visit Abomey. But as time went on, official European agents were generally allowed to go and pay their respects at court. By 1793 the English agent* at Ouidah could report that "from Ouidah to Abomey is perhaps the most beaten track by Europeans of any part of Africa." Most of these visitors to Abomey thought that the king was an outright dictator, but in this they were mis-

* Archibald Dalzel.

taken. Though the king's power was undoubtedly very great, he still needed the assent of his counsellors, and even then he could not act without obedience to traditional customs which placed limits on his power.

Dahomey and Oyo

Formed in self-defence against raids from Oyo and raids from the coast, the Fon rulers had developed a considerable military strength. But dangers from without did not end when Agaja seized control of Ardrah and Ouidah. Agaja still had to face his overlord, the alafin of Oyo, who could not welcome Dahomey's increase of strength, and to whom the coastal states appealed for aid against the Fon.

As a result the alafin sent his famous cavalry into Dahomey in 1726, two years after Agaja's march to the coast. They overwhelmed Agaja's army and repeated their invasions in 1728, 1729, and 1730. But Dahomey still kept a hold on its coastal positions, though forced to sell more and more captives to Europeans in return for guns and gunpowder. All these conditions reinforced the military organisation of the Fon state. They likewise reinforced all those customs which were thought of as protecting or helping the king, since the king was the symbol and guarantee of Fon safety. Royal customs which were believed necessary to the king's welfare had to be maintained at all costs, even when, as for a long time, these customs required the yearly killing at Abomey of a large number of human victims.

This powerful though in some ways peculiar state reached the height of its power under King Agonglo (1790–97) and King Ghezo (1818–58). Its armies continued to ravage nearby lands in search of captives for sale or for use on royal plantations; in the maintenance of Dahomey's authority and safety; and in revenge for real or imagined insults. Even after 1800 the alafin of Oyo, though no longer able to overawe the Fon, was sometimes able to make them pay tribute to him. After 1818, with the power of the Oyo cavalry in decline, the Fon were strong enough to refuse to pay any further tribute and afterwards themselves took the offensive against the Yoruba.

Though controlled by the Fon, some of the old coastal states continued to flourish. By about 1780 Ouidah was the main market for the whole lagoon traffic along the shore. Badagry also became active in business. Westward, other lagoon markets prospered at Grand and Little Popo. These had good defensive positions in their creeks and lagoons, and managed for the most part to escape from Dahomey's control. They dealt largely in ivory. Here is an English description* of one of them at the end of the eighteenth century:

"The houses are well constructed, and generally two storeys high with stone steps. There is a good market with the most abundant supplies of stock of every kind, and many delicious fruits. The [people] and chiefs are respectful, honest, and desirous of trade. Ivory abounds here in endless quantities, being constantly sent from the inland towns."

By this time, in fact, the Slave Coast had ceased to deserve its name.

* That of Lieutenant Edward Bold.

19 THE AKWAMU, ASANTE, AND THEIR NEIGHBOURS

The Akwamu and their rivals

While the early kings of Dahomey were building their power and making ready to push their armies to the coast, comparable developments were in preparation in the forest lands to the west, in the southern area of modern Ghana. Here there occurred a long struggle for power, trade, and security among a number of enterprising peoples. Prominent among these were the Akwamu and the Denkyira, and afterwards the Asante.

The state of Akwamu took shape in the modern region of Akim Abuakwa on both sides of the Birim river during the late sixteenth or early seventeenth century. Traditions say that the Akwamu had previously lived at Twifu Heman to the north-west of Cape Coast. The new state prospered by trade in the gold of the Birim river district, and in other goods. Towards 1650 it became strong enough to look round for allies and for lands to conquer. The underlying problem, essentially, was how to bring relatively large territories within a single system of tax and tribute.

For the Akwamuhene and his advisers the problem was no easy one. To the west and north-west they faced the power of Akim and other states that were allied or subject to the empire of Denkyira. There was only danger from that direction. But to the south and south-east the position looked more promising. Here Akwamu was in contact with a cluster of little states—Aburi, Bunu, and the like—which lay between Akwamu and the Ga and Fante towns and markets of the coast itself.

Now it was from these markets that Akwamu had to buy its guns, ammunition, and other European goods. To

ensure the future of the state, accordingly, the first need
was to break through to the coast, subdue the Ga towns,
especially Great Accra, and forge a direct trading partnership with the English, Dutch, and Danes. The Akwamu
armies achieved this in 1677 under a memorable leader
whose name was Ansa Sasraku. In this the Akwamu set
an example which was to be repeated later by the Fon of
Dahomey to the east and the Asante to the north-west.

Ansa Sasraku brought the whole Ga coast under his
control between 1677 and 1681. He and his successors continued to expand their authority and their trade. Helped by
their commerce with the Europeans, they enlarged their
armies and sent them further afield. In 1679 they subdued
the state of Ladoku east of Accra, and in 1689 the Fante
state of Agona west of Accra.

These were no mean feats. The Ga towns of Great and
Small Accra, for example, could raise an army of 9,000
men in 1646, and their power was not much smaller when
Ansa Sasraku defeated them thirty years later. The Ga,
however, were weakened by internal disputes. They split
up after Akwamu's victory. Led by Ashangmo, successor
to the more famous Okai Koi, some of them left their
homes and went eastward to Little Popo on the Dahomey

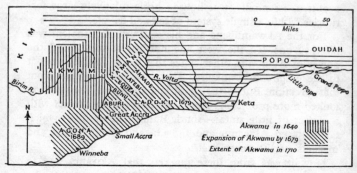

33   Stages in Akwamu expansion

coast. But the majority remained where they were, opposing Akwamu when they got the chance and taking what aid they could from the commanders of the European forts.

There were now two great powers in the forest and coastland of modern Ghana: Denkyira in the south-west and Akwamu in the south-east. Each sought allies. In this way Akim was generally the ally of Denkyira, while Asante, still small and weak, looked rather to Akwamu. Blocked by Denkyira and its allies on the west, Akwamu expanded eastward. In 1702 its armies crossed the Volta river and occupied some of the little states of the Dahomey coast, notably Ouidah. In 1710 they went over the Volta again, and brought the Ewe of the Ho region under their general control. The Akwamu empire had now reached its greatest point of expansion. Its authority reached for more than 250 miles along the coast, and for some way into the inland country.

But this widespread power was short-lived. By 1710 Asante had overshadowed it. Though friendly with Akwamu, Asante was traditionally hostile to Akim. Pushed and raided by Asante, groups of the three sections of the Akim people, Kotoku, Bosome, and Abuakwa, pressed across the borders of Akwamu in search of a safer home. Every Akwamuhene in the past had been worried by the threat from Akim: now, with Akwamu's strength extended over so wide a territory, the threat became a mortal danger. In 1730 there were many battles with the incoming Akim, who were mostly victorious. In a long and straggling war the Akwamuhene was finally reduced to flight. He led some of his people north-west across the Volta and settled there, while the remainder of Akwamu was divided among the Akim and their neighbours. Out of this war came the new Akan state of Akim Abuakwa.

With the eclipse of Akwamu, the little city-states of the Dahomey coast became almost at once subject to the kings of the Fon. Westward from them, along the coast, the

Ewe and the Ga regained much of their earlier freedom of
action. Westward again, between Accra and Elmina, the
peoples of the Fante group of states escaped from the
overlordship of Akwamu only to fall, though not at once,
within that of Asante. Elsewhere, Asante subdued Denkyira
and went from victory to victory.

Origins of the Asante empire

Of all the Akan peoples, the Asante were the most successful in bringing a large region of central Guinea under
the control of a single government. They built an empire
which was much larger than that of the Akwamu or the
Denkyira, and which lasted much longer. This empire became the greatest factor in the politics and trade of central
Guinea for nearly two centuries.

Their capital at Kumasi grew as time went by into a
large and bustling centre of political, commercial, intel-
lectual, and religious life. Here gathered men of action and
men of thought: educated Muslims; chiefs and soldiers
from the forest lands; envoys from many states; Dyula
traders from Bobo, Kong, and Jenne to the west and north;
Hausa merchants from Kano, Katsina, and other eastern
cities, together with a host of other folk.

Let us look ahead for a moment, and see what Kumasi
was like at the height of Asante power. We have a good
description from the year 1817, when some English officials were allowed to visit the city. These were greeted by
nearly five thousand people, most of whom were warriors,
and by a great deal of military music. "There was so much
smoke from the firing of muskets shot off in welcome,"
recalled William Bowdich, "that we could see only what
was near to us . . . We were halted in the midst of a circle
of warriors, where English, Dutch, and Danish flags waved
and flourished all around . . . The dress of the captains
was a war cap, with gilded rams' horns projecting in front,

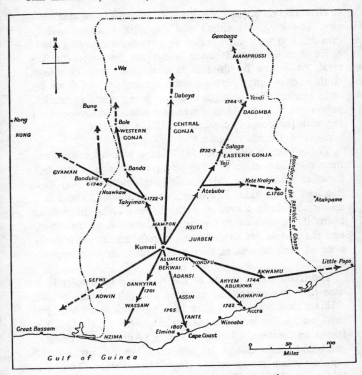

34 The expansion of the Asante empire

the sides extended beyond all proportion by immense
plumes of eagles' feathers . . . [and] they wore a vest of
red cloth that was covered with charms in gold and silver,
and loose cotton trousers with long boots of a dull red
leather that came half way up their thighs . . .

"What we had seen on our way [coming from the coast
to Kumasi] had made us expect something unusual. But
we were still surprised by the extent and display of the
scene which burst upon us here. An area of nearly a mile

in circumference was crowded with magnificence and novelty. The king, his chiefs and captains, were splendidly dressed, and were surrounded by attendants of every kind. More than a hundred bands broke into music on our arrival. At least a hundred large umbrellas, each of which could shelter thirty persons, were sprung up and down by their bearers with a brilliant effect, being made in scarlet, yellow, and the brightest cloths and silks, and crowned on top with [models of] crescents, pelicans, elephants, barrels, arms, and swords of gold."

These English visitors of 1817 found Kumasi much finer than they had expected. "Four of the principal streets," Bowdich wrote, "are half a mile long, and from fifty to a hundred yards wide. The streets are all named. There is a senior captain in charge of each of them. Every household burns its rubbish every morning at the back of the street, and the people are as clean and careful about the appearance of their houses as they are about their own appearance."

The traditions of origin of the Asante empire refer to a time that was nearly one hundred and thirty years before William Bowdich visited Kumasi. These traditions tell how two famous leaders, the Asantehene Osei Tutu and his friend and adviser Okomfo Anokye (Anokye the Priest), combined their efforts in order to bind a number of separate Akan groups into a single strong union. They are said to have done this in about 1695 after Osei Tutu had been installed as ruler of the Asante. Okomfo Anokye declared that he had a mission from Nyame, supreme god of the Akan. Nyame, he revealed, had ordered him to make the Asante into a great people. To spread this message the new Asante ruler, Osei Tutu, who was working closely with Anokye, called a vast assembly of people. At this gathering Anokye "brought down from the sky" a wooden stool that was partly covered in gold, causing this stool to come to rest on Osei Tutu's knees.

Having done this, Okomfo Anokye announced that the

Golden Stool contained the collective soul or spirit of the whole Asante people. He told the chiefs and people that their power and health, bravery and welfare, were all symbolised in this stool; and the chiefs and people accepted this. Osei Tutu then began to make laws for the Asante groups, who were thus welded into a union. Among the first of these laws was one of common citizenship, which forbade anyone to speak about any of the old separate traditions of the now united groups. In this way the Asante acquired a single tradition about their past, and this single tradition was to act as a powerful means of keeping them united.*

The origins of the Asante thus are firmly linked in popular memory to a deliberate if highly imaginative act of statesmanship. This act achieved unity among Akan groups, who had been living side by side but governing themselves separately. When the Golden Stool "came down from heaven," these groups gave up their separate government and united under the single rule of Osei Tutu and his counsellors.

We can probe a little into the truth behind the story of the Golden Stool. The key lies in deciding just *why* these separate groups should have decided to form a union. For it is certain that no act of statesmanship or skilful magic could have persuaded them to make this decision unless they had seen great advantages in doing so. What were these advantages?

At some time not long before and after 1600, it seems, groups of farmers began leaving the Adansi region, where they were then living, and moved some fifty or sixty miles to the northward. Scholars have suggested two main reasons for this movement or migration: first, that these farming groups wanted to find more land in which to cultivate their crops; secondly, that they wanted to win a share in

* Many of the old separate traditions were still remembered, though in secret.

the prosperous gold and kola trade which flourished to the north of them. Of these groups the most enterprising were the Oyoko clan; and they moved north soon after 1600.

They settled not far from a small lake called Bosomtwi in the country known as Amansie. There they cleared farms, gradually took the lead among their neighbours (who spoke Twi as they did), and built a town which they called Asantemanso. They became active in the business of producing and selling gold and kola to merchants from the north as well as to merchants who came from the coast, and were joined by other groups from Adansi. They steadily grew stronger, and called themselves the Asante.

But they still faced two big problems. They were subject to the powerful state of Denkyira, to whose ruler, the Denkyirahene,* they had to pay tax and tribute in goods and slaves. They had serious rivals for land and trade in the Domaa, another Akan people who lived north-west of them. So long as these problems existed, the Asante could be neither secure nor prosperous. And it was to solve these problems that they began to find ways of acting together. This happened soon after 1650.

At first their acting together was no more than a loose alliance of different groups, Juaben, Kumawa, Nsuta, Bekwai, Mampon, and others, each of which formed a little polity of its own. They stood together when it suited them against their common overlord, the Denkyirahene, or against their rival, Domaa. They generally recognised a common leader, the best known of whom is a rather mysterious figure whose name was Obiri Yeboa. But this loose alliance could not solve their problems. They needed to come still closer together, and this need led them, in about 1695, to the momentous act of union associated by tradition with the skill and leadership of Osei Tutu and Okomfo Anokye.

* The suffix *hene* means "chief": Denkyirahene, Asantehene, Akwamuhene.

The Asante empire

Osei Tutu was installed as Asantehene in about 1695 after
Obiri Yeboa had perished in battle against Domaa. He
ruled until his death in about 1712,* and was the first
great builder of the Asante empire.

He began by preparing to throw off the overlordship of
the Denkyirahene, a ruler named Bosianti.

Denkyira was still the biggest power of all the country
that lies in the south-western part of modern Ghana. This
meant that Denkyira controlled the trade with Elmina castle; and Elmina at that time was the wealthiest market on
the Gold Coast, the main source of European goods including guns, and the possession of the Dutch (who had
taken it from the Portuguese in 1637). Needing guns and
ammunition and other European goods, the Denkyirahene
made good use of the Dutch at Elmina.

But in order to buy these guns and other goods the Denkyirahene, like other kings trading with the sea-merchants,
had to pay for them in gold and slaves. He accordingly
imposed heavy taxes, in gold and in captives, on his subject
peoples. Among these subject peoples, as we have seen,
were the Asante.

The Asante therefore possessed another strong reason
for wanting to get the better of Denkyira. So long as they
were separated from Elmina and other coastal markets by
the power of Denkyira, they could never be sure of obtaining regular supplies of guns and other European goods.
Yet war between Asante and Denkyira did not come at
once. To begin with, Denkyirahene Bosianti tried to win
Osei Tutu's friendship. Wisely preferring to negotiate rather

* This revised date, which we propose to adopt, was worked out
in 1960 by Professor Ivor Wilks and Miss Margaret Priestley:
the usual date given for Osei Tutu's death has been 1731.

than to embark on the risks and losses of war, he offered
Osei Tutu compensation for past wrongs. Less wisely, he or
his sub-chiefs even allowed Osei Tutu to buy guns from the
Dutch at Elmina.

But Osei Tutu was not won over. Dominant in his own
country, he went on with his military preparations. War
broke out in 1699 when a new Denkyirahene, Ntim
Gyakari, demanded from the Asante a larger tax than
usual. By about 1701 the power of Denkyira was smashed,
though at the outset of the war Asante suffered a near defeat. United as never before, the Asante then carried their
war into the dominions of Denkyira and brought most of
these under their own overlordship.

They captured much booty. But among the things they
captured and brought home to Kumasi was a piece of paper; and this piece of paper was to matter as much as all
the weapons and gold and other wealth, for it was the rent
agreement for Elmina castle. Signed originally by the Dutch
with the coastal chiefs of Komenda, this Note, as it was
called, had passed into the hands of the Denkyirahene
when the chiefs of Komenda had fallen under his control.
Now the Note belonged to Asante, and the Asantehene
naturally regarded Elmina castle as standing upon his own
soil. The power of Asante, in other words, had reached the
coast. This meant that it had also reached the Europeans in
their seaside castles. Asante and these Europeans now faced
each other directly, as friends or as enemies, an encounter
that was to matter increasingly in the years ahead.

Having defeated Denkyira and made most of its chiefs
into his subjects, Osei Tutu turned his armies against the
main ally of Denkyira, Akim, which had fought on Denkyira's side against Asante and was even said to have lost
as many as 30,000 soldiers in doing so. Osei Tutu marched
against the Akim Kotoku, and obliged them to pay tribute.
But the Akim armies did not give in easily. There had to
be a second war against them.

This second war against Akim is said by the traditions

to have been led by Osei Tutu, who was killed by an Akim marksman while crossing the Pra river in 1731. But modern research in Ghana suggests that Osei Tutu really died in 1712; that the second war against Akim occurred in 1719; and that the name of the Asantehene who was killed on the Pra river was deliberately omitted from the traditional records. These claim, in any case, that the next Asantehene was Opoku Ware, who was probably installed in about 1720, and reigned for thirty years. Under this strong and successful leader, the achievements of Osei Tutu and Okomfo Anokye were made firm and carried further.

Opoku Ware's first big problem was a hostile alliance of the warriors of Denkyira, Sefwi, and Akwapim, who all joined Akim in trying to crush the rising power of the Asante. The allies failed in two harsh wars, during one of which an Akim army even took Kumasi and searched for gold in the royal graves. But the union of the Golden Stool did not break down. Opoku Ware defeated the allies, and also brought the neighbouring states of Takyiman and Gyaaman under Asante rule. In 1744–45 he sent his armies northward, and established his authority over Dagomba as well.

Asantehene Kwasi Obodum came next, reigning from about 1750 until 1764, when the royal stool was occupied by another strong ruler, Osei Kojo, who brought the states of Wassaw and Banda under Asante control. Osei Kojo died in 1777, and was succeeded by Osei Kwame, who reigned until 1801. And after 1801 another ninety-nine years would pass before Asante power was finally crushed by the invading British.

Thus for nearly two hundred years Asante was not only a united nation, but also a large empire. Its kings ruled not only over the present-day Asante region, but over most of the country of modern Ghana, some of the inland country of the modern Ivory Coast, and parts of modern Togo. Here in central Guinea they succeeded in building another

large and unified system of taxation and trade such as
had existed earlier in the Western Sudan, or in eastern
Guinea under Benin and Oyo.

All the important rulers of West Africa recognised the
strength and dignity of the Asantehene; some of them, including the sultan of the Fulani empire centred on Sokoto,
the king of Dahomey, and possibly the imam of Futa
Jallon, maintained diplomatic relations with him. Literate
clerks and archivists were drawn from the ranks of Muslim
migrants from the north, many of whom had accompanied
the Dyula and Hausa traders down the well-established
trade and courier trails from Kano, Kong, Jenne, and
other states and cities within the Muslim zone. Meanwhile
the strength of the executive was steadily reinforced, at
least from the early years of the nineteenth century, by the
raising of long-service soldiers and the appointment of officials closely dependent upon the king.

There was obviously a certain parallel with the executive centralisation which had long since taken place in the
Sudanese states, although, since Islam scarcely gained a
foothold here, the parallel must be drawn with caution.
The fact remains that in nineteenth-century Asante "the
central government had assumed control over a wide range
of activities."* In everyday administration of a complex
imperial system, in taxation, military affairs, and state-
trading the Asantehene was supremely and actively involved in matters great and small. "The king," observed
a Frenchman in royal service, "knows each day what is
happening in the most humble villages in his empire;
from all sides he receives reports and minute details . . .
[and], day and night, [his] orders are despatched in all
directions."

Much of this went a good deal further towards systematic

* For a detailed enlargement on this statement see Ivor Wilks,
Aspects of Bureaucratization in Asanti, Institute of African
Studies, University of Ghana, 1965.

centralisation than other and earlier imperial structures, and here, too, one is repeatedly struck by Asante adaptability. By the last quarter of the nineteenth century the Asantehene was even taking Europeans into his service as technical advisers. One of these, a Dane, was employed in the recruitment of Hausa troops to reinforce the Asante army, then facing British military pressure, while another, who was French, shared the governorship of a province. It would be interesting to speculate what might have happened without colonial invasion. For while Asante was not a modern state when the British launched their seventh and finally victorious war against the empire, there are grounds for thinking that in some important respects it was on the way towards becoming one.

Asante, Fante, and Britain

Southward along the coast of modern Ghana the power of the Asantehene was well known to Europeans in their castles, and, through them, to the courts of European kings and the boardrooms of European and American banks and trading companies. But here in the south there were local developments which it will be useful to notice.

The Dutch and English in Ghana now became an important factor in African plans and policies. Denkyira, and then Asante, had made a trading partnership with the Dutch at Elmina and at one or two other forts. But the Asante and the Dutch were not the only partners in this business. There were also the Fante and the English.

Like the early chiefs of the Asante, those of the Fante, whose territory lay along the coast between Elmina and Accra, now came together in an alliance for their common good. Living near the sea, they made a similar trading partnership with the British at Cape Coast and other castles. So there arose a second "set of partners": the Fante made use of the English, just as the Asante made use of

the Dutch. This soon brought Asante and the Fante chiefs
into collision. In 1806, after years of growing hostility,
war started between them. It led to defeat of the Fante
army at Abora.

Abora was not far from the shore. Pressing on after
their victory, the Asante armies came down to the water's
edge. Their advanced guard occupied Kormantin and demanded the surrender of Fort Amsterdam, then held by
their partners the Dutch, who at once gave in. The Asante
generals next turned their attention to Anomabu, where the
remnants of their Fante opponents had taken refuge under
the walls of an English fort garrisoned by five officers and
twenty men. These decided to help their Fante allies. The
result was a fierce battle for the fort itself.

In this way Asante and Britain came to blows for the
first time. Later on, as British imperialism steadily took
shape, hostilities like these were to break out time after
time. But in 1806 peace was quickly made.

The fort held out against stubborn Asante efforts to
storm its gun-defended walls, and both sides were glad to
leave it at that. The British were far too weak to consider
war against Asante, while the Asantehene, for his part,
wanted only that the British, like other Europeans, should
recognise his authority over this part of the Gold Coast
shore. He was perfectly successful in obtaining this recog-
nition. His armies again entered the coastal country in
1811 and 1814, destroyed the military alliance of the Fante,
placed the Fante chiefs under Asante governors, and subdued Akim and Akwapim further to the east. As for the
Europeans on the coast, by now only the British and the
Dutch, they hastened to make their peace with the Asantehene. Not long afterwards, the Dutch quit the coast altogether. By about 1820 the power of Asante was supreme, and would remain so until British invasion many
years later.

20 WESTERN GUINEA IN THE SEVENTEENTH AND EIGHTEENTH CENTURIES

Gonja, Kong, Bonduku

The story of the northern part of the modern Republic of the Ivory Coast is not unlike that of the northern part of modern Ghana. Both had become linked with the expansion of inland trade since the enlargement of the empire of Mali after about A D 1325.

We have seen how Dyula and other traders pushed their activities south towards the forest country, and how, after 1550, warrior groups from the north founded Gonja in northern Ghana. Much the same thing happened in the open country of the Ivory Coast. There is no doubt that strong trading centres existed in this country long before the founding of Gonja, notably at Kong and Bonduku. These trading centres gradually developed into self-governing towns which built themselves up into small states. They were mainly loyal to Islam, following the lead of their trading rulers; but of course they were also the product of intermarriage and combination between Dyula traders and warriors and the Senufu and other peoples who were already living in the land.

In the seventeenth century these little states became more highly organised. Gonja, established before 1600 in the northern part of modern Ghana, now expanded under a strong chief whom the traditions call Jakpa. Commander of a force of armoured cavalry, Jakpa came south from the region of Jenne, where he and his warriors had long been active in one way or another, and reached Gonja in about 1629. Not long afterwards, later in the seventeenth century, another warrior leader called Seku Wattara likewise came south from the Masina region, along the middle Niger, and invaded the little state of Kong, where he established himself as ruler in place of a chief called Lasire Gombele. Strong in their cavalry, Seku and his successors brought the neighbouring countryside under their rule. Eager for a larger share in the gold and kola trade, they raided their neighbours. In 1725 they even marched as far north as the Niger at Segu, and attacked the Bambara ruler Mamari Kulibali.*

Kong remained an important state until French colonial invasion during the last years of the nineteenth century. Bonduku, another key point on the trade route with the forest lands, had a somewhat different history. It was much influenced by its powerful neighbour, the Asante empire, and was placed under an Asante governor in the middle of the eighteenth century.

The Baoulé

Two other important matters remain to be discussed in connexion with the history of the Ivory Coast. These concern the Baoulé people, and the peoples of the coast itself.

The Baoulé are by origin a branch of the Akan. After the death of Asantehene Opoku Ware in about 1750, there arose a dispute as to who should have the power. A section of the Asante decided to leave home and seek fresh lands to the west. They were commanded by a courageous woman called Awura Poku. She and her followers settled in the country to the east of the Bandama river, which flows from the forestland of the modern republic of the Ivory Coast down to the ocean at Grand Lahou. The people whom they found in possession of the land they gradually pushed out, the Senufu to the north

* See page 267.

and the Guru to the west, although we may be sure that they also took wives and husbands from among these and other Ivory Coast peoples.

Queen Poku died in about 1760 and was buried in her capital town of Warebo, which is near Bouaké. Her niece, Akwa Boni, followed her as queen of this Akan people, who called themselves Baoulé; and under Akwa Boni the Baoulé took over the gold-bearing lands to the west of the Bandama region. Queen Akwa Boni died about 1790. After that the unity of the Baoulé was lost through quarrels between the heads of important families, and they never succeeded in forging the same close unity as their Akan relatives in the empire of Asante. Yet they continued to

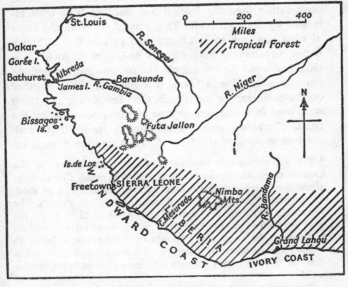

35   Coastline of the Ivory Coast, Liberia, and Sierra Leone in the eighteenth century

rule much of the southern Ivory Coast country until the
coming of the French at the end of the nineteenth
century.

The coast

Here it will be convenient to consider the whole coastline
of the modern Ivory Coast, Liberia, and Sierra Leone.
This long section of seaboard was influenced by trade with
the sea-merchants, but less than other parts of the Guinea
coast.

There were several reasons why the sea-merchants came
here less frequently than elsewhere. They went to the Ghana
coast rather than the Ivory Coast because they were attracted by the gold trade. They tended to avoid the coast
of what was later to be Liberia, and part of that of Sierra
Leone, because the anchoring of sailing ships could be a
risky business.* To this simple picture, however, something
must be added. Sierra Leone had good harbours, whether
on the mainland or on islands near the shore; and these
were used from the earliest time of European trade on the
coast. There was also a small though steady trade with
the lagoon-ports of the Ivory Coast where the French es-

* The old sailing-ship captains had their own names for the
Guinea coastline. These included the Windward Coast, from
about the Gambia river to Cape Palmas (eastern end of modern Liberia); and the Leeward Coast, east of Cape Palmas. The
prevailing winds in this part of the Atlantic blow from the
west or south-west, so that when sailors were on the western
sections of the coast they thought of themselves as being to
windward, and when they were on the central and eastern sections of the coast they thought of themselves as being to leeward.

Part of the Windward Coast, mainly that of modern Liberia,
was also very unfavourable for the safe anchoring of ships, and
was little visited until the nineteenth century.

tablished themselves at Grand Lahou, for example, in 1787. In general, though, the coastal peoples living along the seaboard to the west of Ghana had few opportunities for trade, and were accordingly much less influenced by developments after 1600.

All this changed to some extent at the end of the eighteenth century, as we shall see, with the formation of ex-slave settlements in Sierra Leone and Liberia. Before that happened, however, the region contained many small states, which had been formed in much earlier times and had built up political methods of their own. In the Sierra Leone region, for example, the real rulers of the country were the leading members of the special political and religious societies, of which the most important was the Poro.

These peoples possessed a rich though entirely non-mechanical culture. Mention may be made, for example, of the Kru fishermen and farmers. The Kru were divided into two main groups, one living in the country of the Ivory Coast west of the Bandama river, and known as the Bete; and the other, the Gueré, inhabiting the coastal regions of what later became Liberia. Like their neighbours, the Kru shared in the general trade of the country, sometimes acting as middlemen for the exchange of African and European goods, and sometimes trading on their own. They made a great name for themselves as skilful boatmen.

The foundation of modern Sierra Leone and Liberia was an outcome of the European and American movement to end the slave trade, and will be discussed in the final part of this book.

Gambia and Senegal

Going on westward from Sierra Leone, we find the same story of local African enterprise and varying contact with the sea-merchants. But there the contact was more frequent, and the trade more valuable, than along the seaboard of Liberia or the Ivory Coast, or even of Sierra Leone; and the influence of the sea-merchants became correspondingly greater.

Europeans knew this coastline west of Sierra Leone as *Sene-Gambia,* a composite label drawn from its two main rivers, the Senegal and the Gambia. From early times they found it profitable and possible to establish trading settlements here. The Portuguese had arrived in the fifteenth century and had remained at one or two points along the coast, mainly in the region of the Bissagos Islands. The French had later set up trading stations at one or two places and so had the English. A few details will be useful, because it was from their settlements in *Sene-Gambia* that the French and English were to launch many of their colonial expeditions during the second half of the nineteenth century.

The English were especially interested in the Gambia, rightly believing that this could prove a good channel for trade with the inland country. They occupied an island near the mouth of the river in 1618, and called it James Island after the name of their king at the time; here they built a fort in 1664. Along the banks of the Gambia they found an enterprising peasantry who were in touch with the inland peoples of the old kingdoms of Mali and the empire of the Woloff, and who also had small towns of their own.

Richard Jobson, an English captain, early in the seventeenth century described one of these Gambia towns, which he visited on a trading mission, as being strongly defended by a ten-foot fence. "Inside the fence," he wrote, "they have built various rooms which are like little towers. From these they can shoot arrows and throw spears whenever they are attacked. Outside the fence, too, they have a deep trench which is very broad, and outside that again the whole town is encircled by posts and tree-trunks which are set fast in the ground and joined together, so as to make another fence about five-foot high. Beyond that again they have another fence like this. And the reason, they explained to me, is that they need these in order to defend themselves from the attack of cavalry"—from the raiding horsemen, that is, of the inland country.

Jobson was impressed by the skills of the Gambians. He has left us a lively description that is useful not only for the Gambians, but also for many other folk along the coast, since it is quite certain that these same skills were practised elsewhere as well. Writing in 1623, he says that he found three main kinds of craftsmen: smiths who made weapons and metal tools; leather workers who made shoes, sandals and harness for horses; and clay workers who made many sorts of pots and also built clay-walled houses. But everyone, he adds, also worked at farming.

Bathurst, the later capital of the Gambia, was founded as a British settlement in 1817. This little colony acquired more land along the banks of the river. In 1857 the French trading station of Albreda was transferred to Britain. Gradually, the long and narrow territory of the later colony took shape.

There were important European settlements and forts further north, along the coast of Senegal. These often changed hands according to the fortunes of the many wars that Europeans fought against each other. Thus the old Portuguese establishments on the Island of Gorée and the nearby mainland, where the city of Dakar stands today, were taken by the Dutch in 1621. Between 1677 and 1697 they were held by the French. The English then had them for a few months, after which they went back to the French, who held them until 1758, when they were returned again to the English; and so on back and forth for several times more. Much the same quarrelling among Europeans went on at the settlements near the mouth of the Senegal river, and at Arguin further to the north. None of these quarrels mattered much to Africans. They continued to use these settlements and forts as convenient points of trade with Europeans, caring little which European nation should possess them. Only much later, during the rise of European imperialism, were these coastal forts and settlements to offer any threat to African independence. Then they became the jumping-off places for European colonial invasion. Yet it is also true that here, as in some other places along the coast, the trade in muskets and slaves grew into a means of sowing war among indigenous peoples, weakening their power of resistance to foreign conquest, and undermining their general welfare.

Meanwhile, what counted most for the coastal peoples of western Guinea were their powerful neighbours of the inland country. These included the states of the Fulani of the Futa Jallon hills, and those of the Serer and Woloff peoples of Senegal. Here, once again, the history of Guinea links up with the history of the rest of Africa, and especially with that of the Western Sudan.

21 THE WESTERN SUDAN IN THE SEVENTEENTH AND EIGHTEENTH CENTURIES

Ruin and revival

The seventeenth century saw the rise of new and ambitious political structures in Guinea. While many small city-states crystallised and prospered along the seaboard, much of the inland country became the scene of imposingly great initiatives such as those that built the vigorous empires of Oyo, Dahomey, Akwamu, and Asante. But for large regions of the Western Sudan this was a century of political ruin and decline.

Years of disaster followed the Moroccan invasion of the Songhay empire in 1591. Law and order broke down across wide regions. Trade suffered. Great market cities felt the pinch of hunger; some of them never recovered their old prosperity.

Timbuktu was hard hit; Gao even worse. Such was the fury of the invaders that Gao is said to have been emptied of its inhabitants within a few days. What happened in Gao also occurred elsewhere. With the ruin of these cities there went as well the decay of large farming areas which were attached to these cities, where the complex work of irrigation, of water-supply to the fields, had been the work of many hands. All this was followed by a large and revolutionary shift of power and initiative.

As the power of the cities dwindled and disappeared, the power of the countryside regained strength. But this power of the countryside was that of farming peoples; and these had different ideas from the ideas of the city-folk. They had never accepted Islam, or, if they had accepted it, they had done so half-heartedly. Their Muslim faith, where it existed, tended to be a mingling of Islam with the beliefs and superstitions of West African religion.

Out of this mingling there came many special features of West African Islam, notably the great authority given to marabouts, to "holy men" who combined Islam with ideas that were close to the old faiths of earlier times. So the rising power of the countryside was that of men and women who were non-Muslim, anti-Muslim, or Muslim only in a special way. All this affected their attitude to the more strictly Muslim people of the cities. Often, too, these new leaders of the countryside spoke and fought for the rights of rural populations who had suffered much violence or enslavement from the rulers of Songhay and their like. At any rate at first, they had little interest in trade, especially in the trans-Saharan trade, but hoped for gain from raiding and looting their neighbours.

These country leaders gradually built states of their own. While retaining much of the old tolerance and democracy of West African custom, these tended to be ruled, more and more, by groups of men whose power rested on professional armies. Being increasingly equipped with guns, the armies became more destructive, the soldiers more difficult to control. A succession of military *coups*—most dramatically among the Bambara of Segu—repeatedly emphasised the eruptive dichotomy that now lay between a strengthened executive and a general framework of society which had remained largely traditional. The old types of master-servant relationship were in fact fast breaking down. They had supported much prosperity, but much suffering too; and now, with the collapse of the venerable imperial systems, new types of social organisation began to take their place.

We see them at work soon after 1700; and the eighteenth century is generally a time of revival. Trade is now growing once again, both internally within the region and externally across the Sahara. Some of the old commercial success is recaptured. Islam, too, revives in forms that are not so much new as a restatement under new conditions of religious and political adjustments embarked on long before. There comes, as it were, a late harvest of that old Islamic penetration and conversion of the far west by way of Mauretania which had reached the land of Tekrur—Futa Toro as men called it now—in Almoravid times. By now, moreover, many people are longing for better and more peaceful times, and much of this longing seems imprinted in the revival of Islamic rule and precept. Deeply religious in form, the revival of the eighteenth century was still more profoundly social in its inner drive and meaning.

Destruction of Songhay

Judar Pasha and his Moroccan army of musket-carrying soldiers seized the heart of the Songhay imperial system when they captured the cities of Timbuktu, Gao, and Jenne. This they quickly did, for the Songhay armies could not stand against them.

But the Songhay leaders did not give in. Defeated whenever they attempted a set battle with the Moroccans, they fell back on guerrilla tactics. From their stronghold in Dendi, the southerly part of the old empire, they fought back in this way for more than half a century. In 1608, for example, the Dendi *hi-koy,* or admiral of the Songhay fleet of war-canoes on the Niger, attacked Moroccan garrisons along the whole middle course of the river. A year later the Dendi *fari bar,* a leading Songhay general, led a tremendous raiding march across the wide belt of land enclosed by the bend of the middle Niger, and attacked the Moroccans then in occupation of Jenne. Other Songhay units followed this surprise assault by a series of guerrilla operations against garrisons west of Timbuktu. Hostilities of this kind continued until about 1660. They did nothing to restore Songhay: on the contrary, they only added to the ruin of that once prosperous system. By the second half of the seventeenth century Songhay was reduced to nothing more than a weak alliance of little states in the south-eastern part of the old empire.

It was not so much the strength of the Moroccans that prevented the restoring of Songhay, as the total collapse of the old imperial system once its central power was undermined. That system, as we have noted, had rested largely on the strength and prosperity of the cities; and this strength and prosperity of the cities had relied, in turn, largely on the subjection or enslavement of many peoples of the countryside. For them the Moroccan invasion was a chance for freedom. They seized it eagerly. Many subject peoples or groups of peoples, of whom the strongest were called the Doghorani, rose in revolt against their masters. They took advantage of Songhay defeats to lift the banner of their own interests, and these interests were in direct opposition to the restoring of the empire. Only a widely popular war against the invaders could have restored Songhay; and no such war was possible.

Timbuktu and Jenne

Early in the seventeenth century the rulers of Morocco began to tire of their Songhay adventure. It had brought them much loot in gold and other goods, but not as much as they had expected; and it had cost them dear. Sultan Mulay Zidan, successor of Sultan Mulay the Victorious, complained that as many as 23,000 Moroccan soldiers had died in this effort at conquest. Although Mulay Zidan had taken the title of king of Gao, Timbuktu, and Jenne, the Moroccans decided to stop reinforcing their garrisons there.

After 1621 these cities along the middle Niger were left to the rule of locally recruited governors, called pashas, who were generally powerless to do more than offer a feeble and not always successful defence of the cities and nearby lands they were supposed to protect. These pashas and their soldiers intermarried with the local population. They gave birth to a group of people who were partly Moroccan in origin, and were called the *arma*. By 1700 the *arma* had little effective power left to them.

Timbuktu and Jenne became the target for attacks from the Bambara in the west.* But they and Gao also became targets for an old enemy, the raiding warriors of the Saharan Tuareg. In about 1680 a section of these Tuareg, called the Wulliminden, seized Gao and made a camp there. From this base they turned westward up the Niger, warring continually with the defenders of Timbuktu. By 1720 the Wulliminden and Tadmekkei Tuareg had won control of much of the middle Niger country, and in 1737 the Wulliminden actually captured Timbuktu for a time and made the local pashas pay them tribute. In about 1770 they made a permanent settlement at Gao.

These Tuareg were more than mere raiders. They were also interested in the trans-Saharan trade, and set about trying to restore it. In this they were not very successful, partly because they were often at war with the peoples of the Niger country, and partly because these peoples were often at war with each other. Yet it would be wrong to think that the trans-Saharan trade disappeared even in this time of troubles. In spite of all dangers and obstacles, traders found ways of carrying on their business. In 1635, for example, some English merchants in Morocco were able to tell their colleagues in London that they were sending many English goods by camel-caravan to Timbuktu, Gao, and other parts of West Africa, and were buying West African gold in exchange. Yet the great days of the gold trade across the desert were over.†

* See next section.
† See the discussion on pages 193–94.

New Niger states: Segu and Kaarta

Among the country folk who now began to raise their heads in the country of the middle and upper Niger were West African populations who had lived here under various empires in the past. Some, like the Soninke or Sarakolle, were descendants of people who had lived in Ancient Ghana. Others who belonged to the large and various Mande or Mandinka language-family had been loyal to Mali. Others again, like the Dogon, had lived on the verge of these old empires. Spread among them in groups of varying size were the Fulani. All, we may be sure, had greatly intermarried with each other, and it will be well to remember that the only racial distinction between them, from a scientific point of view, lay in the different languages they spoke.

In the troubles that followed on the destruction of Songhay, some of these peoples began to seek new fortunes of their own. Foremost among them were the Bambara. Under energetic leaders, the Bambara now formed a state that was based on the Niger market-town of Segu and its surrounding lands. Somewhat later they built a second state in the countryside of Kaarta to the north-west of Segu.

The traditions say that the Bambara state of Segu was founded by two brothers, called Barama Ngolo and Nia Ngolo, soon after 1600. These two men were possibly at first little more than leaders of a well-organised band of raiders from the countryside. They took advantage of the confusion of the times in order to enrich themselves at the expense of their neighbours, building what the merchants of the cities no doubt regarded as a robber gang. But success brought them bigger and better ideas. Under their Ngolo chiefs, these hard-riding Bambara farmers settled down and formed their own system of law and order.

We do not know exactly how they did this. Towards

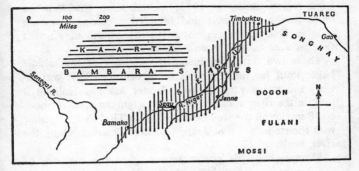

36   The Bambara states

1650, however, they were established in the Segu region, mainly on the south bank of the Niger, and were led by an energetic chief called Kaladian, who seems to have ruled them until about 1680, and, in doing so, to have extended Bambara authority over a wide belt of the central grasslands of the Western Sudan. This "empire" even briefly included the city of Timbuktu.

Mamari Kulibali and Ngolo Diara

Kaladian's empire evidently fell apart with his death. This seems clear from the fact that the next important figure in this region, the famous Mamari Kulibali—Mamari the Tiguiton or Biton, Mamari the Commander—began his career with no more than a handful of followers.

Mamari the Commander reigned from about 1712 until 1755, and was the true founder of the state of Segu. He got the better of his Bambara rivals soon after 1712, fought off an attack by the king of Kong in about 1730, drove out another set of Bambara rivals a few years later, and left his successors with a considerable power.

The Bambara rivals whom Mamari drove out of the

Segu region, in about 1753, moved some two hundred miles to the north-west and founded a second Bambara state in Kaarta, the region where the capital of Ancient Ghana, Kumbi, had once flourished.

These two states dominated the country of the middle Niger until far into the nineteenth century. Segu was always the stronger of the two. Under Mamari Kulibali it took in the river country from the neighbourhood of modern Bamako all the way downstream to Timbuktu, together with the trading city of Jenne and many markets along the river itself.

Mamari built his power according to the methods of the Songhay emperors after Sunni Ali. He relied on long-service soldiers and sailors. He formed a professional army many thousands strong, and also a professional navy on the Niger, from war-prisoners who, reduced to a type of slavery, became regular soldiers and canoe-men. With these troops he defeated all his rivals and neighbours—Soninke, Fulani, Malinke, Mossi, and others. Yet in building this military power, Mamari helped to ruin his family. After his death in about 1755, events took a new turn. His son Dekoro became king of Segu, but had ruled for less than two years when the generals took over. According to the traditions, King Dekoro was killed by the professional soldiers, bound together as they were in their condition of being a caste or group of "slaves"; and his power was taken by the Ton-Mansa, or senior general of the army and "commander of the slaves."

But this Ton-Mansa, like other ambitious generals then and since, fell victim to their own methods. He set an example which others could repeat. Three years later the soldiers killed him too, and elected in his place another general called Kaniuba Niuma, Kaniuba the Handsome, who was commander of the cavalry at Segu. Kaniuba's reign was likewise no more than three years. Then the soldiers overthrew him in his turn and elected yet another king, Kafa Diugu, from among their number. Not until about 1766 would this irresponsible soldiers' rule come to an end. At this point a man of far greater capacity, Ngolo Diara, seized the throne. Ngolo Diara reigned for more than thirty years, put an end to the soldiers' political plots and plans, and restored the empire of Segu to its position of former power.

Segu under King Ngolo became a large and prosperous city. In 1796, two years after Ngolo's death, the English traveller Mungo Park, the first European to come this way,* estimated that Segu contained as many as thirty thousand people. He found them living in four closely adjoining towns which consisted of clay-built houses with flat roofs, sometimes of two storeys. Segu's prosperity and size greatly impressed Park. "The view of this extensive city," he wrote, "the numerous canoes upon the river, the crowded population, and the cultivated state of the surrounding country-side, formed altogether a prospect of civilisation and magnificence, which I little expected to find in the bosom of Africa."

The Fulani reforming movement

The Bambara states of Segu and Kaarta were a part of the political recovery in the Western Sudan after the collapse of Songhay and the final decline of Mali. But they were by no means the only part. Another of much importance was the rise of a new set of states under Fulani leaders, and, combined with this, a renewed effort to strengthen the cause and the ideas of Islam.

Most of the Fulani, as we have seen in earlier pages, were cattle-breeders who followed a wandering way of life. Now and then, linked with other peoples, some of

* At any rate for some three centuries, though it is possible that a few stray Portuguese had travelled the same route in earlier times.

them had settled down and grown used to living in towns. Mixed with Mandinka allies, the Fulani of Tekrur had done this in the middle of the sixteenth century.* Other groups of Fulani had also done the same, and, in doing so, had likewise changed their social organisation. Living in one place for long periods, they had accepted the authority of some of their ruling families; and these families regularly elected men to rule them as chiefs. In this, of course, they behaved like many other wandering peoples who have settled down and found that they needed chosen men to rule over them. Many Fulani ruling families now took part in a movement for the revival of Islam.

Scholars differ on the precise reasons for this. Broadly, however, we can perceive in this Fulani acceptance of Islam the same kind of motives as had inspired earlier kings and peoples in the Western Sudan. Islam's unified system of ideas about religion, law and order, and trading customs, could promise much to men who suffered from the confusion of the times, for it offered a way of overcoming conflicts and rivalries. And many men undoubtedly remembered how the empires of Mali and Songhay had become strong under Muslim rule, or at least under Muslim influence.

Among the Fulani the new faith had a revolutionary effect. Not only did it begin to give them a new unity among themselves; it also brought them into touch with the whole tide and drive of Muslim thought, whether from West Africa, from Egypt, or within the Western Sudan itself, and made them think about far more than their own local affairs. They became fired with new ambitions. At their best, these held out a common vision and idea of how men should behave and live together, and of what men should strive to do for the betterment of life.

This new vision and idea aimed at a grand revival of the power and law of Islam throughout the Western Sudan.

* See page 113.

Little by little, Fulani leaders gathered warrior bands and began to set up new states in the countries where they lived, in those same countries which had suffered so many troubles since the decline of Mali and the ruin of Songhay.

Two general points may be emphasised. The first is that although this Muslim revival was often the work of Fulani people (or their close relations, the Tucolor), these were by no means alone. Others also took part. Among them the most important were probably the Mandinka, whose ancestors had built the empire of Mali, and whose traders, the Dyula, had done much for the commerce of West Africa. The Mandinka will generally have understood, far better than the Fulani, how to revive trade and why it was desirable to build up the strength of the market-cities once again.

A second point to bear in mind is the sheer inner complexity of this revival or reforming movement. It looked back, as other Muslim reformers had looked back at other times and in other places, to the great ideal of the "divinely guided caliphate," the golden age of justice and equality associated with the rule of the Prophet and his immediate successors nearly a thousand years earlier. In the minds of its best leaders the intention was to reopen a period of peace and prosperity among all who shared the teachings of the Faith. The whole of the Western Sudan should come within this reformed Dar al-Islam, this ideal home of Islam where men obeyed the laws of Allah and lived in good community together. But the social and political reality—here as in other lands where men had felt the fire and inspiration of the same millennial vision—could not respond. The ideas of the past proved once more inadequate to solving the problems of the present.

Across the years that followed there was indeed much progress in several directions. Trade, education, the acceptance of law and order: all these expanded. The Western Sudan regained its old international connexions. Schol-

ars once more travelled from capital to capital, and there
were many amongst them who came from distant lands.
Yet this progress was increasingly purchased at a bitter
cost to many non-Muslim populations who were raided,
plundered, or reduced to slavery. Later, in the nineteenth
century, the wars spread still more widely; and not a few
of them were conducted by kings and warrior-leaders who
used their call to jihad, to holy war for the conversion of
the heathen, as little or nothing more than a cover for the
seeking of loot and privilege. In the eighteenth century,
however, the progress was often impressive.

The western imamates

The earliest of these reforming states, of these Fulani-led
enterprises in Muslim revival, was the imamate of Futa
Jallon, so called because it was ruled by an almamy or
imam. It lay in the hillside country that is now in the central part of the modern Republic of Guinea. Muslim reformers of the Fulani—mujaddadin, "revivers of Islam"*—
together with allied groups of Mandinka, Susu, and other
peoples, founded this state in about 1725. They subdued
the non-Muslim farmers who were living in the neighbourhood, members of a branch of the Mandinka language-
family called Dialonke.

This was a state of a new kind. Organised in nine
provinces (*diwal*) and many sub-districts (*miside*), its political power was wielded by a religious leader, the almamy,
while its military power, likewise commanded by the
almamy, was based on a strict system of compulsory service. But the imamate of Futa Jallon was more than a mere
dictatorship of religious leaders. It retained many traditional features of West African political life, and these in-

* Mujaddadin must be distinguished from mujahiddin, warriors
of Islam.

cluded a measure of democracy. The almamy was very powerful, and claimed to rule in the name of God, but he still had to listen to the opinions of his counsellors; and these counsellors, at least when they were good men, were bound to listen to the complaints and needs of the population.

But the part of democracy grew less with time. A new almamy was chosen every two years, at least after about 1800; but the election was always from one of two ruling families, the Alfa or the Sori. With this narrow method of choosing their ruler, the leading families steadily increased their privilege and wealth. In the nineteenth century this was to lead to many revolts and changes. Here we need only note that the imamate of Futa Jallon, strong in its defensive hills, survived more or less intact until French colonial invasion at the end of the nineteenth century.

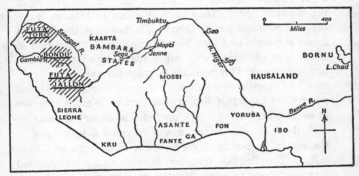

37 The western imamates

Roughly the same thing happened in Futa Toro, in the land of old Tekrur far to the west, among the northern neighbours of the Woloff. Here along the south bank of the Senegal river the Denianke kings had ruled since the

Fulani-Mandinka invasion of 1559.* Yet here too the influence of Islam had remained alive, though the Denianke
kings were not Muslims; and Islam now acquired new
power. In the 1770s there arrived in Futa Toro a group
of Muslim reformers who belonged to the clan of the
Torobé, and were led by a famous marabout, or religious
leader, called Suleiman Ba. This almamy or imam defeated
the ruling silatigui (a Mande word which means "commander," and was the title of the Denianke rulers) at a
decisive battle in 1776. The Torobé then formed the
imamate of Futa Toro, electing their kings after the death
of Suleiman Ba from the members of a small number of
leading families.

These conquerors were the Tucolor, a West African people closely related to the Fulani. Once established in Futa
Toro, they began to expand the trade with French sea-
merchants who came up the Senegal river, as well as with
other Muslim centres of trade in the western region of
the Western Sudan. They gave attention to Muslim learning and founded many schools for teaching the laws of
Islam although, like their Fulani neighbours, their belief in
Islam was combined with other ideas drawn from traditional customs. This included a great reverence for "holy
men" or marabouts who were supposed to possess magical
powers, an aspect of life in that part of West Africa (as
in some other parts) which may still be observed today.

A third Muslim imamate was founded a little later in
the region of Bondu, lying between Futa Toro and Futa
Jallon. The English traveller Mungo Park, who passed
through Bondu in 1795, has left us a good description of
the country. He found it prosperous and at peace, though
threatened by many dangers. The king, who lived in a set
of clay-built houses surrounded by a high wall, received
him hospitably and introduced him to his wives, who found

* See page 113.

their first sight of a European very surprising.* Park also found Bondu well provided with village schools, and visited many of them. He thought the children well behaved and attentive. The cattle-breeders of the countryside, he observed, were quite wealthy, "and enjoy the necessaries of life in a high degree," including excellent horses.

Park met with many difficulties through the actions of some of the kings through whose lands he travelled—not surprisingly, for he reached them through the territories of rival kings, and was easily suspected of being a spy. But he also met with much kindness from some of the people and one of his stories about this deserves telling here. Arriving at Segu for the first time, he had to wait on the bank of the Niger opposite that large and flourishing city, while the king of Segu decided whether or not to let him go across. He was hungry and alone. At sunset, while he was sitting under a tree and wondering whether he would ever see his own homeland again, a woman who had been working in the fields came up and spoke to him. She asked him why he looked so sad and tired. When he explained, "she took up my saddle and bridle, and with looks of great pity, asked me to follow her." Leading him to her hut, she lit a lamp and spread a mat upon the floor, and told him that he should rest there until the next day. Meanwhile she would find some food.

In a little while, Park recalled, this kindly and hospitable woman returned with well prepared fish, which she baked on the embers of her fire and gave him to eat. After this she told the other women members of her family to go on with their spinning, and they worked through most of the night. While they were spinning, they made a song about

* They teased him good-humouredly about the whiteness of his skin and the size of his nose, saying that both were artificial. "The first, they jokingly said, was produced when I was an infant, by dipping me in milk; and they insisted that my nose had been pinched every day till it had acquired its present unsightly and unnatural conformation."

their hungry visitor. This song "was sung by one of the
young women, the rest joining in a sort of chorus." The
words, Park tells us, went something like this: "The winds
roared and the rains fell. The poor white man, faint and
weary, came and sat under our tree. He has no mother to
bring him milk, no wife to grind his corn. Let us pity the
poor white man: no mother has he . . ."

In this moving little episode one may perhaps see how
misleading an impression can be given by the bare record
of events. Wars and dynastic rivalries, the clenched ambition of kings and generals, the lamentation of prophets:
all these suggest an everyday life that was replete with
misery and violence. But in times of peace it was not like
that; and the times of peace were more frequent than the
times of war.

Other reforming movements

While these three new Muslim states were taking shape in
the west, others of a similar type or inspiration were emerging further eastward. Here, too, the Fulani and their allies
played a leading part.

Some of these Fulani lived in the Masina plains which
lie in the neighbourhood of the Niger market-town of
Mopti. Like their Bambara neighbours, with whom they
were sometimes on good terms and at other times on bad,
they made a bid for independence. In about 1629 their
chiefs, the Ardo, who were not yet converted to Islam,
broke away from the overlordship of the Moroccan pasha
or governor of Timbuktu, allied themselves with the Songhay of Dendi, southernmost province of the old Songhay
empire, and waged war on every Moroccan or part-Moroc-
can garrison they could reach. Afterwards they became
subject to the overlordship of the rising power of Segu.
Much later, in the nineteenth century, Muslim Fulani in

these Masina plains built a new Islamic state or miniature empire of their own.

Further eastward again, beyond the Masina plains, other Fulani groups established themselves on the plains to the south-west of Gao. In 1690, or thereabouts, they also set up a little state of their own. Other groups went on down the banks of the Niger. Not long before 1800 the religious leader of some of these, a marabout called Alfa Muhammad Diobo, founded the town of Say, not far from modern Niamey, capital of the Niger Republic today. Alfa Muhammad's idea was to make Say into a centre for Muslim revival. With the foundation of Say, as a glance at the map will show, the Muslim revival movement had moved right across the Western Sudan as far as the borders of Hausaland. This movement now took an imposing form. It gave birth to a vast political revolution that was to make Uthman dan Fodio the founder of a new empire.

Events in Hausaland: Katsina and Kano

A wavering balance of gain and loss, with trade generally
expanding but internecine wars growing more costly and
erosive, continued to govern the fortunes of the Hausa
states. On the credit side there was the fact that Songhay
collapse proved no disaster here. On the contrary, it re-
lieved the western Hausa rulers—notably those of Gobir
and Katsina—of a major source of outside danger, since the
Songhay armies, or such as remained of them, were fully
occupied with the Moroccans, and the Moroccans were far
too weak to thrust their interfering hand much beyond
Timbuktu.

If many Hausa communities prospered increasingly from
their farming, handicraft industry (especially cotton weaving), and enterprise in trade, the endemic lack of unity
among their kings and ruling groups occasionally cost them
dear. The main bone of contention was the possession of
the lion's share of control over the northern trading routes.
For this, Katsina and Kano fought each other during almost a hundred years, with Katsina slowly gaining the upper hand, at least until threatened by Gobir after the latter's
victory over Zamfara in 1764. Yet it would be a mistake
to see these wars as more than sporadic nuisances. They
cut into Hausa prosperity, but they did not ruin it; so much
is proved by the remarkable general prosperity of Kano
observed by Heinrich Barth in the 1850s. Kano gradually
emerged as a major centre of production and exchange,
and as a great magnet for traders from the whole Sudan.

Jukun raids continued from the south, and Zaria's

strength waned. After about 1750, adding to these troubles, the western states had to face bold incursions from the Tuareg now established on the left bank of the Niger near Gao; among the eastern states, meanwhile, the pressure of Bornu continued to be felt. Internally the trend towards social stratification continued and deepened; and it was in this period that the Hausa kings widely sowed those popular discontents from which the Fulani reformers were soon to profit. In the 1720s, for example, we find King Muhammad Sharifa of Kano (1703–31) imposing fresh labour-services and heavier taxes on the merchants and the poor alike. Monarchy became more oppressive. Its means of plunder widened.

Yet even this, one may repeat, failed to do more than check the prosperity of Kano and its surrounding countryside. Such was the condition of the cotton-weaving industry in the 1850s, Barth concluded, "that Kano ought to be one of the happiest countries in the world; and so it is so long as its governor, too often lazy and indolent, is able to defend its inhabitants from the cupidity of their neighbours, which of course is certainly stimulated by the very wealth of this country."

The Fulani empire: Uthman dan Fodio

Such was the general situation when Uthman dan Fodio began to preach his holy war in Gobir during the last years of the eighteenth century. Launched in 1804, this revolt carried all before it. Kings whose ancestors had ruled the Hausa cities for centuries were rapidly removed from power. By 1811 the Fulani leaders were masters of all Hausaland, and the movement for Muslim revival had acquired a strong new base in the east, a base from which other Muslim forces were afterwards to set forth on fresh conquests in the Western Sudan.

Why did this revolution succeed, and succeed so quickly?

An answer to such questions will throw light on the way people were living in Hausaland during the eighteenth century. Fortified in their cities, and often at war with one another, the Hausa kings had come to rely increasingly on their personal armies and courtiers. The division of society into "masters and servants" had grown sharper. The masters had become more oppressive, being themselves continually threatened by rival masters in other cities, while the mass of the people, whether farmers or craftsmen, suffered heavier taxes and careless government. There was much wealth in the cities, but it flowed into fewer pockets. And so it came about that when Uthman dan Fodio* (1754–1817) launched his revolution against the Hausa kings, he and his fellow-leaders found some sympathy among the Hausa population.

We have to be careful about this. Most of the written evidence comes from the Fulani side of the case. Uthman dan Fodio and his flag-bearers or commanders made war on the Hausa kings in the name of far-reaching reform—religious but also social—and it was part of their case that Hausa government was unjust and bad. Having triumphed, they destroyed most of the Hausa state papers and documents. We know little of the Hausa side of the argument.

Yet the fact remains that many Hausa people did respond to the revolutionary appeals of Uthman and his followers. Much may therefore be learned about the true situation in Hausaland from seeing what these appeals actually were. Here we are on firm ground, for the Fulani leaders were scholarly men who wrote many books. One of the most useful is the *Kitab al-Farq*, probably written by Uthman dan Fodio himself. This book thundered against the unjust customs of the Hausa kings.

"One of the ways of their government," it said, "is to

* The Fulani generally have three grades of Muslim clerks or learned men: *modibo, tierno,* and *fodio* (or *fudi*), the highest grade.

arrange succession to the kingship by birth and by force, and without consulting anyone. One of the ways of their government is to build their royal power on three things: on the peoples' persons, honour, and possessions. In pursuit of their greed, the kings kill or exile or dishonour or take the wealth of anyone they wish . . ."

Uthman's ideas

Many such accusations were made by the revolutionaries. They denounced the Hausa kings for corruption, luxury living, selfish or unjust government. And they founded their main appeal on the claim that they, the revolutionaries, would sweep away these evils and give the common people a better life. Here is how the author of the *Kitab al-Farq*, no doubt Uthman dan Fodio himself, couched this appeal:

"And I say—and help is from God—that the foundations of government shall be five things. The first is that power shall not be given to one who seeks it. The second is the need for consultation. The third is the doing away with harshness. The fourth is justice. The fifth is good works.

"And as for the ministers of government, they should be four in number. The first is a trusty *wazir* [or chief secretary] to wake the ruler if he sleeps, to make him see if he is blind, and remind him if he forgets; and the worst misfortune for government and people is to be denied honest *wazirs*. Among the qualities of a *wazir* is that he should always be compassionate and merciful towards people.

"The second of the ministers of government is a judge whom the blame of the blamer cannot overtake in the affairs of God [who is, that is to say, above fear or blackmail]. The third is a chief of police who shall obtain justice for the weak from the strong. The fourth is a tax collector who shall do his duty and not oppress people."

Now in making appeals of this kind Uthman dan Fodio was not saying anything very new in the Western Sudan of his day. They were in fact the essence of the Muslim reforming movement as it developed towards the end of the eighteenth century. What proved to be new and decisive, in this case, was the response of ordinary Hausa people. For Uthman dan Fodio himself was fifty years old when he called for his holy war against the Hausa kings. He had long preached the same lessons in Kebbi and Gobir, yet with little success. Only when his appeals went further into Hausaland did he begin to gather a mass of supporters.

Of course there is more to the story than bad government by the Hausa kings and a resulting eagerness for change among their peoples. Uthman dan Fodio could count on the fervent support of Fulani cattle-folk among whom his preaching had much success. He could also ask and receive military aid from Fulani and other allies further to the west and north; many such warriors came to fight under his banner.

The question as to how far the Fulani leaders were actually successful in building a more just and democratic way of life lies outside our survey. What must be noticed here is that they were quite largely successful in one great matter over which their Hausa predecessors had failed. They brought internal wars among the states of Hausaland practically to an end. They united these states under the general authority of a single supreme ruler; and this empire, with the sultan of Sokoto at its head, prevailed for nearly a hundred years, being brought to an end only by British colonial invasion.* They beat off the Jukun and put an end to their raids. Not strong enough to swallow Bornu, they pushed south-eastward round the frontiers of Bornu, and founded the state of Adamawa. They went south into Ilorin, then in revolt against the failing power of the alafin of Oyo; came to the aid of the rebellious Yoruba general

* The British established their colonial rule over Northern Nigeria, which includes most of the Fulani empire, during the first ten years of this century.

there; and proceeded to make Ilorin another Fulani-dominated state.

This work of unification had clearly beneficial effects in reducing internecine warfare, raiding, and the interruption of security along the trade roads; and it was now that Kano, above all, entered on its great epoch of prosperity. Yet the nineteenth century was soon to show that Fulani rule could be even more oppressive than the "unjust society" it had overthrown. Like other Muslim reformers, Uthman found almost at once that theory and practice could not be made to meet. Having followed the banners of reforming idealism, Fulani lineage leaders threw themselves upon the fleshpots of Hausaland with a furious hunger that carried all before it. They fastened on these countries a kind of royal absolutism which cut ruthlessly through the oligarchical checks and balances by which the Hausa kings had generally exercised their strong but quasi-constitutional power. Yet the beginning was a brilliant one, not least because of the quality of the senior Fulani commanders, with Muhammad Bello at their head.

Muhammad Bello

Bello undertook the main work of political reconstruction, and, as the first sultan of Sokoto, pulled together the conquering Fulani groups into a loosely organised empire. Like his father Uthman dan Fodio and his uncle Abdallah, he was a distinguished scholar as well as a successful man of action. Writing continually for the benefit of his distant governors and vassals, instructing them, exhorting them, arguing with them in a flood of letters and directives, he also did much for education and learning in the Hausa cities. "The Hausa country flourished greatly under Muhammad Bello's rule," wrote one of his admirers.* "He

* Al-Hajji Said, who served as a state official at Sokoto under Bello's son and successor.

spread respect for learning, and scholars came from different countries. He looked after them well . . . and he himself spent much time in writing.

"He supported himself by the fruits of his work, without asking for upkeep from the public purse . . . He was sympathetic to the people and full of thought for them, calm, patient, not caring for the wealth of other men. A skilful administrator, he watched over the work of the judges, quashing their judgments if these had been given under the influence of passion . . . Ruddy of complexion, tall, bald of head, wearing a long and tufted beard, such was his appearance."

Though written by a courtier, this description may be taken as it stands, for there is much other evidence to show that Bello was a ruler of outstanding merit. He and his fellow-scholars worked in the great tradition of the sixteenth century. They were interested in many things. Their outlook was world wide. We catch a glimpse of this from a report of 1824. In that year the English traveller Clapperton visited Sultan Bello in Sokoto and found him reading Euclid's geometry. When Clapperton arrived, the sultan was "sitting in the inner apartment of his house, with the Arabic copy of Euclid before him, which I had given him as a present. He said that his family had possessed a copy of Euclid brought by one of their relations, who had procured it in Mecca; that it was destroyed when part of his house was burnt down last year; and he observed, that he could not but feel very much obliged to the King of England for sending him so valuable a present."

Though Clapperton was the first European traveller to visit Sokoto, Bello was already interested in foreign lands. Clapperton wrote afterwards that the sultan asked him "a great many questions about Europe." He also started a discussion about Christian and other religious problems which were too difficult for Clapperton; the sultan continued to ask questions until, Clapperton writes, "I was obliged to confess myself not sufficiently versed in religious subtle-

ties to resolve these knotty points." Few other leaders
of the Muslim revival of the nineteenth century would
prove so wise, merciful, or modest in their personal demands.

Bornu after Idris Alooma

It remains in this necessarily brief survey of political events
to complete the story of Kanem-Bornu down to the beginning of the nineteenth century.

The great Mai Idris Alooma had come to power in about
1580. By about 1600 his rebuilding of the Kanemi empire
was complete. He died in 1617, having brought its peoples
many peaceful years. Bornu traditions then speak of three
reigns, those of Mai Muhammad (1617–32), Mai Ibrahim
(1632–39), and Mai Omar (1639–57), during all of which
the empire remained at peace within itself, and often with
its neighbours. These rulers carried on the work of Idris
Alooma, and on the whole they did it well.

This long period of security, more than half a century
disturbed only by occasional frontier battles or minor
quarrels at home, was the ripe and smiling "harvest time"
of Kanem-Bornu civilisation. While confusion and upheaval
struck and pounded many other peoples of the Western
Sudan, those of Kanem-Bornu had few such troubles. And
although we know little of the detailed way of life of ordinary people, we may well imagine that they made the best
of these years. Farmers could work their fields in safety.
Travellers and pilgrims could follow the roads without
fear. Those who lived in towns and market-villages could
prosper with the spread of trade that came both from
everyday security and from unified rule over a wide
country. There was growth of learning in the towns, and
of schools in the villages. There was regular traffic between
Kanem-Bornu and the Egyptian and Tunisian provinces of

the Turkish empire in North Africa. Mai Ali, who succeeded Mai Omar in 1657, even made three religious
journeys to Arabia.

Decline of Bornu

But Mai Ali, who reigned until 1694, had to face a different situation. It was while returning from his third pilgrimage, in 1667, that the first grim warnings reached him of
harsher times ahead.

The danger this time was not from the peoples to the
east of Lake Chad, the Bulala nobles and their warriors
who had rebelled so often against Kanemi rule. It came
from the Tuareg of the Aïr oases in the north, and, at the
same time, from the Jukun in the south. Both came raiding
into Bornu, just as they went raiding into Kano and other
Hausa states, their common motive being to seize some of
the wealth of flourishing towns; and both gave Mai Ali and
his armies some bitter days and hard defeats. Twice he was
besieged by these two enemies in his capital at Gasreggono.
In the end he managed to deal with each of them separately, and drove them back. The traditions say that a great
famine struck Bornu in the later years of Mai Ali's reign,
a disaster no doubt caused by these destructive raiding and
defensive wars.

The great days of the Kanem-Bornu empire were now
at an end. After Mai Ali the traditions list seven rulers
(or perhaps six, for one of them is in doubt) down to Mai
Ahmad, who came to power in 1753 and later faced the
first of Uthman dan Fodio's attacks. All these rulers saw
the strength of their empire gradually decline. There occurred here the same general process as further to the west:
central government broke down and failed in the face of
revolt or independent action by this or that subject people.

Throughout the eighteenth century there were likewise
many political changes to the east of Lake Chad. The rulers

of Baguirmi and Waday, backed partly by Fulani warrior
groups settled there in earlier times, fought each other for
control of Kanem, while the ancient authority of the
Bulala kings and nobles vanished from the scene. In this
vast region, too, there now arose a movement for Muslim
conversion and Muslim rules of government. On the ruins
of the old Christian Nubian province of Darfur, a line of
kings known as the Tungur had built a non-Muslim
kingdom in the distant past; and this kingdom now fell to a
new line of Muslim rulers. The tall ruins of their red-brick
palaces and mosques, especially those of Sultan Muhammad Teirab (reigned 1752–87), may still be seen
among the foothills of Jebel Marra, half-way between Lake
Chad and the Nile.

Yet this time of troubles in the eighteenth century was
not the end of the old friendship and alliance between
Kanem to the east of Lake Chad and Bornu to the west.
When the Fulani of Hausaland made the second of their
three attacks on Bornu in 1808, they drove Mai Ahmad
from his capital of Gasreggono. He appealed for help to
the Kanembu living east of the lake; and the Kanembu sent
an army to his relief under their leader Amin, a renowned
scholar as well as a skilful diplomat and soldier. Amin
drove the Fulani back, arguing meanwhile in letters to Sultan Bello that he and his followers were every bit as good
Muslims as the Fulani; indeed better, for they did not attack their fellow-Muslims. Amin then took over the real
leadership of the state from the ageing Mai Ahmad. With
the death of the latter Amin became Shehu or Sheikh of
Bornu, and a little later, in 1846, the thousand-year-old
dynasty of the Sefuwa kings drew finally to a close.

23 1800 AND AFTER

In 1807 the British Government decided that British citizens and ships must cease trading in slaves. This decision did much to change the course of history in many lands, but notably in Guinea. Northward in the plains of the Western Sudan, meanwhile, another train of events was set going by a further extension of the Muslim revival movement. In 1810 a reforming group led by Sheik Ahmadu bi Hammadi (Seku Hamadu) overthrew the non-Muslim rulers of the Masina plains along the middle Niger, seized Jenne, captured Timbuktu for a while, and founded a strong new state with their capital at Hamdallahi ("God Be Praised"). Later again, the same movement was carried further by another outstanding political and religious leader of the Western Sudan, Al-Hajj Umar Tall, who became caliph of the Tijaniyya tariqua or brotherhood* of Islam, conquered the non-Muslim states of Segu and Kaarta in 1861–62, and afterwards the Muslim state of Hamdallahi. His son, Ahmadu, reigned after him at Segu.

All these events were to have many consequences of profound importance for West Africa. This is not the place to follow them in detail. To round off our story, though, we may briefly consider the general condition of West Africa in 1800 and after; summarise the results of the Atlantic slave trade and its abolition, including the foundation of the modern countries of Sierra Leone and Liberia; and, lastly, note how the rise of European colonialism, the nineteenth century's most powerful challenge to West Africa, was itself the outcome of what had happened in the past.

* Formed by a North African leader, Ahmad al-Muktar al-Tijani (1737–1815), but much modified and radicalized in the Western Sudan.

Strength and weakness

Within all these changes and chances, the way of life of
most West Africans remained true to the traditions of their
past. Most people went on living by the rules and laws
laid down in the time of their ancestors. These laws and
rules came from the long slow growth of their civilisation,
and they offered what could often be a calm way of life,
prosperous and easy-going, peaceful and self-confident.
They pointed repeatedly to the interests of the whole community of the dead, the living, and the yet unborn; and
they bade men and women serve the interests of their community. They knew little of that god of the modern world,
individual competition. On the contrary, they discouraged
any individual who might try to get more than his due share
of wealth.

These laws and rules, the ideals of traditional African
civilisation, were strong and valuable. They were the creation of many centuries of steady growth, and had helped
to build the civilisation of West Africa. But this civilisation
also had its side of weakness. This was of two kinds. One
kind of weakness lay in West Africa's lack of unity. Against
the threat of foreign invasion and conquest, West Africans
seldom or never stood together. Religious beliefs and customs often pushed one people against another. There was
no "common front" against invasion, and this greatly weakened African resistance to the challenge of the nineteenth
century. Another and still more important weakness, and
one already noted, lay in the methods by which people
worked and produced wealth. These methods, as we have
seen, were largely the methods of subsistence economy.*
Most people grew or made only what they needed for
their own families, together with a little extra for trading

* See pages 151 and 152.

at local markets. Having enough, they saw no need to improve their ways of producing; they went on producing goods by the same simple methods as before, and with little or no aid from the mechanical inventions of Europe, so that by 1800, when compared with the strong countries of Europe, West Africa had fallen far behind in technology.

This is not in the least to say, one may perhaps repeat, that most Europeans were therefore happier or better off than most West Africans. On the contrary, the majority of the peoples of Britain and France, to mention only the most powerful nations of the nineteenth century, paid a harshly high price for their material progress. People of the rural areas in England and France were forced into the hunger and disease of grey and comfortless towns. Women and children were thrust without mercy into mines and factories. Countless numbers of industrial workers were starved or worked to death. Their lives were turned into a kind of slavery that was little different, in practice, from the slavery of the Africans across the Atlantic. This very suffering, however, put into the hands of rich and powerful men in Europe a strength and wealth which enabled them to conquer half the world. Much of this new strength and wealth came from mines and plantations in the Americas, where Africans and their descendants toiled and suffered as slaves. Between 1600 and 1800 (and even after 1800), Europe drew enormous benefits from the Atlantic slave trade. But what did this trade do for Africa, and especially for West Africa?

24 THE ATLANTIC TRADE: A SUMMING-UP

It is well to remind ourselves, at this point, that West Africa traded with the sea-merchants in many goods besides slaves. Gold and ivory were important in early times, and continued to be in high demand throughout the long period we have studied. There was always some trade in other exports, too, notably in pepper, ostrich feathers, gum, and various other products of West Africa. After 1600, however, it was increasingly the European demand for slave labour that dominated the coastal markets and sent its influence far inland.

The main consequences in West Africa

The slave trade was generally very bad for the peoples of Africa. But it was bad in different ways at different places. It was worst of all for the victims themselves. Once delivered to the captains of European and American ships, they were stripped, branded, and pushed into airless underdecks, crushed together, often chained by hand and foot. Like this they crossed the Atlantic in harsh weeks of sailing. Perhaps as many as one in every six captives died on their voyage across the ocean. Often they rose in brave revolt against their masters.

Back in Africa, though, the slave trade had effects of another kind. Many millions of strong and youthful men (with a small proportion of women) were forced out of Africa during the slave trade, and a number of African peoples were crippled by loss of population. Yet this was not always the case. Very large numbers were taken from areas like Iboland, where the vigour and fertility of local populations quickly filled the gaps. This, after all, was just what happened in certain parts of Europe. Millions of European men and women were driven across the seas by hunger and unemployment during the nineteenth century; but there were always enough people left at home to make good the loss.

The main consequences of the slave trade for African life lay in the field of production and in the field of politics.

The slave trade damaged local production in two ways. First of all, it obliged West Africa to export its most valuable raw material, which was human labour. Year after year, for more than three centuries, tens of thousands of African farmers and craftsmen were shipped away to work in American plantations, mines, and cities. With their labour they created vast wealth and profits, but seldom for themselves and never for Africa. All that Africa received in exchange were the manufactured goods of Europe; and this was the second way in which the slave trade damaged Africa. It is easy to see why. West Africa, like other parts of Africa, possessed its own craftsmen. Often they were highly skilled. They produced goods which were sold from one end of West Africa to the other. But they produced them by old-fashioned hand-methods. Increasingly they had to face the competition of much cheaper goods made by machinery in Europe.

Cheap foreign cottons, produced by Europeans or Indians forced to work for very low wages, began to ruin the market for cotton stuffs produced by self-employed and often prosperous African craftsmen. Cheap European metalware, machine-made, competed with the hand-work of African metal-smiths. Understandably, African craftsmen suffered from this rivalry. Yet they were unable to meet it by going over to European factory methods, since they had neither the necessary money nor the knowledge, while their way of life kept them faithful to traditional methods. So the slave trade removed African labour from

Africa, and did much to ruin the livelihood of African craftsmen.

A minority of Africans, of course, gained from the trade. These were the kings, chiefs, or rich merchants who went into the trade as dealers. They built up the prosperity of their towns and city-states just as their European partners brought new wealth to the ports and cities of western Europe. Yet even they suffered from the dangers and risks of the slave trade, and, although the transition could not be made without much difficulty and adjustment, they quickly shifted to other forms of business when the European and American demand for slaves came, after 1807, step by step to an end.

Other consequences, perhaps even more serious, were felt in the field of politics. These resulted especially from the very large import of guns and gunpowder. We have touched on this in an earlier chapter.* Being more efficient than spears and swords, firearms were soon in wide demand by African chiefs and kings. But they could generally be bought from the sea-merchants only in exchange, or part-exchange, for slaves. Thus the demand for captives usually went hand-in-hand with the demand for guns. This double pressure helped to spread war and conflict over many lands; and when the hammer-blows of European colonial invasion struck West Africa, as other parts of the continent, they did so at a time of fierce internal divisions. Politically the slave trade helped to open the way for European conquest.

Resistance to the slave trade

We have noted how the slave trade grew out of the traditional customs of chiefs and kings who were accustomed to regard all war-prisoners as property that could be sold,

* See pages 216–17.

exchanged, or simply given away. We have looked at some of those forms of political life in which certain groups of people were turned into permanent servants or house-slaves of rulers and rich men. We have seen how the lords of old West Africa indulged in the buying and selling of men and women—sending many across the Sahara both before and during the ocean slave trade—in the same way as did the lords of Europe and Asia. We have discussed how the massive export of millions of Africans to the Americas was founded on customs such as these.

One might have expected, though, that there would be African efforts to cut down the ocean slave trade, or even to stop it altogether, when the damaging effects of this trade became clear. And such efforts were indeed made. They failed, because the pressure of European and American demand was too great for them, but they are none the less worth remembering. Here are three examples.

The first occurred as early as the sixteenth century. In 1526 a famous king of the Bakongo state of Congo, near the mouth of the river of that name, wrote an angry letter of protest to the king of Portugal. King Nzinga Mbemba, whose Christian name was Affonso, complained to the Portuguese king, his ally and partner in trade, that the slave trade was doing great harm to his country. Together with certain Bakongo "thieves and men of evil conscience," he wrote, Portuguese traders were "grabbing and selling" his people, even including members of his own family. He wanted nothing from Portugal, he went on, except "priests and people to teach in our schools, and no other goods but wine and flour for the holy sacrament." Above all, he demanded that the Portuguese king, who was himself deep in the business of the slave trade, should recall his traders from the Congo, "because it is our will that in these kingdoms of Congo there should not be any trade in slaves nor any market for slaves." But the advantages and temptations offered by European-made goods, for which the sea-merchants increasingly demanded slaves, were too much for many of King Affonso's chiefs and sub-chiefs. They went on with the trade.

Another example occurred on the Dahomey coast of West Africa, the stretch of seaboard which the Europeans knew as the Slave Coast. When King Agaja sent his armies to capture the city-states of Ardrah and its slave-dealing neighbours, in 1724, he seems to have had it in mind to bring the slave trade to a halt. He sent a message to the British government, by the hand of an Englishman whom his generals had found in one of the coastal towns, telling it that he wanted to stop the export of people from his country. The Fon of Dahomey, after all, had every reason to know the damage that was done by the trade, for they had greatly suffered from it. King Agaja was no more successful in ending the trade than King Affonso two centuries earlier, though he certainly checked it for a time.

A third and similar example was noted in 1789 by a Swedish traveller who visited the imamate of Futa Toro in northern Senegal. A year before his visit, wrote this traveller, the almamy of Futa Toro had passed a law, "very much to his honour," which declared that no slaves were to be taken through Futa Toro for sale abroad. But the almamy was up against a powerful trading system which yielded great profits; and this system defeated his good intentions. Waiting in the Senegal river, as usual, were several French slave ships. Their captains, seeing they could not now hope to buy any slaves in Futa Toro, complained to the almamy, asking him to change his mind and do away with the law.

The almamy refused to do so, and followed this refusal by sending back to the agents of the French slave-trading company a number of presents they had given him, adding that "all the riches of that company would not make him change his mind." Faced with this refusal, the French captains discussed among themselves what they should do next. Then they found that the inland slave-dealers, also damaged by the almamy's new law, had worked out another route for taking slaves to the coast. So the French captains weighed anchor and sailed down the coast to this new market; and there they supplied themselves with the captives whom the almamy had prevented them from buying in the Senegal river.

There were other such acts of resistance, or attempted resistance, at Benin and elsewhere. They all failed. And they failed because the slave trade, until the early years of the nineteenth century, was a central part of the commercial system of the western world, the system to which large regions of Africa increasingly belonged. Only a change in this system could stop the trade in slaves. The beginnings of this change occurred in the closing years of the eighteenth century and led, among other things, to the foundation of Sierra Leone and Liberia. Before considering these events, however, another main consequence of the Atlantic trade needs at least to be touched upon. This happened outside Africa, and yet it is in many ways a large and inseparable part of African history. Great populations of African origin were implanted in the lands beyond the Atlantic. Their toil, skills, and achievements played a large and even essential role in building the civilisations of the Americas. Without Africa's contribution, those civilisations could not have become what they are today.

Africans beyond the seas

By 1800 about half the population of Brazil was of African descent. So was about half the population of Venezuela. So was a smaller but still large part of all the populations of the trans-Atlantic republics, whether in North, Central, or South America, or in the Caribbean islands. These were men and women who conquered the wilderness in the lands where they were taken, clearing and working countless farms and plantations, founding and opening innumerable mines of iron or precious metals. Harsh and painful as it was, the overseas slave trade (like the not much less harsh and painful movement of millions of hungry or jobless men and women from Europe) helped to lay the foundations of the American republics. And these Africans beyond the seas deserve their place in the story of Africa, and especially the story of West Africa, if only by reason of the fact that what they attempted and achieved was also a reflection of the strong and independent civilisation from which they came. Consider, for example, the heroic and successful struggle for independence conducted by the slaves of the Caribbean land of St. Domingue. In 1789, at the moment of the French Revolution, this French colony in the Caribbean was probably the wealthiest colony in the world. Its tens of thousands of African slave-workers produced enormous quantities of sugar; whole European communities lived off the profits.

When news of the Revolution in France reached St. Domingue, these slaves claimed their share in its ideals and benefits. They demanded their freedom. Denied this, they rose in revolt against their masters. In years of hard fighting against large armies sent by France, and afterwards against large armies sent by Britain, these men of St. Domingue won their freedom and founded the Republic of Haiti. Yet more than half these soldiers of freedom had made the "middle passage" across the Atlantic. More than half, in other words, had been born in Africa, had spent their childhood in Africa, had learned in Africa their respect for freedom; while nearly all the rest were the children of parents or grandparents born in Africa. And they were led by Africans: by men of genius and courage such as Boukman, Toussaint L'Ouverture, and Dessalines. Raised by Toussaint and his Africans, the banner of revolt was carried from people to people. Many threw off their bondage. Large numbers of men of African origin fought in the Northern armies of the American Civil War. It was a general of African descent, Antonio Maceo, who led the military struggle for Cuban independence against Spain in 1868.

Like other men of vision, Maceo had no time for racialism. Some of the whites of Cuba disagreed with him. They were Spanish settlers who thought that white was going to be better than black even in an independent Cuba. One day Maceo was approached by a Spanish Cuban who suggested that the regiments of the independence army should be divided into whites and non-whites. Maceo made him a reply which became famous in Cuba. "If you were not white," Maceo said to this man, "I would have you shot on the spot. But I do not wish to be accused of being a racialist as you are, and so I let you go, but with the warning that I shall not be so patient another time. The revolution has no colour."

In Europe, too, West Africans who had gained their freedom had begun to gain honours and respect as well. One of them, whose name was Ibrahim, became personal secretary to the Russian emperor Peter the Great. Another, a young Nzima from Axim in modern Ghana whose name was Anton Wilhelm Amo, entered the ancient German University of Halle in 1727. After studying philosophy and law, Amo passed on to Wittenberg University and was there crowned with a doctorate of philosophy in 1733. On that occasion the Rector of Wittenberg University, after praising the scholars of the African past, welcomed Dr. Amo as a man of rare gifts, morality, and civilisation. A third African to make his name in the world of letters was Olaudah Equiano, an Ibo who wrote in 1789 the first English book about Iboland and one which played its part in the English anti-slavery campaign of the late eighteenth century. Yet all these even had been formed in their different ways by the ideas and values of their native land.

25 SIERRA LEONE, LIBERIA, AND THE RISE OF COLONIALISM

Introduction

When Europeans first began to think about abolishing the Atlantic slave trade, during the closing years of the eighteenth century, two main lines of action gradually emerged.

The first of these aimed at setting up new settlements on the West African coast by means of which men and women of African descent, freed from American slavery, could be sent back to Africa and could there build lives of their own. The second, which came into effect somewhat later, aimed at increasing the number of European trading stations so as to profit from new types of West African production which developed after the end of the slave trade.

These lines of action, both European and American, affected different parts of the Guinea coast. The Windward Coast was selected for the first kind of settlement,* and here there now emerged the origins of modern Sierra Leone and Liberia. The rest of the coast, that of Sene-Gambia in the west and of modern Ghana, Dahomey, and the Niger delta in the east, became the scene of increased trading activities in palm-oil and other products.

All this was to have great influence on the future of West Africa. The experiment of sending back freed slaves to Sierra Leone began in 1787, and to Liberia some thirty years later; but the big change really came in 1807, when the British abolished their trade in slaves and brought strong pressure on other European nations to do the same. Any full discussion of the reasons why the British did this must lie outside the limits of this book; generally, however, there were two reasons of central importance.

* See footnote to page 256 above.

The first reason was that British businessmen and manufacturers were no longer very interested in the fate of West Indian and North American plantations. Having used the profits of the slave trade to help them build new industries, British industrialists and merchants faced new economic needs. Their interest now was to find labour for their new factories; and they had to find this labour inside Britain. They became less and less concerned with buying and using African slaves.

This change inside Britain meant that the British or American owners of slaves across the Atlantic enjoyed less and less political influence. Their voice in Britain grew weaker. They went on shouting that the end of slavery would ruin them, but fewer people cared. What is more, fewer people listened, for at this point there emerged a second reason for British abolition. Liberal Christian opinion began to condemn the slave trade as inhuman and disgraceful. There arose a great and popular movement in Britain, and afterwards in other countries, which demanded the end of this cruel commerce in human beings, a movement that was led by Granville Sharp, Thomas Clarkson, and William Wilberforce in Britain, and by the Abbé Gregoire and a number of leaders of the French Revolution in France. Free Africans abroad were also active in the movement, notably the Ibo writer Olaudah Equiano.

Founding of Sierra Leone

Those Englishmen who thought it right to end the slave trade began with the idea of sending free Africans back to Africa. But why, it may be asked, were there any free Africans then in Britain? The answer is that in 1772 an English Chief Justice, Lord Mansfield, declared in a famous legal judgment that no men in England, no matter from where they came, could be slaves. After that judgment all the African slaves in England became legally free men, and there were probably about fifteen thousand of them. This number grew larger after the North American colonies had won their independence. Runaway slaves made for Canada, and from there they made for Britain.

These former slaves had their freedom in Britain, but they found it hard and even impossible to find acceptance in society and regular work. In 1787, trying to do something to help them, a group of Englishmen banded together with the aim of sending three shiploads of Negroes to the coast of Sierra Leone. Like the Negroes from the United States who arrived in Liberia a little later, the pioneers in Sierra Leone were badly equipped and poorly prepared for the difficulties they would have to face. A total of four hundred and eleven of them sailed in the first two ships. They settled on a stretch of coast about nine miles long. This piece of land was sold to the Englishmen who were in charge of the settlement for the sum of £59 1s. 5d., paid in various kinds of goods, including arms and ammunition, cotton cloths, metalware, tobacco, and rum. The chief who made this sale, King Tom, ruled over a section of the Temne people living on the seaside, and his senior chief, King Naimbana who lived about six miles up the Sierra Leone river, also seems to have had some hand in the sale.

On 14 May 1787, the colonists cut their way through the bush to the top of a hill which overlooked the spot where they had landed. There they raised the British flag and made ready for their first village, which they called Granville Town after Granville Sharp, one of the best-known leaders of the British anti-slavery campaign. Their troubles began almost at once. Many died of fever or other sickness. Supplies were hard to obtain. Money soon ran short. Yet the men who came to settle here included not a few who were determined to make a success of it, who valued their freedom and were not prepared to see it wasted.

Prominent among the second wave of pioneers was a former slave called Thomas Peters. He was one of those who had escaped from his American plantation-owner and had won his freedom by joining the British army, in which he rose to be a sergeant. He was also one of many former slaves to whom the British had promised to give land in the colony of Nova Scotia. When this promise was broken, Thomas Peters took the bold step of sailing to England as the spokesman of his fellow-Negroes in Nova Scotia. In London he was offered land in Sierra Leone. Together with a British naval officer called John Clarkson, brother of Thomas Clarkson of anti-slavery fame, Peters went back to Nova Scotia and gathered a group of volunteers among the landless Negroes there. In 1792 they sailed for Sierra Leone. They numbered as many as eleven hundred and ninety men and women. With their arrival, the fortunes of the little colony took a more hopeful turn.

Yet its miseries were far from ended. The port of Free-town, founded in 1791, was invaded and looted by a French naval force in 1794. Fever killed many of the new settlers just as it had already killed many of those who had come from England. The survivors somehow held on. They persevered. They demanded from the British Sierra Leone Company, which had started the colony and continued to direct it, a large control over its laws and in this they were successful, thanks to the wisdom of a governor called Zachary Macaulay, who ruled the colony for the company between 1794 and 1799.

In 1808 there came another change. The Sierra Leone Company could no longer pay its bills. The infant colony, still numbering fewer than two thousand people settled on a narrow strip of land along the coast, was taken over by the British Government and became a Crown Colony, with its governors sent out from England. The good anchoring-places of Sierra Leone now acquired a new value. They offered a secure base for British warships which had been sent to police Guinea waters so as to prevent the ships of other maritime nations—those that had not yet abolished the trade—from carrying away slaves. Many liberated captives

were now taken into Sierra Leone ports.* Here they tended
to stay, partly because they lacked any means of transport
whereby they might return to their native lands, and
partly because they feared recapture if they tried to go
home. Later, however, a number of enterprising Sierra
Leoneans did find their way to other parts of West Africa,
and built up business enterprises at such places as Abeokuta
in Western Nigeria. In this way the population of this
coastal colony, composed of the descendants of many West
African peoples, grew and gradually spread its influence
over the inland country behind the Sierra Leone coast.

Founding of Liberia

The origins of Liberia were rather similar to those of Sierra
Leone except that the former had its roots in America.
In 1790 as many as sixty thousand Negroes in the United
States had managed to gain their freedom. Their number
continued to grow, and by 1820 they totalled a quarter of
a million. Yet it continued to be hard or impossible for
them to win acceptance as free men. Here, too, some individual efforts were made to help them, though with small
success, and here too it was decided to try to find a West
African home for at least a few of these unfortunate people. Among whites who pursued this idea was a liberal-
minded though characteristically paternalist clergyman
called Robert Finlay. He thought that "sending Negroes
back to Africa" would help to "civilise the Africans,"
whom he curiously described as "the wild and wandering
people who now roam over that great section of the globe."

Led by Finlay, and with the interest of a number of
leading Negro Americans, a small group of men accordingly met in Washington in 1816, on 28 December, and

* By about 1850, some 70,000 Africans liberated from slave-
ships had been put ashore and settled in Sierra Leone.

founded a society for sending free Negroes back to Africa.
This was the American Colonization Society, or, to give it
its full title, the American Society for Colonizing the Free
People of Colour in the United States. At first the Society
sent a few Negroes to Sierra Leone, where it was hoped
that they would be able to find the opportunities denied to
them at home. This expedition failed. Then, after many setbacks, some land was purchased in 1821 from a local chief
at Cape Mesurado on the Windward Coast, and one hundred and thirty Negro settlers were established there.

This tiny American colony was named Liberia after the
Latin word for a free man, *liber*; and the colonists decided
to call their first settlement Monrovia after President Mon-
roe, who was then in office. From their earliest arrival the
colonists had a hard time. They were joined by others from
the United States, but survived only with the greatest difficulty. Nearly everything went wrong for them, mainly because these pioneers were badly equipped and knew nothing
of West African conditions. Yet somehow they hung on.
Later in the nineteenth century, after many adventures,
their little settlement of Monrovia grew into a city, and
became the capital of the Republic of Liberia.

New kinds of trade

A second line of European action was to strengthen and
expand their trading stations on other parts of the coast.
This took effect only gradually. It was caused by a new
interest in African trade; and this new interest came from
the realisation that Africa might well be a wealthy continent which could provide many types of crops and goods
for export. Africans likewise found that the end of the
slave trade, during the first half of the nineteenth century,*

* Here and there the Atlantic slave trade continued even after
the 1850s.

opened new opportunities for them, and these they grasped with skill and energy.

Palm-oil became a valuable export. With their factory towns growing ever larger and dirtier, Europeans found for the first time in history that they needed large quantities of soap. Such soap as they had was made from animal fat, and there was not enough of it. Better soap, it was discovered, could be made from palm-oil. Businessmen in great ports such as Liverpool, once so busy with the slave trade, began sending out orders to their agents in West Africa to buy this valuable vegetable product, and African palm-oil growers eagerly responded.

We should notice this response because it, too, was part of African civilisation. Once they knew that they could make a good living from palm-oil, West African growers and traders quickly adjusted themselves to this new trade. They had no need to be organised by anyone else: they organised themselves. Almost from its beginning, the new trade boomed. In 1800 the whole of West Africa from the Gambia river to the Niger delta supplied England with only a few tons of palm-oil. Yet within a dozen years this quantity had grown to several hundred tons. By the 1830s the West African coast was exporting many thousands of tons of palm-oil every year. Hundreds of African merchants were busy in the trade. Thousands of African farmers were at work in African-owned palm-oil plantations. The palm-oil growers of the Niger delta became especially famous for their enterprises. Energetic "House companies" cleared land, planted palms, dealt in thousands of pounds' worth of trade every month; and the Niger delta became known to Europeans as the Oil Rivers.

Events were now moving fast, for this revolution in West African trade went hand-in-hand with another development, the huge and rapid growth of industry in western Europe. Europeans began to look to Africa for the raw materials they needed in ever-increasing quantities. They made it their business to buy these raw materials and turn them into finished goods. Very soon, not content with buying from West Africans, Europeans began to think of the advantages they could gain from possessing the sources of Africa's wealth. There came the rise of colonialism. Meanwhile their curiosity and their ambitions had been fed by the reports of European explorers, more and more of whom had penetrated into the unknown lands behind the coast.

Explorers from Europe

By 1800 Europe's traders and sailors had learned much about the seaboard of Guinea; but their ignorance of West Africa, like West Africa's of Europe, was profound. Of the whole inland country, its peoples and their achievements, their history and their civilisation, little or nothing was understood in Europe or America; and most of what was thought to be understood was in fact wrong. It was even strongly suspected until Mungo Park's journey of 1795–97 that the Niger flowed from east to west, and joined the Atlantic Ocean by way of the Senegal.

A few attempts had been made in earlier times to solve these "inner mysteries" of Africa, but they added little to knowledge. Several early Portuguese travellers probably got as far as Timbuktu; the records of what they had seen and heard were long since lost or laid away forgotten in the Portuguese archives. There now followed a new and far greater enterprise of exploration, at first designed merely to satisfy the curiosity of scientists and geographers in Europe. In two bold journeys from the Gambia river, begun in 1795 and 1805, a young Scots surgeon named Mungo Park marched successfully to the middle Niger. Another extraordinary and still younger man, this time from France, soon followed him. His name was René Caillié, and he walked from the coast of western Guinea in 1823, disguised as a Muslim, all the way to Timbuktu and afterwards across the Sahara to Morocco. Others followed. Several Englishmen—Denham, Clapperton, Oudney—came south from Tunis into the Fulani empire during the 1830s. Not much later, the two Lander brothers followed the Niger from Hausaland down to the delta. A German traveller called Heinrich Barth travelled through the Sahara and the Western Sudan for five years between 1849 and 1855 and brought back a great harvest of information.

Meanwhile attempts were being made to go up into the inland country by way of the coast, and especially by way of the Niger. To begin with, malaria killed most of the Europeans who tried this route. Now a medical discovery helped them. It was shown that quinine could save lives threatened by malaria-carrying mosquitoes. In 1854 a British expedition under William Baikie went up the river Benue as far as Yola and returned to the coast without losing a single man. More and more was learned of the inland country. By the 1860s a great deal of the shape and geography of inland Africa was, at least in outline, broadly understood.

Rise of colonialism

Little by little, the explorers were followed by the invaders. There came the military penetration of West Africa from European bases along the coast. And the most important bases or "jumping-off points," we may note, were precisely those trading stations which earlier Europeans had founded in western Guinea on the coast of Sene-Gambia, in central and eastern Guinea along the Ivory Coast and on the seaboard of modern Ghana, Togo, Dahomey, and Nigeria.

The effects of colonial invasion were many and profound, and we cannot discuss them here. They closed one long epoch of West African history and opened another. In 1800 Europeans were ruling nowhere in West Africa, except within a few thousand square yards of soil on which their castles stood, and, indirectly, along a short strip of the Sierra Leone coast. But in 1900 they were ruling or were about to rule the whole of West Africa except Liberia.

One may well ask how this swift change could come about. For hundreds of years, after all, West Africans had dealt with Europeans and Americans as their equals. Attacked from the sea, they had successfully defended themselves. Threatened from foreign-held castles, they had stormed and captured these castles. Deceived by foreign traders, they had brought such men to order and punished their deceit. Yet now, within less than a hundred years, this power of resistance seemed to collapse.

African technological inferiority and political disunity provide two obvious explanations. But there was also another reason which belonged to European history. The late eighteenth and early nineteenth centuries had greatly transformed the structure of society in the leading nations of western Europe. With the onward drive of industrial revolution, the great edifice of private capital accumulation and investment was now in place. Its very process of internal growth acquired a dynamic of its own that soon proved irresistible. Even while British and French governments continued to oppose territorial expansion across the seas, or at any rate to consider such expansion more as a liability than a gain, the new men had their way. From Egypt and North Africa their ambitions turned gradually to the tropical lands of the south.

This new imperialism grew rapidly during the middle decades of the nineteenth century, and reached an explosive point in the 1860s. Thereafter it was repeatedly powered and impelled by sharp and violent rivalries between the leading European competitors. But in Africa, for the most part, the imperialists were careful not to come to blows with each other, at least until the First World War, for they saw that if they did they might well lose their chance of conquest. Generally, they found it both wise and profitable to reach agreement, or rather many agreements, on how they could best cut up their African elephant even before they had shot it. They accordingly "shared" Africa into "spheres of interest," setting aside some parts of the coast and inland country for the French, others for the British, and others again for the Portuguese, Germans, Italians, Belgians, and Spanish. This "international share-out," as it came to be called, was no mean factor in helping the colonialists to crush African resistance.

All the same, there was much African resistance. Built over so many years, African independence found brave defenders. Driven by their fury for conquest, their desire for colonies, the European governments assaulted West Africa from many directions. But they faced no simple task. The traditional civilisation of West Africa was not quickly overcome.

The past and the future

Yet the challenge to West Africa, as to other regions of the continent, was not simply one of military invasion. It was also, as we have seen, the challenge of the modern world, of those machine-using industries and scientific discoveries out of which European strength had largely grown.

Having fought the armies of invasion, Africans still faced this second part of the challenge. Their task now was to modernise their way of life. But to do this they had first to regain their freedom of action. The best of their leaders turned their thoughts in that direction, reflecting in this the deep influence of traditions which had taught the value of independence. Now that this independence was lost, they sought to win it back again. In order to succeed, they saw that they must attain a clear understanding of the modern world, and they therefore tried by every means they could to exploit the benefits of modern education. But they also remembered the history of their ancestors and drew strength from that memory. They strove to build a new and free future on the foundations of the past. And so it was not for nothing that the early nationalists of West Africa were historians as well as political thinkers. "To put it shortly," wrote J. E. Casely-Hayford, one of the best-known spokesmen of West Africa during the early colonial period, "before ever the British came into relations with our people, we were a developed people, having our own institutions, having our own ideas of government." This was to be one of the great themes of later African renaissance.

There was to be another great task as well as the regaining of African independence, and the modernising of Africa. This was to assert the natural equality of Africans with all other branches of the family of man. After 1800, with gathering industrial and military strength, Europeans began to feel more and more superior to Africans not only in technology and civilisation, but also in natural gifts, intelligence, and moral value. This racialist approach was boldly answered by men who had studied African history, such as Edward Wilmot Blyden, a West Indian of African descent who had become an adopted son of Africa. Blyden was among those who argued powerfully against the European belief, very common then, that Africans had done nothing great or important in the past. "On the contrary," he said as early as 1880, at the very outset of the colonial period, "Africa is no vast island, separated by an immense ocean from other portions of the globe, and cut off through the ages from the men who have made and influenced the destinies of mankind." Far from this, he went on, "Africa has been closely connected, both as source and nourisher, with some of the most potent influences which have affected for good the history of the world."

Today we live in a new time. Africans have won back their right to rule themselves. They have begun to modernise their continent. They have renewed their independent history from the point where the colonial period broke it off.

And with all this, the history of the African continent must take on fresh and vivid meaning for us all.

What kind of history this was and what manner of experience it enclosed, its strengths and weaknesses, its failures and achievements: such have been the central themes of this brief and introductory survey. At least at this stage of knowledge, very incomplete in many ways, these themes can be followed in their detail only through the lives and ambitions of kings and rulers, men of power and wealth. Yet perhaps we should remember, while future scholars prepare to give us the more capacious histories which we need, that the full and rich story of the past, here as elsewhere, concerns much more than the lives of famous or outstanding men. For it is the ordinary people whose names are so often absent from the records of history who were and are the true creators of kings and rulers, the true founders of wealth and progress, the true builders of the past and inheritors of the future. That is why we may end as we began, with the words of an Akan saying which celebrates the importance of ordinary people:

> I call Gold,
> Gold is mute.
> I call Cloth,
> Cloth is mute.
> It is Mankind that matters.

A RELATIVE DATING GUIDE

TABLE FOR PART ONE

BC	WEST AFRICA			ELSEWHERE
	WESTERN REGION	CENTRAL REGION	EASTERN REGION	
4000		The three or four Old Stone Age languages used in West Africa begin to split up into the four hundred or more different languages which are now spoken there		Early farming in Egypt. New Stone Age comes to an end with spreading use of copper for many purposes
				Early states in Egypt
3500		New Stone Age farming and cattle raising in the Sahara, at this time green and fertile		
		Old Stone Age (without farming) continues in the forest lands		
3200		The Sahara and Sudan are still green and fertile		Unification of two states of Upper and Lower Egypt. Beginning of the civilisation of pharaonic Egypt
				Building of the Pyramids
2500	Sahara begins gradually to dry up			Great period of Egyptian history
2000	Gradual movement of farming peoples out of the Sahara, where water is now growing scarce			Asians, called Hyksos, invade Egypt. They introduce use of horses and chariots.
1700–1600				

WEST AFRICA

BC	WESTERN REGION	CENTRAL REGION	EASTERN REGION	ELSEWHERE
1575				New Egyptian empire under pharaohs of 18th dynasty.
1500				Rise of Berber civilisation in North Africa
1000	Carts and chariots drawn by donkeys or horses begin to be used for crossing the Sahara between North and West Africa			
800				Rise of civilisation of Kush on middle Nile. Soon Kush invades Egypt and holds most of it for a century.
814				Traditional date of foundation of Carthage by Phoenicians
500	Farming begins to develop in the forest lands			
200	Iron-working begins to appear in West Africa south of the Sahara. The Nok Culture. Trade continues between North and West Africa across the Sahara			Greek kings (the Ptolemies) in Egypt. Wars between Rome and Carthage. Rome wins and destroys Carthage

Date			
105	More Sudanese peoples learn how to make iron		Romans defeat King Jugurtha of the Berber Kingdom of Numidia. Much of Tunisia and Algeria are brought within the new Roman empire
100	Trans-Saharan trade now using increasing numbers of camels		Iron-working begins to appear in central South Africa
AD 300	Spread of iron-working through West Africa		Many fine and prosperous cities flourish in Roman North Africa
550			Emergence of Christian kingdoms in Nubia on middle Nile
750	Ancient Ghana grows important		Muslim conquests in North Africa and Spain far advanced
800	Ghana commands the international trade in gold and salt. Becomes a powerful empire	Islam begins to appear in West Africa through Muslim Berber traders from the Sahara. Traditional date for founding of early Kanem empire (about 850)	Egypt becomes a great centre of Muslim civilisation
1000	Ghana at height of its power	Traditional dates for foundation of Timbuktu, Jenne, and Gao	Kanem expands. Founding of early Hausa and Yoruba states
			Fatimid Kalifate in Egypt (969–1171)

WEST AFRICA

AD	WESTERN REGION	CENTRAL REGION	EASTERN REGION	ELSEWHERE
1050				Bani Hillal devastations begin in Tunisia and eastern Algeria
				Almoravids set up new Muslim states in Morocco and Spain (1061–1147)
1054	Almoravid Berbers capture Audaghost from Ghana	Early Songhay state of Gao; its rulers, the Dia line of kings, have accepted Islam		
1076	Ghana begins to collapse under Almoravid attacks: its capital is taken by them			Arts and early sciences flourish in Muslim Spain and North Africa
1086			King of Kanem accepts Islam	
1200	Time of confusion	Early state of Benin under Ogiso rulers (very approximate dating)		Almohads set up new Muslim state in North Africa and Spain (1147–1289)
				Ayyubids rule Egypt (1171–1250)
1230	Sundiata becomes king of small Mandinka state of Kangaba: defeats his enemy Sumanguru: founds empire of Mali			

1255	Mansa Uli (dies 1270) continues to build empire of Mali	Growing commercial power of Gao	Kanem a small empire to east and west of Lake Chad	Mamluk soldier-kings rule Egypt (1250–1517)
1300	Woloff states founded in Senegal	Early states in forest country	Yoruba states under spiritual lead of Ife (very approximate dating)	Christians reconquer most of Spain. There remains only the small Muslim kingdom of Granada (1232–1492)
1312	Mansa Musa comes to throne of Mali. Dies in 1337 after expanding Mali far across both western and central regions of West Africa. Takes Gao into Mali empire in 1325			Beginning of Hundred Years' War between English and French
1335	Mali continues at height of its power	At Gao, dia line of kings followed by first of a new line, called the sunni kings		
1375	Mali begins to decline	Sunni Suleiman-Mar of Gao wins back independence from Mali. Gao begins to grow in power	Bulala dominate Kanem east of Lake Chad. Kanem rulers temporarily much weakened	First detailed map of West Africa is drawn by Cresques of Majorca
1400		Songhay of Gao raid Niani, capital of Mali. Bono-Manso and Mossi states in existence	Hausa and Yoruba states grow stronger and wealthier. Nupe founded at this time	

WEST AFRICA

AD	WESTERN REGION	CENTRAL REGION	EASTERN REGION	ELSEWHERE
1415		Timbuktu and Jenne are great centres of Muslim scholarship		Portuguese, raiding overseas for first time, capture Ceuta, a port in north-western Morocco
				Egypt ruled by strong Mamluk sultan Baybars (1422–37)
1434	Portuguese begin sailing down Atlantic coast of West Africa. They are soon followed by other Europeans in small numbers who engage in more or less peaceful trade with many coastal states		Benin is now a big empire Islam reaches Zaria (1456)	
1464	Mali continues to decline	Sunni Ali comes to throne of Gao and begins to build the Songhay empire	Muhammad Rumfa of Kano (1465–99)	
1472		Songhay captures Jenne (1473)	Portuguese reach Bight of Benin. Christian missionaries soon follow them	Portuguese and Spanish attacks on Morocco, which is much weakened by them
1482	Much European trading on the coast of Sene-Gambia	Portuguese build Elmina castle on Gold Coast		Portuguese make contact with Bakongo kingdom near mouth of Congo river
1492		Sunni Ali dies		Columbus reaches Caribbean
1493		Askia Muhammad becomes ruler of Songhay	Al-Maghili of Tuat at Kano and Katsina	

TABLE FOR PART TWO

WEST AFRICA

AD	WESTERN REGION	CENTRAL REGION	EASTERN REGION	ELSEWHERE
1507		Big expansion of trade between Sudan and Guinea. Jenne becomes prosperous	Mai Idris Katakarmabe becomes king of Bornu. Wins battle of Garni-Kiyala and gains control of Kanem	Spanish conquests in Caribbean and Central America
1517			Kebbi gains independence from Songhay empire. Attacks Gobir and Katsina	Ottoman Turks conquer Egypt and move west along the coast of North Africa
		Mahmud Kati of Timbuktu starts writing *Tarikh al-Fattash* (1519)		
1528		Askia Muhammad deposed by Askia Musa in Songhay		
1534	Mali sends ambassador to Portugal			Martin Luther dies (1546)
1550	Trading partnerships between European sea-merchants and African coastal states become established firmly in this period			
		The state of Gonja founded by Mandinka warriors at this time		Religious wars in Germany

WEST AFRICA

AD	WESTERN REGION	CENTRAL REGION	EASTERN REGION	ELSEWHERE
1553			English visit Benin for first time	"Bloody" Mary ascends English throne
1559	Tengella Koli establishes new line of kings in Tekrur (Futa Toro). They were called the Denianke	Gold trade expands		
1575			Hausa states revolt against Songhay	Portuguese invasion of Morocco defeated by Mulay the Victorious, who becomes king (1578)
1580			Mai Idris Alooma becomes ruler of Kanem-Bornu and establishes the new empire by the time of his death in 1617	Spanish Armada fails to invade England (1588)
1591	Mali empire in last stages of collapse	Songhay empire begins to collapse under Moroccan invasion		
1600				Judar leads the Moroccan army across the Sahara and defeats Songhay

TABLE FOR PART THREE

WEST AFRICA

AD	WESTERN REGION	CENTRAL REGION	EASTERN REGION	ELSEWHERE
1600	Woloff states prosper	Gonja fights Dagomba	Kanem under Idris Alooma is most powerful state in this region	Dutch emerge as strongest European sea-power. European powers now form their early chartered companies for trading with Africa and other distant countries
1650		Early Bambara state of Segu Rise of Denkyira	Rise of Oyo	Dutch make small settlement at Cape of Good Hope (1652): origins of modern South Africa
		Rise of Fon state in Dahomey under King Wegbaja, who reigns until 1685	Oyo empire extends over most Yoruba states and Dahomey	British fight the Dutch for supremacy at sea (1653–54 and 1665–67)
			Rise of new city-states in Niger delta	British fight the Spanish and the French for supremacy at sea (1655 onwards)
1659	French found St. Louis in Senegal			

WEST AFRICA

AD	WESTERN REGION	CENTRAL REGION	EASTERN REGION	ELSEWHERE
1664	English build Fort James on Gambia river	Beginnings of Asante Union		
1677–81		Expansion of Akwamu under Ansa Sasraku	Kanem enters period of confusion which leads to its gradual decline	
1705		Asante a strong power under Osei Tutu	Tuareg and Jukun raid N. Nigeria (1670–1703)	
1713	Europeans expand trade with Woloff and Tekrur	Founding of Bambara empire under Mamari Kulibali (1712–55)		With Treaty of Utrecht between Britain and France, British become the biggest buyers and carriers of slaves from Africa. Europeans in West Indies now making tremendous profits out of sugar grown by African slaves
1725	Foundation of Imamate of Futa Jallon	Fon take control of city-states on Dahomey coast. End of Akwamu empire (1730)		
1750	Spread of Muslim revival	Asante predominates in central Guinea. Emergence of Baoulé state in Ivory Coast	Muhammad Teirab is sultan of Darfur (1752–87)	Britain enters her industrial revolution with invention of many important machines: 1733. Kay invents mechanical weaving shuttle 1738. Paul invents mechanical spinning roller

1753		Foundation of Bambara state of Kaarta	Niger delta city-states at height of their trading expansion	1768. Hargreaves invents the "spinning jenny" 1776. Watt invents his mechanical pump 1803. Trevithick builds a steam locomotive to run on iron rails
1775	Foundation of imamate of Futa Toro: end of Denianke line of rulers (1776)	Asante empire at its height		American Revolution
1789			Decline of Benin. Oyo still powerful	French Revolution. George Washington becomes President of the United States
1791	Foundation of Freetown			Toussaint declares freedom in Haiti
1798	Mungo Park at Segu (1796)			French under Napoleon invade Egypt
1801				Thomas Jefferson becomes President of the United States
1804	Church Missionary Society in Sierra Leone. Methodists and others soon follow	Fulani revolts and conquest of Hausaland (1804–11)		British and French at war

WEST AFRICA

AD	WESTERN REGION	CENTRAL REGION	EASTERN REGION	ELSEWHERE
1806		Britain clashes with Asante, but peace is at once restored. Asante continues to dominate the greater part of central Guinea and neighbouring grassland countries	Mai Ahmad reigns in Kanem (1793–1810)	
1807	Sierra Leone a British colony (1808)		Fulani conquer N. Nigeria but not Bornu. Bello is first sultan of Sokoto	British abolish their trade in slaves. Soon institute naval patrols to prevent all slave ships from operating on the Guinea coast. Battle of Waterloo (1815) ends the first French Empire
1816				Foundation of the American Colonization Society
1817 1821	Foundation of Bathurst Foundation of Liberia	Dahomey revolts against Oyo		Peace is made in Europe. Big growth of capitalist system. Beginning of European overseas imperialism
1827		British clash again with Asante, and are defeated	Many wars in Yorubaland	

ONE HUNDRED KEY SOURCES
for West African History

This short list aims only at suggesting, out of a very copious possible total of books and papers, a manageable bibliography of key sources and commentaries which may best carry the reader more deeply into the history of West Africa up to the eve of the colonial period.

IFAN   *Institut Français d'Afrique Noire*
JAH   *Journal of African History*
JHSN *Journal of the Historical Society of Nigeria*
THSG *Transactions of the Historical Society of Ghana*

Archaeological Papers

Clark, J. D. "The Prehistoric Origins of African Culture," JAH 2 of 5, 1964

Connah, G. "Archaeological Research in Benin City," JHSN 4 of 2, 1963

Fagg, B. A. B. "The Nok Culture in Prehistory," JHSN 4 of 1, 1959

Fagg, W. and Willett, F. "Ancient Ife: an Ethnographic Survey," *Actes du IVe Congrès Panafricaine de Préhistoire*, 1962

Goodwin, A. J. H. "Archaeology and Benin Architecture," JHSN 2 of 1, 1957

Leboeuf, J.-P. "Prehistory, Proto-History and History in Chad," JHSN 4 of 2, 1963

Ozanne, P. "Early Historic Archaeology of Accra," THSG 1962

Shaw, T. "Field Research in Nigerian Archaeology," JHSN 4 of 2, 1963

Shinnie, P. and Ozanne, P. "Excavations at Yendi Dabari" (Northern Ghana), THSG 1962

Willett, F. "Investigations at Old Oyo 1956–7," JHSN 1 of 2, 1960

———— "Ife and its Archaeology," JAH 1 of 2, 1960

Some Principle Arabic Sources in
English or French Translation

Abdullah ibn Muhammad *Tazyin al Waraqat,* c. 1810 (Fulani conquest of Hausaland), trans. M. Hiskett, Ibadan, 1963

al-Bakri, Abdullah Abu-Ubaid *Al Masalik wa'l-Mamalik,* Córdoba 1067, trans. M. G. de Slane, 2 vols., Paris, 1859

al-Idrisi, Abu Abdullah Muhammad *Nuzhat al-Mushtaq fi Iktiraq al-Afaq,* Palermo 1154, trans. R. Dozy and M. J. de Goeje, 2 vols., Leiden, 1866

al-Maghili, Muhammad ibn Abd al-Karim (Answers to Muhammad Askia) partial trans. by J. O. Hunwick in B. Davidson, *The African Past,* 1964

al-Omari, Ibn Fadl Allah *Masalik al Absar fi Mamalik al Amsar,* Cairo, c. 1342, Gaudefroy-Demombynes, Paris, 1927

Anonymous *Tedzkiret en-Nisian,* Timbuktu (history of, c. 1650–1750), trans. O. Houdas, Paris, 1901

Bello, Muhammad *Infaq al-Maysur,* trans. E. J. Arnett in *The Rise of the Sokoto Fulani,* Kano, 1929

Fodio, Uthman dan (attrib.) *Kitab al Farq,* trans. M. Hiskett in *Bull.* School of Oriental and African Studies, London, part 3, 1960. (See other partial translations in T. Hodgkin, *Nigerian Perspectives,* 1960.)

Ibn Batuta, Muhammad ibn Abdullah *Tuhfat al-Nuzzar fi Ghara'ib al-Amsar wa Adja'ib al-Asfar,* Marrakesh c. 1355, partial trans. H. A. R. Gibb, London, 1929

Ibn Fartua, Ahmed (Kanem War of Idris Alooma), trans. H. R. Palmer, Lagos, 1928

Ibn Khaldun, 'Abd al-Rahman *Kitab Tarikh ad Duwal al-Islamiyya etc.,* (towards end of fourteenth century) trans. as *Histoire des Berbères et des Dynasties Musulmanes de l'Afrique Septentrionale* by M. G. de Slane, Paris, 2nd ed., 1925

Kano Chronicle trans. H. R. Palmer, *Sudanese Memoirs,* Lagos, 1928

Kati, Mahmud *Tarikh al-Fattash,* Timbuktu, completed by successors c. 1655, trans. O. Houdas and M. Delafosse, Paris, 1913

Leo Africanus (Hassan ibn Muhammad al-Wazzan as Zayyati)

Déscription de l'Afrique, original in Italian 1526, corrected and published by G. Ramusio, Venice, 1550; trans. A. Epaulard, 2 vols., Paris, 1956

Sadi, Abdulrahman as- *Tarikh al-Sudan,* Timbuktu, c. 1655, trans. O. Houdas and Edm. Benoist, Paris, 1900

Early European Travellers

Azurara, G. E. de *Crónica dos Féitos da Guiné,* trans. C. R. Beazley and E. Prestage, *Chronicle etc.,* 2 vols., London, 1896

Cadamostro *Voyages,* Eng. trans. G. R. Crone, 1937

Dapper, O. *Description of Africa,* first published Amsterdam, 1668, in German 1670 and French 1686. German version preferable to French. Useful extracts from latter in Hodgkin, *supra*

Fernandes, V. *Déscription de la Côte Occidentale d'Afrique,* 1506–10, and based on information relating largely to 1499–1507 for Sierra Leone sections: French ed. by Th. Monod, A. Teixiera da Mota, and R. Mauny, Bissau, 1951

Hakluyt, R. *The Principal Navigations, Voyages, Traffiques and Discoveries of the English Nation* 1598–1600, especially volume VI

Pereira, Duarte Pacheco *Esmeraldo de Situ Orbis,* French trans. R. Mauny, Bissau, 1956, for parts relating to West African coast as far south as Gabon, with Portuguese original. Complete English trans. by G. H. T. Kimble, Hakluyt Society, London, 1937

Pina, Ruy de, and other early European voyagers translated extracts in *Europeans in West Africa,* ed. J. W. Blake, 2 vols., Hakluyt Society, 1942

Secondary Sources and Commentaries etc.

mainly for Period before A D 1600

Armstrong, R. G. *The Study of West African Languages,* Ibadan, 1964

Bradbury, R. E. "Chronological Problems in the Study of Benin History," JHNS 4 of 2, 1959

———— "Historical uses of comparative ethnography with special ref. to Benin and the Yoruba," in *The Historian in Tropical Africa,* 1964

Davidson, B. *The Lost Cities of Africa,* 5th impr., 1963

Egharevba, J. *A Short History of Benin,* 3rd ed., 1960

Fage, J. D. *Atlas of African History,* 1958

———— *Ghana, A Historical Interpretation,* 1959

———— "Reflections on the Early History of the Mossi-Dagomba Group of States," in *The Historian in Tropical Africa,* 1964

Goody, J. "The Mande and the Akan Hinterland," in *The Historian in Tropical Africa,* 1964

Greenberg, J. H. *The Languages of Africa,* revised ed., 1963

Hau, K. "Evidence of the Use of pre-Portuguese written characters by the Bini," *Bulletin* of IFAN, 1–2, 1959

Hunwick, J. O. "Ahmad Baba and the Moroccan Invasion of Songhay," JHSN, 3 of 2, 1962

———— "Religion and State in the Songhay Empire," International African Institute, 1963

Jones, D. H. "Jakpa and the Foundation of Gonja," THSG, 1 of 2, 1961

Leboeuf, J.-P. *La Civilisation du Chad,* 1950

Levtzion, N. "The Thirteenth and Fourteenth Century Kings of Mali," JAH, 2 of 4, 1963

McCall, D. F. "The Traditions of the Founding of Sijilmassa and Ghana," THSG, 1 of 5, 1961

Mauny, R. trans. of Pereira *supra*

———— *Les Navigations Médiévales sur les Côtes sahariennes antérieures à la Découverte portugaise,* 1960

———— *Tableau Géographique de l'Ouest Africain au Moyen Age,* IFAN, Dakar, 1961

Olderogge, D. *Zapadni Sudan v XV–XIX vv.,* Moscow, 1960

Oliver, R. and Fage, J. D. *A Short History of Africa* (down to modern times), 1962

Person, Y. "En Quête d'une Chronologie ivoirienne," in *The Historian in Tropical Africa,* 1964

Rouch, J. *Contribution à l'Histoire des Songhay,* IFAN, 1953

Ryder, A. F. C. "The Benin Missions," JHSN, 1 of 2, 1961

Smith, M. G. "The Beginnings of Hausa Society," in *The Historian in Tropical Africa,* 1964

———— "Historical and Cultural Conditions of Political Corruption among the Hausa," in *Comparative Studies in Sociology and History*, The Hague, 1964

Suret-Canale, J. *Afrique Noire Centrale et Occidentale*, vol. 1, 2nd ed., 1961

———— "Zur historischen und sozialen Bedeutung der Fulbe-Hegemonie," in *Geschichte und Geschichtsbildung Afrikas*, Berlin, 1960

Trimingham, J. S. *Islam in West Africa*, 1959

———— *The History of Islam in West Africa*, 1964

Urvoy, Y. *Histoire des Populations du Soudan Central*, 1936

———— *Histoire de l'Empire du Bornou*, 1949

Secondary Sources, Travellers, etc.
mainly for Period after A D 1600

Ajayi, J. F. A. *Christian Missions in Nigeria 1841–91*, 1965

Ajayi, J. F. A. and Smith, R. *Yoruba Warfare in the Nineteenth Century*, 1964

Ba, A. H. and Daget, J. *L'Empire Peul du Macina (1818–53)*, 1955

Barbot, J. *A Description of the Coasts of Northern and Southern Guinea*, (in Churchill's *Voyages*, 1732)

Barth, H. *Travels in North and Central Africa*, 5 vols., 1857–58

Boahen, A. A. *Britain, the Sahara and the Western Sudan*, 1964

Bosman, W. *A New and Accurate Description of Guinea etc.*, English trans. London, 1705

Bovill, E. W. *The Golden Trade of the Moors*, 1958

Bowditch, T. E. *Mission from Cape Castle to Ashantee*, 1819

Clapperton, H. with Denham and Oudney: *Narrative of Travels and Discoveries etc.*, 1826; and also *Journal of a Second Expedition etc.*, 1829

Claridge, W. W. *History of the Gold Coast and Ashanti*, 1915

Crowder, M. *The Story of Nigeria*, 1963

Curtin, P. *The Image of Africa: British Ideas and Action, 1780–1850*, 1965

Dalzell, A. *History of Dahomey*, 1793

Davidson, B. *Black Mother: The African Slave Trade*, 1961

———— *The African Past: Chronicles from Antiquity to Modern Times*, 1964

Dike, K. O. *Trade and Politics in the Niger Delta,* 1956

Donnan, E. *Documents Illustrative of the History of the Slave Trade to America,* 4 vols., 1930–35.

Dupuis, J. *Journal of a Residence in Ashantee,* 1924

Forde, D. (ed.) *Efik Traders of Old Calabar* (Diary of Antera Duke), 1957

Fyfe, C. *History of Sierra Leone,* 1962

Hargreaves, J. D. *Prelude to the Partition of West Africa,* 1963

Hodgkin, T. *Nigerian Perspectives* (anthology of extracts from many sources), 1960

————— "The Islamic Literary Tradition in Ghana," Int. African Institute, Dec. 1963

Jones, G. I. *The Trading States of the Oil Rivers,* 1963

Lander, R. and J. *Journal of an Expedition to . . . the Niger,* 1832: abridged and ed. R. Hallett, London, 1965

Newbury, C. W. *The Western Slave Coast and Its Rulers,* 1961

Oliver, R. and Fage, J. D. *Short History, supra*

Priestley, M. and Wilks, I. "The Ashanti Kings in the Eighteenth Century: a revised chronology," JAH, 1 of 1, 1960

Smith, M. G. *Government in Zazzau,* 1960

Smith, R. See Ajayi *supra*

Staudenraus, P. J. *The African Colonization Movement 1816–65,* (Liberian origins), 1961

Tauxier, L. *Histoire des Bambaras,* 1942

Ward, W. E. F. *A History of Ghana,* 1958

Wilks, I. "The Rise of the Akwamu Empire, 1650–1710," THSG, 2 of 3, 1957

————— "The Northern Factor in Ashanti History," Legon, 1961

————— "The Position of Muslims in Metropolitan Ashanti," Legon, 1963

————— "The Growth of Islamic Learning in Ghana," Legon, 1964

————— "Aspects of Bureaucratization in Ashanti," Legon, 1965

ACKNOWLEDGMENTS

I should like to express my warm thanks to my Ghanaian col-
league Mr. F. K. Buah, and to Professor J. F. A. Ajayi of the
University of Ibadan, Nigeria, for his guidance and encourage-
ment. Among other historians to whom thanks are due for
many valuable suggestions and corrections are Mr. Christopher
Fyfe of the University of Edinburgh and Professor Ivor Wilks
of the University of Ghana; while many more, mentioned in
the bibliography, will recognise the influence of their pioneering work.

For some of the maps Mr. Buah and I found sturdy guidance
in Professor J. D. Fage's invaluable *Atlas of African History*
(Edwd. Arnold Ltd., 1958); while for other maps we have followed those in Professor K. O. Dike's *Trade and Politics in
the Niger Delta, 1830–85* (Oxford, 1956); Dr. Colin Newbury's
The Western Slave Coast and Its Rulers (Oxford 1961); Professor Raymond Mauny's *Tableau Géographique de l'Ouest Africain au Moyen Age* (IFAN 1961); M. Jean Rouch's *Contribution à l'Histoire des Songhay* (IFAN 1953); Professor Jean
Suret-Canale's *Afrique Noire* (Editions Sociales, 1958) and
Zur Geschichte und sozialen Bedeutung der Fulbe-Hegemonie
(Akademie Verlag, 1960); the late Louis Tauxier's *Histoire des
Bambara* (Paul Geuthner, 1942); the late Yves Urvoy's *Histoire de l'Empire du Bornou* (IFAN 1949); and Professor Ivor
Wilks's "Rise of the Akwamu Empire" in the *Transactions of
the Historical Society of Ghana*, 1957, while Professor Wilks
has also kindly provided our map of Asante expansion. To all
these and their publishers we tender our thanks. At the same
time we should like to explain that our maps are not intended
as more than broad guides to comparative positions, frontiers,
and lines of movement.

BASIL DAVIDSON

INDEX

Abd al-Rahman as-Sadi, 160, 168

Abdullah ibn Yasin, 48

Abdullahi Burja, 141

Abomey, 231, 234, 235, 236

Abora, 252

Abu Abdallah Muhammad, 66

Abuakwa, 241

Abu Bakr, 48, 50

Aburi, 239

Accra, 131, 214, 240, 242

Adamawa, 283

Adams, John, 227n.

Adansi, 76, 131, 245, 246

Adrar, 67

Affonso, King Nzinga Mbemba, 296–97

Africa: "African civilisation," 5–6, 11; life of early men, 9–13; early great regions, 21

Africans abroad, 298–300

Africanus, Leo. See Leo Africanus

Agadès, 125, 194

Agaja, 234–35, 236, 297

Agona, 240

Ahmad Baba, 167

Ahmadu bi Hammadi, 289

Aïr, 125, 135, 136, 194, 287

Akan, 9, 13, 75, 76, 77, 130–33, 156, 160, 171, 241, 244–46, 254–55, 313; ancestors of, 75; states, 76–77; gold trade and expansion, 122, 130–33

Akim, 131, 239, 241, 248, 252

Akim Abuakwa, 239, 241

Akim Kotoku, 248

Akwa Boni, 255

Akwamu, 76, 131, 214, 239–42, 261

Akwapim, 249, 252

Al-Bakri, 41–42, 43, 46

Alfa Muhammad Diobo, 277

Al-Fazari, 19

Al-Hajj Umar Tall, 289

Ali Ber. See Sunni Ali

Al-Kwarizmi, 19

Allada. See Ardrah

Al-Maghili, 141, 191

Almoravids, 48–49, 84, 107, 150, 263

Al-Murabethin. See Almoravids

Al-Omari, 58, 181

Alooma. See Mai Idris Alooma

Amayaa, 76

Amina, 143

Amo, Anton Wilhelm, 300

Ancient Ghana. See Ghana, empire of

Anokye the Priest (Okomfo Anokye), 244–45, 246, 249

Ansa Sasraku, 240

Aoukar. See Ghana, empire of

Archaeology, 21–22, 39, 94, 97

Ardrah, 232–33, 234, 236, 297

Armies. See Professional armies

Art and religion, 169–72

Asaman, 76, 77

Asante, 75, 77, 130, 154, 156, 174, 239, 240, 241, 242–46, 254, 255, 261; origins, 242–46; empire of, 247–51;